Mike Wimpenny, 28

Len Hunt, 26

Nigel Davies, 32

Chris Hurran, 28

Gordon Turnbull, 28

John Highton, 41

Dave Monteith, 25

John Chuter, 28

Clarence Island Party

Elephant Island

Chris Furse

Elephant Island
An Antarctic Expedition

Anthony Nelson

First published in 1979 by Anthony Nelson Limited
7 St John's Hill, Shrewsbury SY1 1JE, Shropshire, England

ISBN 0 904614 02 6

Photographs by expedition team members as initialled in captions.
Drawings by Chris Furse.

Royalties from the sale of this book are to be donated to the
Royal Geographical Society, London

For convenience of description, some unofficial place names have
been used in this book. These are shown in inverted commas. To
avoid confusion in the future, these names should not be quoted in
subsequent literature. All official place names are to be found in the
Gazetteer of the British Antarctic Territory published by Her
Majesty's Stationery Office.

Designed by Alan Bartram and printed in Great Britain by
Livesey Limited, Shrewsbury, Shropshire

Contents

Appendices

List of Maps

Foreword

To read this story is to realise that there is still plenty of adventure left in the world for those who seek it. Few people have ever landed on the precipitous shores of Elephant Island and its associated group. Elephant Island itself became famous in 1916 when Sir Ernest Shackleton and his party, struggling for their lives, made the first known landing; and thence later, with five picked companions, he made his epic open boat journey to fetch help from South Georgia.

During the next fifty years four or five visits have been made to the group, but almost all we know about them has resulted from two Joint Services Expeditions in 1970-71 and 1976-77. Chris Furse was a member of the first, and leader of the second. When he first approached me about his proposed expedition I was somewhat astonished, indeed perturbed, to hear that he intended to use canoes as his main means of transport around the islands. The Antarctic seas, and particularly the Drake Passage, are notorious for violent storms which can so quickly turn a placid sea into a turmoil of wind and wave.

Finally I was persuaded that his plan was practical, if risky, and I was delighted to see the careful preparations and training that went into the preliminary work in this country. In mid-December 1976 two parties of eight men were landed by helicopter from HMS *Endurance*, one on Clarence Island, the other on O'Brien Island. Later they moved on to the other islands, and this book tells the story of their adventures, both on land and water.

During twelve weeks they had more than their fair share – 100 knot winds, tents flattened by waves or torn to shreds, canoes destroyed by icefalls or damaged by falling rock. Of the twenty-three tents taken, they brought back seven; of the ten canoes only three survived. But despite the hazards nearly all the plans were fulfilled, and geological, botanical and zoological collections were made. So science went hand in hand with the adventure of first ascents and the challenge to Nature's violence.

V. E. FUCHS

Antarctic Peninsula region – Shackleton's journey, 1914-16.

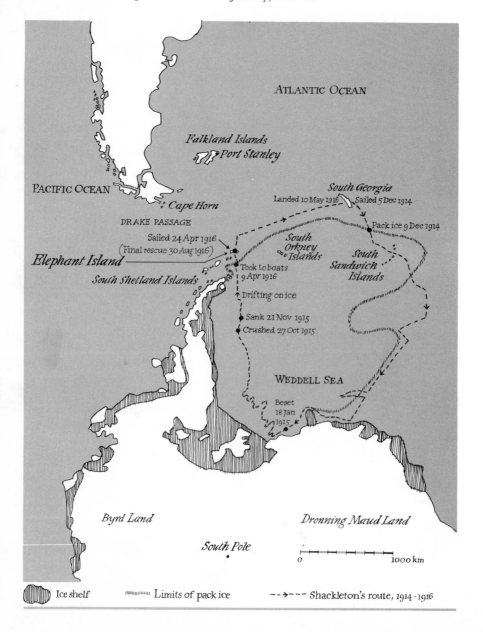

ATLANTIC OCEAN

Falkland Islands
Port Stanley

PACIFIC OCEAN

South Georgia
Landed 10 May 1916   Sailed 5 Dec 1914

Cape Horn

DRAKE PASSAGE

Pack ice 9 Dec 1914

Sailed 24 Apr 1916
(Final rescue 30 Aug 1916)

South
Orkney
Islands

South
Sandwich
Islands

Elephant Island

South Shetland Islands

Took to boats
9 Apr 1916

Drifting on ice

Sank 21 Nov 1915
Crushed 27 Oct 1915

WEDDELL SEA

Beset
18 Jan
1915

Byrd Land

Dronning Maud Land

South Pole

0   1000 km

Ice shelf   Limits of pack ice   Shackleton's route, 1914-1916

Introduction

'Do you talk as much as you write?'

I had just walked the hushed stone corridors of the Royal Geographical Society and sat now on one side of the great table of the Council Room. Far away on the other side a panel of distinguished explorers sat with my application before them and the man on Mwanga's throne was waiting for my answer. I blushed and stuttered.

'No, but I so desperately want to go to Elephant Island.' I answered their questions: they weren't technical probes but personal queries. Would I feel the old man of the team? I was thirty-four, an engineer officer in the Royal Navy, I was rugby fit, no I didn't feel old at all. Why did I want to join the expedition? There would be everything I loved most, mountains, snow, islands, boats, sea and wildlife (especially birds), plus the romantic chill of Shackleton, and still unexplored today! How could I help with the bird work? From a child I had watched, studied and drawn birds; I showed them my paintings of seabirds. What did I know about climbing? Over the years I had spent many weeks walking, camping and skiing in Scotland and Norway, and skiing in the Alps; but I had always been alone, so I was not a climber, and there had been fewer opportunities for mountaineering in six years of marriage. What did my wife think of my going? Faye wanted it for me; while I was gone she would take our sons Ralf Thor and Paul Roald to see her parents in Australia.

Then I went to Plymouth, and waited, with little hope, for the result. It was October 1969.

I was selected! Now I would realise the dream, snatched from the very turnstiles of middle-aged spectatorship. I was to be a member of a Joint Services Expedition led by Commander Malcolm Burley to be the first explorers of Shackleton's Elephant Island. Malcolm Burley had led an expedition to South Georgia in 1964-65, to follow Shackleton's route over the island. Now at forty he was leading his last expedition to his beloved Antarctic. The fifteen team members became friends over a year's training. My task was to survey the island's birds, and after our winter fortnight in the Cairngorms I was made Deputy Leader. Over that year I saturated myself in knowledge of the region: it filled my life.

The first sight of Antarctica for many is Elephant Island smothered in a caul of cloud. Ships' logs record the island's grim presence as they meet the first growlers, sight the grounded icebergs and desolate icecliffs through unwelcoming snowflurries, and pass on. It was not so for us. Early on the morning of 4 December 1970 the whole of Elephant Island sparkled in the sunshine to the south. The next four months were to be the most exciting of my life, and after this, my first introduction to Antarctica, I was in thrall to its magic. I longed for more time, but by April 1971 we were back in England and I knew that my only chance of returning was to organise it myself.

I took up my new job as senior engineer of HMS *Ark Royal,* but I thought and dreamed of Antarctica day and night, and when I left my ship I started to set up my own Antarctic expedition. And that is what this book is about.

I take this opportunity to thank my team again, for making this expedition both memorable and successful. However, we realise that ours was the enjoyable part. The expedition would not have been possible without the unstinting help we received from many organisations, and individuals at home, whose interest, encouragement, advice, material and financial support, and above all enthusiasm, made it possible. My difficulty here has been how to thank people in the little space available. I finally decided in the acknowledgements to list either individuals or their organisations, but never both. That criterion leaves out many of those who helped us most, such as the crew of HMS *Endurance,* the Joint Services Expeditions Trust, the Stores authorities and many servicemen's clubs and societies, which I have included under the umbrella of the Ministry of Defence, and also our many friends in the British Antarctic Survey. Doubtless others who helped us have been omitted in error. To all our helpers, whether named or not, go the heartfelt thanks of all the expedition. I hope that this book will give you pleasure, and show that your help was appreciated.

That I can so thank you is due to my publisher, Tony Nelson. This book would not have been begun without his enthusiasm. It would not have been completed without his constructive criticism, and the professional expertise of Carol O'Brien, who managed to halve my overweight manuscript, Alan Bartram, who designed the layouts and redrew my 'Swallows and Amazons' maps, and Jo Christian, who polished the text, all without hurting my feelings.

This book is dedicated to all of you who made it possible, and most especially my own family – Faye my wife, Ralf and Paul my sons, my parents Paul and Polly, and to my aunt Beet.

OPPOSITE: THE ELEPHANT ISLAND GROUP

Top: Before the Joint Services Expeditions. From the Directorate of Colonial Survey's map published in 1948. All other maps in this book are from the map published in 1972 using the aerial photographs taken in 1956-57 and the ground control we established in 1970-71.

Bottom: The main expedition movements by ship, and dumps of food and stores established by ship's helicopter.

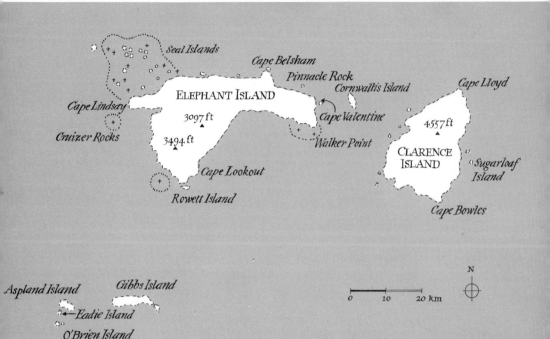

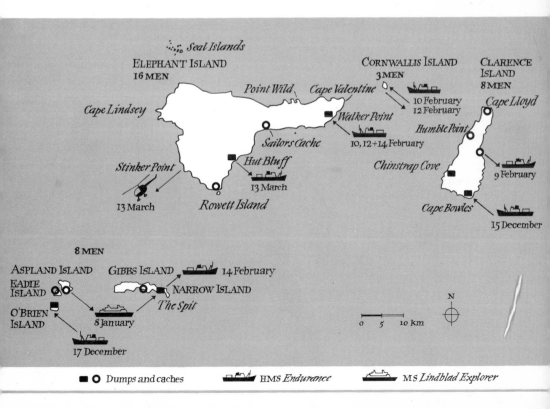

■ O Dumps and caches   HMS *Endurance*   MS *Lindblad Explorer*

1 Preparations

1

Conception of an Expedition 1973-75

Everybody knew Shackleton well, and we very sorry he is lost in ice with all hands. We not know three terrible looking bearded men who walk into office off the mountainside. Manager say: 'Who the hell are you?' and terrible bearded man in the centre of the three say very quietly: 'My name is Shackleton.' Me I turn aside and weep. I think Manager weep too.
WHALER AT HUSVIK, SOUTH GEORGIA

Through two years in HMS *Ark Royal* I dreamed of returning to the Antarctic. I wrote up the results of the 1970 Elephant Island expedition and in September 1973 I drove up from Devon to the British Antarctic Survey (BAS) unit near Cambridge, to deposit a file of detailed maps and observations on the island's birds. The thick report was my offering to certain gods in the academic pantheon.

A few weeks later I was waiting nervously in the corridor outside the Director's office at the rather poky but bustling BAS headquarters in Pimlico. I had come by appointment, to ask: 'Where in British Antarctic Territories can I take a Services expedition that would be useful to BAS?' I felt like a schoolboy in the headmaster's study as I asked my question, and I probably talked like one. My letter had suggested the South Sandwich Islands or the Elephant Island group. BAS scientists had recently visited most of the South Sandwich group; these islands were anyhow scattered over hundreds of kilometres and often unreachable because of pack ice: somewhat regretfully, I dismissed them as a possibility. The choice converged upon the islands of the Elephant Island group. There was much that I would enjoy doing on Elephant's unexplored satellite islands. There would be the satisfaction of learning more about this whole island group than anyone else in the world; I could look at that name on every schoolboy's globe with a proprietary glow. As a Services expedition we offered Dr Laws a highly mobile party to reconnoitre a very hostile group of islands within his territory. He seemed to welcome the proposal, with guarded reservations. My offering had appeased the first and vital academic god.

In September I visited Roger Morris at the Hydrographers (the branch of the Navy who produce charts), who planned the survey tasks for HMS *Endurance*. Here I met an enthusiast who had been south himself. The ship would be undergoing her long refit in the summer of 1975, and only minor maintenance in 1976 and 1977. My rough programme seemed reasonable. *Endurance* is the Royal Navy's ice patrol ship, sailing south each summer for six months. She is the only Naval ship coloured red, and has patrolled the Antarctic waters in the old Falkland Islands Dependencies Survey territories for many years.

Next I saw my appointing officer, Standish Branfoot. My new job as a Naval Overseer at Yarrow Shipbuilders Ltd would terminate in two-and-a-half years, give or take a bit. I asked him to 'give a bit' so I would finish by November 1976, to lead a four-month expedition. He agreed, subject to those ever-present handmaidens of the fates, the exigencies of the Service.

Now I had the three basic necessities: I could go myself, I could get there and back, and I could expect a measure of approval from the British Antarctic Survey.

I went off to Rhu on the Gareloch to start my new job on Clydeside, and spent the autumn evenings crystallising my first rough plan, tossing it to and fro on paper with Dr Laws. The outline closely resembled the 1970-71 expedition with the important exception that I planned to move around by canoe. Canoes 'violated the BAS boating regulations', but eventually a compromise was reached with canoeing limited to coasting movements. I had never before organised an expedition on this scale, and first I had to discover the people who were well placed and well disposed to help. Living on the fringe of the Highlands was marvellous for walking and skiing, but it was a handicap when it came to contacting the hundreds of people whose help would make the expedition possible. Whenever my work took me south I rushed around London, Taunton, Portsmouth or Cambridge to see people. Between these flying visits, I wrote letters and more and yet more letters. Faye, hammering out series of letters, budgets, prospectuses, scientific summaries, etc, etc, wore out our typewriter. I borrowed my parents' typewriter: she had no respite. With no reputation as a successful expedition leader, I had to convince in turn each new person or organisation that here was something worthwhile for them, as well as for me. One experienced press agent warned me that my plans were too 'worthy' to catch the public imagination. It appeared that the best news I could offer might be 'Grampus eats Naval Officer'.

Success came in bursts, followed by plateaux of consolidation. One day out of the blue Crispin Agnew rang me at my office, from Belfast. 'Would you like four Arctic Pyramid tents?' he opened. 'They are worn and faded after four months on the Patagonian icecap, but only need some minor repairs.' He went on to give me a score of useful contacts of whose existence I might otherwise have remained forever ignorant. In remote corners of the War Office and the Admiralty I found his contacts eager and willing to lend cameras and radios for evaluation trials. Best of all he told me of Don Grieve, the RAOC Major whose desk at the Admiralty I found nostalgically labelled 'War Office'. Crispin introduced Don as the 'Funny Rations Man', and he proved to be the man for all rations. And when I went to pick up the tents in Edinburgh I found that there were five of them, worth about £200 each when new, and solving our base camp tentage problems at one stroke.

The all-important matter of team selection would not start until 1975, but I wanted to set up the arrangements early. I had been so impressed by the selection of the 1970-71 team that I wanted to repeat not only the method of interview but also the panel. I wrote to Surgeon Commodore David Dalgliesh, asking him to chair the Selection Committee in 1975. He was then Deputy

Medical Director General of the Navy, apart from being a noted Antarctic explorer and expedition leader. He agreed to do so. My greatest secret delight was that he congratulated me 'on being selected as leader of the expedition group'. At that time the whole expedition consisted only of me, a £5 note, a great deal of hope, and (evidently) some bluff.

Late in 1974 a bank account was opened for the Expedition Fund. The first deposits followed at once from selling some of my bird paintings. About that time I gave up smoking after twenty years (to avoid frostbite and poverty, rather than cancer and depravity). On the strength of this I put £500 into the Expedition Fund as the 'Leader's Non-smoking Fund'. Getting rid of paintings and tobacco gave the expedition an air of respectability and personal commitment, which I am sure helped to win support.

We would need sea transport to get around the islands. After the gemini (inflatable craft, about 4 m long and flat bottomed) in 1970-71 I decided that the paddle-power of canoes would be safer, but I had no experience. At the nearby swimming pool I tried a slalom kayak. The sensation of having an integral nether half floating like a water centaur was for me a thrilling new experience. As a virtual non-swimmer, it was the first time that I had ever been part of the water, yet swift and powerful. I sought advice on touring canoes. Tom Shenton of the Royal Marine Special Boats Company recommended a rigid GRP double canoe called a Tasman. Three months later my mother launched my first one with a bottle of cider from her own Kent apples. We named the orange canoe Willy Nilly after a penguin in a children's book and Ralf and I nearly capsized her among the waterlilies of the farm pond. In October we drove up to the Inter-Services Kayak Championships at Aberfeldy with Willy Nilly on the roof, to persuade establishments to buy Tasmans and lend them to us. The Navy was so short of crews that Willy Nilly and I were co-opted the next day to race down the Tay to Perth. I spent a frightened evening in the pub being regaled by back-slapping hearty tales of smashed boats at every waterfall, while I reassured a nervous Faye that really this was the safest way to learn, with divers at each fall to pull one out. Next day, after learning too late that Willy Nilly should have had a rudder, I watched the field draw steadily ahead of us over my worried skipper's shoulders. Wild geese flew overhead, and great salmon leaped to right and left of us as we raced down past intent fishermen. Willy Nilly happily ploughed through the haystacks of each fall with never a wobble, though sometimes we seemed to be submerged. I feared the last and most notorious fall, but learned that we had been passing through it when that stranger had shouted some rude comment about a yellow submarine. We even beat a few boats, although some of those who capsized managed to remount and overtake us; one pair did so twice. I myself had become an enthusiast, and promptly ordered a second Tasman.

I was still slightly worried that BAS were unhappy about our canoes. 'Oh of course,' said a friend, 'but some of the bases have one or two tucked away. We had a couple at Stonington. Bunny Fuchs would support you, he was always for having a go at something like that.' I drove home turning this over in my mind, nibbling at the information like an eel at the bait. It dawned on me that I could perhaps ask him to be Patron of our expedition: Sir Vivian Fuchs, Fellow of the Royal Society, leader of the first crossing of Antarctica in 1957, the man who had suggested Elephant Island to Malcolm Burley, the first and (until just previously) only Director of the British Antarctic Survey, as well as its predecessor the Falkland Islands Dependencies Survey. Gosh! I wrote to him that night. Very soon he replied, encouragingly: he might be willing if my group really wanted him. He asked me to call.

He took me to lunch at his house in Cambridge, where a great green topiary penguin sat on the lawn gazing out over the high hedge at Cambridgeshire. Everything he spoke of with enthusiasm and infectious boyish delight. I ranged over Africa and the Ruwenzori, where Sir Vivian and Lady Fuchs had been before the war. I followed conventions of dignified scientists to America and to Japan, throwing their problems away as spinning plates across a misty gorge. At frequent intervals he would put down his pipe, leap to his feet and rootle around in bowls of strange objects to find one more pertinent or fascinating than the rest. One cannonball as light as a balloon was a glass fishing float fretted to opacity on the sands of Jan Mayen. A fist-sized white object, like a cowrie shell full of lead, was a Blue Whale's earbone. Did it help that I had guessed both fishing float and whale's ear correctly? He particularly advised me in both planning and execution to advance on a broad front, so that, where there was a holdup somewhere, other things could progress, and opposition or technical difficulties could be over-run or bypassed. Yes, he would agree to be the Patron of the expedition: I drove home to Rhu that evening rejoicing, and thereupon had a new expedition letterhead printed, with 'Patron Sir Vivian Fuchs FRS' emblazoned proudly across it.

I contacted the Foreign and Commonwealth Office in late 1974 to give them outline plans. The Elephant Island group is claimed by Britain, Argentina and Chile, but is south of 60°S in the Antarctic Treaty Area, where all such claims are in abeyance until 1989. I entered the portals of the FCO for the first time in my life and waited my turn to be quizzed, assessed and organised by the incredibly efficient, blonde majorette domo. Then a pleasant middle-aged Cockney woman in a shopgirl's overall led me apace down tiled corridors from whose lofty walls notables in vast gilt frames gazed down. We travelled up a small staff lift in the back because the front lift had an uncertain temper; a few half-levels up and odd steps down, through a skylighted courtyard and I was delivered to 'Polar Regions', regretting that I had not left a trail of breadcrumbs to lead me back. I met John Heap: my ideas of devious diplomats protected by civil-service protocol vanished in shreds within a few minutes. Here was a man who was keen to extend scientific work in Antarctica, was interested in the Elephant Island expedition, and, best of all, was prepared to give me helpful practical advice, with the gist of the diplomatic background. I am afraid that thereafter I tried to call on him whenever I passed through London, a bothersome compliment which he accepted with good humour. Indeed at one bad point later on, he seemed to be my only ally, the only person still really supporting the expedition.

Nevertheless the Foreign Office required me to meet stringent criteria before they would make diplomatic arrangements. Being a Services expedition made things harder. We would carry no firearms, even for self-protection, but the most important factor was the scientific value of the expedition. The Foreign Office sought BAS opinion on this. BAS were less encouraging than I had naïvely expected: botany and geology would be worthwhile only if I engaged graduates; furthermore Dick Laws wanted assurance that I would have ship support between Aspland and Gibbs Islands. It took another five months' work to overcome their reservations, but it was worthwhile: I ended with detailed briefs for my scientific specialists, and also made early contact with several operators of ships in the Antarctic.

As 1974 drew to a close I submitted my application for Sponsorship to the Joint Services Expeditions Trust Committee. Every second year they select one expedition for sponsorship. I was in competition with the Army Mountaineering Association expedition to climb Everest, and they had a lot of big guns on their side. The choice was delayed, but in January 1975 the committee 'endorsed' both expeditions. This was a useful badge of viability, and now I could start to collect tangible assets within the Services, stores and people. I had already put notices in various Services newspapers, canvassing interest (I emphasised the geology, ornithology, geomorphology, meteorology, ichthyology, botology, and all the other ologies so that the scientists wouldn't be put off by snow and ice, precipices and canoes). Now the official notice was published by Defence Council Instruction, calling for applications.

2
The Hovering Axe

Difficulties are just things to be overcome.
SIR ERNEST SHACKLETON

I was looking for someone to join the expedition now as Equipment Officer.
One spring morning a phone call came to my office at the shipyard. It was an
old acquaintance, John Highton. 'What are my chances of being selected?' he
asked. The following evening we went through to Rosyth; I outlined the
expedition plan. Later, with permission for John to come, I made him Deputy
Leader and Equipment Officer. Now there were two of us!

Applications to join the expedition had been pouring in, listing interests,
qualifications and experience. Faye and I scrutinised them, building up mental
images of faces. I was looking for men of twenty-five to thirty-five who came out
on paper as CREAM (Canoeists; Recommended characters; Expedition
experience; Academic qualifications; Mountaineers). My short list grew and
grew. They had such qualifications, there might be no room for me, though
oddly there were rather few climbers. Early in September I went south for the
three days of selection interviews in the Royal Geographical Society.

Five of us sat on one side of the great table in the Council Room, where it had
all started for me six years before. I knew how the candidates felt as they
entered through the tall double doors. David Dalgliesh waved them to a chair
opposite and set the scene before handing over to Malcolm Burley. What a
panel! David Dalgliesh (two Polar Medals, Leader of the Royal Society
Expedition that established Halley Bay in 1956, one of the few men to winter
under canvas in Antarctica) scrutinised them hawklike throughout, spectacles
against his teeth, watching their Adam's apples, watching their fingers,
watching their eyes, watching their reactions to each question, watching their
hesitations. Alfred Stephenson (Surveyor on the British Grahamland
Expedition, member of Gino Watkins' Arctic canoeing expeditions) asked them
questions after Malcolm. After my own few queries David Dalgliesh gave each
man a chance to ask his own, then watched them as they left the room.
Immediately the door closed, he would sum them up, sheep or goats. We agreed
a mark out of 100: over 70 was very suitable. Anyone that I did not personally
like and approve was out, no matter what the others thought; it was I who
might share a tent with him for three months. On the evening of the third day
we put names to my skeleton team, starting with the essential posts: doctor,
geologist and botanist, and working out from there to get adequate canoeing
and mountaineering experience, and to cover the various special skills and

sciences. We picked ten with eight reserves. At last my team was no longer imagined shadows: now I knew their names and faces!

During those three days, David Dalgliesh had mentioned a rumour that *Endurance* was to be scrapped. Earlier rumours had proved groundless, but this, it seemed, was true. *Endurance* would be scrapped before the expedition. The bottom dropped out of my world, and just as I got a team. After a day or two of empty bitterness, I began to think of possible ways round. I canvassed anyone I knew in the Services and London about alternative expeditions or alternative transport. The Services were being torn apart by defence cuts. An expedition smacked of fun and no one could afford to support us.

I found one friend and ally: John Heap. After shuddering at the diplomatic nightmare of British servicemen in the disputed border zone at Cape Horn, he gave me the dates and routes of the tour-ship MS *Lindblad Explorer*. Even more important, he counselled me not to despair: the mandarins would argue over *Endurance* for months, like dogs over a bone; the decision might be reversed. My team was about to meet for the first time, strangers preparing for a venture to the other end of the world. He advised me not to let them know that the expedition might be dead. I am a guileless man: this was my first experience of mass deceit. Yet I knew if I told them the truth, the expedition would be destroyed for certain. I took John Heap's advice.

In October I went down to Capel Curig Training Camp in Snowdonia. I set out maps, reports, pictures and other information ready to brief my team. First impressions are so important. It was vital that this first meeting went well. (It was especially important that I made the reserves feel wanted and hopeful.) Through Friday evening they trickled in, some kitted out for a month in Romsdal, others with cravats. Everyone was quiet, nervous, unsure, not knowing each other, not knowing about the expedition, not knowing what would happen this weekend. I was the only one who had met everyone, at least all but one: one place had been earmarked blind for our botanist, Jem Baylis, and he was the most nervous of all.

JEM BAYLIS

Dusk is gathering as the train clatters along the North Wales coastline. The gloom outside and the blank closed expressions of the other travellers leave me feeling isolated and demoralised. I am tired and a little apprehensive. Llandudno Junction, bleak and grey, as though expecting redundancy and anticipating rusted nails and creaking corrugated iron in its windows. In the street outside a few late homegoers move purposefully while I wait aimlessly. A Land Rover turns into the station yard. My mood changes driving up, as I prepare for introductions and the exchange of nervous trivia that attends such occasions. There are introductions, faces, first impressions half-remembered, and names instantly forgotten. Now to meet the leader, the man who will tell me whether or not I join the expedition. I have unconsciously formed an image from his letters: a prosperous-looking, pipe-smoking 'officer-type', casually dressed in expensive and carefully selected clothes. That expectation is instantly vaporised by a new impression founded on well-worn jeans and desert boots, a broken nose and a hand which belies the concept that all manual tasks should be delegated. The interview followed a familiar pattern.

That evening I briefed them on the islands, expedition programme, organisation, money, training, and so on. I gave each man a scientific task entirely his own and also an expedition task like photography or travel documents to co-ordinate. On Saturday the plan was to walk over Tryfan and the Glyders in two groups, and then to canoe in Willy Nilly.

JEM BAYLIS

Saturday dawned cool, pale blue. Beyond the camp the woods tossed jumbled reds and golds across the valley and behind these the rounded green hills eased one's eyes up to the jagged greys and purples of the tops. Even more striking was the smell: the cool, moist, fruity smell of autumn pushed to the back of my memory by the parched heat of Hong Kong but now rushing back to remind me that this was home. The grime and tedium of the journey and the uncertainty of selection were washed away as though they had never been. The process of getting to know everyone really began. The canoes were the major topic of conversation; everybody seemed very knowledgeable (though from the motley collection of kit, they were not all ace mountaineers!). It was crisp and clear on top, with views across Anglesey. The Moelwyns, Carneddau, and Snowdon presented great upsurges of skyline on all sides. Dropping down towards the lake that afternoon, spread like a petticoat below the green skirt of Moel Siahod, the rest of my group were like old companions; the other group standing at the water's edge with a bright orange canoe were strangers by comparison.

The easy walk had been a success. The point of this weekend had been to get to know each other, and this had happened as people walked in pairs, then changed pairs and talked, talked through the day. I was delighted. Later on Saturday evening we all went up to the pub; by now friendships were forming, everyone was relaxed and smiling; people were arranging to meet and do things just for fun. I reached home the following night elated. For two years the 'expedition' had meant just me and Faye, now there were twenty of us. While together there was no question in my mind of future success; worries about *Endurance* simply did not exist. I had concealed my despair from them; their corporate strength had lifted my own spirits. The specialists had been given my outlines of their aims, with references and contacts. Now each of them was beginning his year's preparations.

Through October and November I stepped up our fund-raising attempts: could we gather enough to charter with a well-disposed company? No one was available. Finally Lars Eric Lindblad generously offered to bring us back at $50 a head. Though we still had to get out there, it enabled me to fabricate an appearance of viability. Confidence was essential to attract support. Not to buy canoes would have exposed my real expectations to the rest of the team, so I let the first be built, the James K. Caird, and in January 1976 it was rafted together with Bunny (Willy Nilly had been rechristened for our Patron) on the Royal Navy stand at the Boat Show. I felt a complete fraud. I knew that we would not be taking canoes south with us, and I hated the pretence.

It was 30 January, and my last day at work before going into the RN Hospital at Haslar. For months I had been suffering from stomach aches, and blood tests showed that I was either anaemic or leaking. I came back from a late meeting to a dark and empty office. On my desk was a telephone message from a friend on the Naval Staff in London.

It said: '*Endurance* is running on to 1977.'

We were saved!

At least, the expedition was saved. I myself had to go into hospital. They kept me in for two weeks. My worst fears were exploded: there was nothing wrong with me. I was not even anaemic according to English rules – only according to Scottish ones! I came out feeling as though the sun had come out after six months' darkness. At last I felt confident that Elephant Island was not just a dream. One team member and two reserves had withdrawn in January; it looked now as though most of the remaining fifteen men (listed in Appendix A, pp. 212-15) would reach the Antarctic with me after all.

3
The Team Emerges

Men wanted for hazardous journey. Small wages, bitter cold, long months of complete darkness, constant danger, safe return doubtful. Honour and recognition in case of success. It seemed as though all the men in Great Britain were determined to accompany me.
SIR ERNEST SHACKLETON

In mid-February I left Haslar and two days later we arrived in the Cairngorms with three canoes, five tents and a Land Rover full of climbing gear. A dozen of us were there for our fortnight's winter mountaineering training, a week at the Joint Services Mountain Training Centre at Tulloch, sandwiched between weekends camped by Loch Morlich. After hauling our canoes over snow, sledging them over ice, and several practice climbs, we ended our week in snowholes on Mary's Coffin on Cairngorm, which was a new experience for many. Evenings in pubs had drawn the team closer and closer together; by the time we had our last beers sconced in a tight cluster down in Aviemore, we were a strong group. Then we went our separate ways, with seven months to go.

Our fishing plans were growing with Frank's enthusiasm. In April Nigel tried out the canoe rafting arrangements which would make the fishing possible, during a family holiday on Shuna. The two Tasmans were set side by side with a gap of about 10 cm between them, three poles were laid across the brackets forward, midships and aft and then lashed down; then a special rafting board was set on the after two poles and a canvas dodger laced across the gap between there and the forward pole. Finally a 4-hp Johnson outboard engine was fitted to the back of the rafting board: with two children aboard we raced around calm seas at nearly 10 knots looking for gulls' nests on the skerries.

Endurance came back from the south in May, bringing a marvellous series of oblique photographs of the satellite islands showing the beaches and dumpsites: there were so few landing beaches that we had to change our plans slightly. She also brought aerial photographs for large-scale maps of two points on Elephant. Best of all, the ship agreed to carry a sixteen-man team! A mountain of stores was now growing in Portsmouth Dockyard. John Highton took the increase to sixteen in his stride and Nick Martin now took over the Portsmouth end for us. Over the next few months they worked wonders, locating strange items from screws edge ski to housewives, with obscure catalogue numbers in four different Services' systems. Someone had warned me that radios needed a lot of senior officer backing to obtain, ending with the helpful comment that: 'Most things can be obtained by the right mixture of tact, influence and perseverance, with a sprinkling of obsequiousness.' We had been offered two brand new lightweight radio transceivers, but later they were loaned to a Round the World Yacht crew instead. After a quick count of stars and stripes, we lost our little radios and gained two 10 kg Second World War spy sets straight from the bed of the Zaire and still working. I brushed up on my obsequiousness. In the end we managed to get most of what we wanted, and all that we needed.

In June we gathered at the Joint Services Mountain Training Centre at Tywyn for two weeks to learn sea canoeing. Surf rolled lazily in on kilometres of beach as Cardigan Bay basked in a heat wave. We started in slalom boats. Few of the team had experience: the river and surf were soon littered with orange upside-down kayaks, while men in glistening wetsuits tried to empty them, handicapped by ridiculous spraydecks hanging like ponderous watery sporrans. We had launched each Tasman with a name: James K. Caird, Bunny, Mischief, Scaf, Bosscat, Tigger, Bear Pooh, Tarka, Happy Haggis and Bilbo Baggins. The names proved a master stroke: they somehow crystallised peoples' feelings. After a few days' practice we went down to St David's Head and paddled out to Ramsey Island. Nearing the southern tip we met a party of sea kayaks: they said the waves outside the island were 6 m high and they had all been capsized. We laughed and one by one shot down the flood through a small gap between two islands. I was in Tigger's bow, with John Chuter behind. Beyond the gap were towering waves, humping in great greeny grey hillocks, though with little white water. We felt as if utterly alone. Each canoe was too busy staying upright to look for others in trouble. Down in the troughs I could see nothing but water. As the bows speared into the foot of the next wave I expected to be engulfed, but then the canoe lifted with an awkward wriggle a moment later. As we balanced precariously over the crests we could see other canoes on distant waves out towards the horizon. Remarkably, all of us came through that sea without capsizing. Next morning we launched the canoes at six and paddled out to the South Bishop light.

Nothing could stop us after Tywyn.

Endurance's programme south gradually crystallised, though we still did not know where we would join her in South America, which made it difficult to book air flights. I decided to book to Rio. MS *Lindblad Explorer* arranged to mother us across from Aspland to Gibbs on 8 January. With just the one chance of getting across, I prayed the weather would be good that day. With the big cost of shipping taken care of by *Endurance*, the money situation was getting better, and I was able to loosen the purse strings a little, to get oddments like buoyancy bags and more photographic equipment. Many of the institutions I had approached earlier were now making us grants and the team members were putting in their contributions also, a third of their pay for the period, which totalled a bit more than the Treasury Grant.

In October I received the list of stores in each crate and it was a nasty surprise. Having only room for six boxes at a time, the stores people had been forced to pack things as they arrived at the store, so there was an inglorious hotchpotch in each box. It must have been difficult to manage in the comfort of a store. What would it be like hunting for the round file in a blizzard on

Elephant? Case D67 typified our 241 stores boxes. Amongst other things, it contained: 3 anoraks; 50 drawing pins; 1 groundsheet; 1 roll muslin for fish; 2 kg candles; 1 toolbag; 1 length of codline; 1 wrench; 1 iceaxe; 2 pick handles; 1 pair goggles; 6 pairs bootlaces; 1 hacksaw; 8 string vests; 5 pairs gloves (of 3 different sorts); 22 polybottles; 2 wetsuit trousers; 36 hexamine blocks; 1 steel ruler. This would create problems later.

In October I finished my job in Glasgow, drove the family south to my parents in Kent, and then went back to the Lakes for the final meeting with the team. We stayed in the grand Fylde Mountaineering Club hut at Stair, in the wettest valley in Britain. We practised ropework climbing on wet rock, hoisted and lowered each other as casualties over boggy ledges, prussiked up into dripping trees, briefed each other on our sciences, and gave blood samples to Gordon. It rained for a week, but nothing dismayed Len Hunt. He led his first V. diff. up streaming slabs: standing in the rain, half a jam butty in his hand and the other half in his mouth, he bubbled over enthusiastically: 'Until I met you blokes, I wouldn't even climb the top deck of a bus.'

Once arrived at Elephant, the plan was to split initially into two parties, one on Clarence Island, one on Gibbs. I had long ago worked out who would be in which party, but had purposely avoided telling people to ensure we were a single team, not two. These team training periods were crucial to that. On the last evening of that week Nigel arrived from a diving job and all sixteen team members were together for the very first time. I told them then how I planned to divide over the first two months, so they could make more detailed preparations for the sciences. Then we all went down to the pub. Next morning we departed our several ways. There was one month to go before our flight.

Later in October *Endurance* sailed with all our stores and canoes on board, and Tim as one of the Ship's Officers. Early in November Nick flew out to South America as our advance party, with £120 and *carte blanche* to arrange our accommodation and transport. The Foreign Office could not yet tell me whether we would join *Endurance* in Buenos Aires, Montevideo or Rio. Nick revelled in that sort of challenge and arranged all three.

Then all the preparations were behind. All the farewells were submerged. The expedition held a party on the eve of departure, on board the *Discovery* alongside the Embankment, rich in the atmosphere of Scott's expedition, with the names over the cabin doors: Wilson, Cherry-Garrard, Skelton, Shackleton. We each had one guest of our own, wife, girlfriend, or parent, and there were a dozen expedition guests. Malcolm Burley with Fiona was smiling as always, but admitting to great nostalgia; Dick Laws brought with him from Cambridge some last-minute notes on ornithology and geology. A nice unobtrusive couple I had not met turned out to be Admiral Hearn, the Chairman of the Joint Services Expeditions Trust Committee, and his wife. It was a great privilege to be among such distinguished Antarctic explorers in this crowded and memorable little cabin, yet everything passed in a dream for me, a prelude. Only two things lodged in my memory afterwards. One was David Dalgliesh meeting Patrick Pirie Gordon for the first time in years: 'I remember the last time we met: you gave me £1000 to go up the left-hand side of Greenland to buy dogs for the Antarctic.' The other was the girl from the Foreign Office handing me an envelope containing instructions to join *Endurance* at Buenos Aires.

After the party Faye and I caught the train from Charing Cross down to my parents' farm in Kent. Clickety-clank went the train's wheels as we rumbled past damp and ill-lit platforms. It was a curiously numb night, hanging between the party in *Discovery* and our departure next day.

At last the long awaited day of departure, 20 November 1976, had come! Saying goodbye to my black labrador was bad. Faye and I arrived at Victoria Air Terminal very early and joined Nigel, Jem and Len. At four, as dusk fell, the bus broke down beside the motorway. We sat patiently. Time went by. We tried hitch-hiking, unsuccessfully. After nearly an hour a rotund little Indian gentleman got out, set down his prayermat and made obeisance south-westward towards the lights of Heathrow. Five minutes later Frank's bus picked us up and whisked us to the airport. After half an hour of frenzied goodbyes, distribution of films round hand baggage and pushing through screaming pop-group fans, we found ourselves all fourteen on the plane.

I fell asleep before we took off. Three years of organisation were finished.

As the sun rose next day we landed in Rio de Janeiro, and stepped out into a soft, warm envelope of heat. Walking to the airport building sweat prickled under my belt and began to percolate through my armpits. From here we were to catch a bus. For two days we travelled fast, stopping every four hours at a bus station where we all debouched. Nick Martin met us in Buenos Aires with a list of kind hosts. We scattered for two days, John and I to Alan and Yvonne Roberts, who proved perfect hosts. Buenos Aires is a lovely spacious city of great buildings, open spaces and civilised bustle. People smiled in the streets; doves mated in the trees of the plazas. The streetsellers' flowers smelt of Christmas. There was the music of tangos and old slow lovely railway engines simmered in laybys. In cafés poets sang their songs; vast steaks smoked richly on asado fires; polo ponies heaved in dusty mêlées. Without machismo you were lost.

On 25 November we embarked in HMS *Endurance* and ten minutes later she sailed down the lifeless, turgid Mar del Plata. For five days we journeyed south to the Falklands through calm seas and open skies. We sorted our stores, stacked up almost to fill the hold below the foredeck hatch. We issued clothes, photographic gear, briefed about the Falklands. We discussed the programme in the islands. We did PT daily. We ate standing crowded in the chart room. We slept scattered through cabins, schoolrooms, passages, cells, store rooms and hold, wherever Tim had found a cranny. We talked, laughed, teased and joked. I spent time watching and photographing the seabirds, for now the albatross came sailing by, and many other petrels. Once a pair of Killer Whales cruised past a kilometre off, the great black triangle above and a stripe of white below as they rolled.

At six on the morning of 30 November the Falklands lay clear and low 5 km to starboard, flat undulating moor the colour of faded hay, ending in low cliffs, with rocky ridges breaking the monotony. The changing sky is the delight of these islands, the whole vast sweep unfettered by tree or major vertical, the

HMS *Endurance* lies at anchor in Port Stanley. (DM)

clouds endlessly changing in their serried battalions, releasing shafts of sunlight to bathe yellow campgrass or blue water. Mollymawks and nellies zoomed playfully round our stern in a fresh breeze; King Shags and Kelp Gulls came out to meet us, and a solitary Antarctic Fulmar moped in our wake as a herald of the far south.

We entered Port Williams and then through the narrows into Port Stanley. The town lay scattered up a low slope from the shore, white houses topped by red and green corrugated iron roofs, a tremendous splash of colour with the few crouching banks of yellow gorse. Even a few trees nestled in the lee of the houses. The shores were a litter of old wrecks. We had over a week ashore while *Endurance* prepared for Battle Day on 8 December. The days passed happily, in canoeing, exploring, watching birds, and sorting our stores; evenings were spent in the Rose, our favourite of the town's three hostelries, where the islanders looked us in the eye and talked with knowledge about boats. After the guns and parades of Battle Day we paddled out to the ship.

The long journey now was almost over.

The expedition was about to begin.

4
Into the Antarctic

Beyond this flood, a frozen continent
Lies dark and wild, beat with perpetual storms
Of whirlwind and dire hail.
MILTON

10 December   As the ship heads out of Port Stanley and Port Williams into
Drake Passage the sky lifts. The low islands behind us are swept by rain
showers and lit by occasional flashes of sun, we are escorted by a crowd of Giant
Petrels and Kelp Gulls. There is a large gentle swell remaining, the ship lifts to
it and rolls with a lovely ponderous shippy movement. As we draw beyond sight
of land the last Kelp Gulls leave us and several Black-browed Albatrosses join
the heavy dark Giant Petrels around the stern. One Wanderer sweeps
majestically around and around the ship half a kilometre off; he sticks low to the
surface of the water, slower than his smaller relatives. The last lingering
reminder of the Falklands is the distilled water on board. As I run my tap before
supper it smells fresh and deliciously of iced oysters – the taste of kelp.

11 December   At half past six thirteen of us have breakfast, standing half
awake around the chart room table, looking out at a gentled sea, with two
prions weaving across it. Chris Brown is feeling less seasick today, but has
nevertheless kept away. Frank has caught blue maggot disease from Len, who
misses breakfast as ever. (The army's green maggot disease has been
rechristened to suit our blue Polywarm sleeping bags.)
   In the afternoon I am able to spend quite a lot of time up on the flight deck,
photographing the little flitting Wilsons Storm Petrels and slow Wandering
Albatrosses. Greatly exciting, two slender grey Light-mantled Sooty
Albatrosses pass by and inspect the wake. They are the same size as the Giant
Petrels, and not dissimilar in tone, but body and wings are slender, there is no
neck between broad shoulders and rounded head, and their texture is soft and
smooth. They are the greatest of all fliers.
   In the evening I point out a prion to the Clarence birdmen: 'That's a
whalebird.' As if on cue there is a white blast a quarter of a mile off and a great
black shape slides down again with a backward hooked fin. It is probably a Sei
or Fin Whale, moving fast in the opposite direction, and surfacing quite
frequently. It is gone within a minute. In the hour between supper and our
evening meeting I go to the flight deck to photograph the occasional prion
which joins the other petrels over our wake. Alan Milne is up there meditating,
having just got through to Moira on the radio telephone; he sent my love to

Faye, which is great. We stand around talking quietly and ecstatically about this sunlit weather with an almost greasy sea as we approach Antarctica. We expect to cross the Convergence tonight or tomorrow morning. Alan leaves me to my low-lit creamy albatrosses. A kilometre or two ahead, below a line of yellowish cloud, hangs a white veil trailing on the sea like a curtain. This side of the veil the sea is blue-grey: beyond, it looks white with a tinge of pale green. It looks very odd. It needs a wide angle colour photograph to show the colour change and the line extending far to the right and left across the ship's path: a few minutes later I see a line of white far off on the port bow, like the cliffs of Dover from across the channel: it is the first iceberg, a big one 30 km ahead. My curtain of cloud is actually the Antarctic Convergence! The meeting place of cold Sub-Antarctic waters with colder Antarctic waters, this is the barrier which rings the whole of Antarctica, and is the universally acknowledged boundary of the Antarctic, today rather further north than usual. We hope to sight Elephant Island in the evening tomorrow. We have arrived in the Antarctic.

12 December   It is foggy when we wake at six. Soon the fog lifts a little, as the wind rises to Force 4 from the south-east, and flurries of snow and sleet drift up a little on the decks. After breakfast it clears to a sunlit day of crystal clarity with glittering white horses upon a rich blue sea. The sea is carpeted by scattered birds feeding, fulmars, prions, and a few penguins (always difficult to identify specifically).

We expect to reach Prince Charles Strait between Elephant and Clarence soon after eight this evening. Tomorrow we plan to start flying the dumps into Elephant itself at five in the morning – crack of dawn it seems, though actually sunrise will be 0300. As the morning passes we sight a few icebergs scattered about the azure sea. Excitement mounts in the team. At 0845 we get our flight briefing on helicopter safety equipment, and drills in case of ditching. At 1000 there is a little church service: I read a lesson from Acts, chosen by Chris Hurran: 'Howbeit, we shall be cast upon a certain island.'

Through the afternoon we pass more bergs, some closely. At three o'clock we sight Elephant and Clarence, faint dark ghosts in the cloud ahead. We close through the dogwatches, and the weather holds, so there is yellow sun on snow, fading confusingly into yellow snow cloud, and grey unlit snow, and grey cloud. These are the north-eastern cliffs from Point Wild to Cape Valentine. Cornwallis shows ahead, and there are more bergs about. Around us now flit a host of Cape Pigeons, they cross our bows closely, one so close I brush his wingtip with my outflung fingers; we all vote them our favourite bird, the lovely soft creatures in clowns' dress, with their rich purpled black heads, fat white bodies and checkerboard wings. There are also Black-bellied Storm Petrels heading home for their Elephant stronghold.

After supper we all go up on the forecastle. The clouds have lifted to 700 m and are breaking apart on Clarence Island as we approach its northern tip; the snow ridge above occasionally peeps through the sunlit clouds, and the whole west coast is printed clear in photograph after photograph. It is staggeringly beautiful. Everyone is gaping and chattering. I feel full to bursting that all now

The islands at last! *Endurance* steams into the sunset, towards Gibbs Island. On Elephant Island the snout of Endurance Glacier just catches the sun, while closer at hand looms an eroded tabular iceberg. (DM)

realise why I have striven to return here. Five small tabular bergs are grounded off Clarence and others in the strait near Cornwallis. The ship turns west and passes south of Cornwallis, and along the south coast of Elephant. As she does, the clouds descend on Clarence, which retires into dark gloom; at the same time the clouds on Elephant evaporate and disperse until the ridge crests above Cape Valentine all stand out in shades of white, piled incredibly above and behind each other in a close and towering confusion. Now the whole fantastic 16 km of Pardo Ridge passes in procession down our starboard side, clear and beautiful, flushing as it catches the low sun on points and crests and the icecliffs below, then losing the sun to become plain cold whites. We stand on, looking and looking and looking, until suddenly it is eleven o'clock, bedtime. It has been an unbelievably lovely arrival. The team seem awed by the stark beauty, and the steepness of the hills. I feel somehow proud of these islands I have dreamed of these six years, as if they were 'mine'. Over these next months they will come to belong to the sixteen of us, and no one else. Perhaps their first fresh impressions are more realistic than mine, so overlaid with old memories and recent plans.

JEM BAYLIS

I never realised it was this terrific: by now icebergs have become almost commonplace, but none the less fascinating. They vary in shape, size and colour; many are fantastically sculpted by the waves with crystal powder white tops, and glassy blues and greens near the water. Imagine the Alps flooded to glacier level, and you've got half of it; add to this penguins and seabirds and an indescribable feeling of splendid isolation, and you have a little more. It is one of the very few times that reality has exceeded my imagination. I stayed on deck for hours as we steamed slowly into the sunset towards Gibbs, which showed as a smudge on the horizon.

JOHN CHUTER

We came close by an iceberg. It was a cathedral of ice, high as a tower block of flats; one can get no idea of the size of these bergs until one actually sees them. One tabular berg was several kilometres long. Through the low cloud Clarence Island became visible. Endurance sailed between Clarence and Elephant and we began to get some idea of the scale of the islands. I could make out the prominent glaciers and peaks and the setting sun made the ice and snow look like icing sugar; it was extremely pretty. In Greenland you tramp 30 km across a glacier to reach a mountain; here they all jostle each other and crowd the sea below.

NICK MARTIN

By 2000 we were entering the straits between Elephant and Clarence with the sun blazing through a fine lattice of clouds and the ship steaming through gilded shimmer on the waves. The effect was memorable. The islands are spectacular; an alpine range which has been flooded. The mountains fall to the sea with no foothills or any satellites: amazing whiteness of the snow; stark vertical pitches of rock; forbidding menace; high vertical icecliffs; Endurance Glacier, an enormous great wall of ice 8 to 10 km long bulging into the ocean. One would not expect any life to be there, yet it teems with life. As the sun sank lower, the mountains took on a pinkish glow. None of us could really believe our eyes. We had expected

*to see nothing but heavy cloud and mists shrouding the islands throughout our stay; yet here
we saw them first in all their glory.*

13 December   The grey light is coming in through the cabin porthole, it forces
my tired eyes open. I lie there. Suddenly I remember what is happening today
and look at my watch. It is half past four! I must have overslept, rolled over
after being shaken. The whole expedition will be late for the first flight ashore,
proving to the ship that we are just a bunch of layabouts. I dress in a frantic
rush and get up to the bridge. John Draper, the navigator, just smiles: 'It was
too claggy to fly, so we didn't wake you.' Relief floods over me. I go back to my
bunk, lie thinking, then drop off, to awake with a similar feeling at seven-thirty.

By eight the low cloud is lifting to a characteristic flat pall shrouding
everything above 700 m. We start bringing the food and remaining boxes up
from the hold and aft to the hangar, so that the helicopters don't beat us and
empty the hangar stock. Gordon is boss of the foredeck crew. He has not got his
plans ready, so there is a delay opening the hatch and rigging the hoist. I curse
him for being ill-prepared. Gordon feels aggrieved: 'How can you expect me to
be ready when the winch goes wrong?' I leave, hoping that he will work the
harder for being furious.

John and I get into orange rubber immersion suits for the recce flight; you get
in through the facial opening and then pull up a draw string, as if in a sleeping
bag but with arms and legs. Tight between crown and crutch, we look like
Wombles or dancing dayglo bears. I am rather frightened of flying, but this is
too exciting to worry. We sit side by side in the back of the little Wasp: the rear
doors have been removed so we sit strapped in and able to lean out and look
straight down on grey sea and drifting ice. We go around Rowett Island:
looking down at the birds fluttering off the cliffs below, I realise how high we are
(they are so tiny, I cannot be sure whether they are Cape Pigeons). We circle
around and go in low over the beach cache site; Chinstrap Penguins run
frantically away from the great noisy skua in the skies; Elephant Seals hump off,
brown, dirty and belching defiance, there are several soft grey pups among
them. The grey scree and rock is much more bare than my memory, which had
clothed it in a thin fur of lichen.

Then we are away. A day's journey over the glaciers is done in five minutes to
reach the Hut, still there intact, though bare of paint; the dry-stone annex intact,
half full of food boxes and amazingly almost empty of snow. Quickly we whirr
away across the glacier to 'Sailor's Cache', then on to Walker Point where we
are buffeted by turbulence. We head back over the sea toward Gibbs: bergs
litter the area. I do not realise their size until the pilot points out *Endurance,* a
tiny red dot beyond a great white slab. It has all been too quick. I cannot
comprehend having flown in forty minutes over 30 km of coast, where I lived for
four months, and which had stayed for six years since in my mind. It is all
recognisable, but the south end above Rowett Island is much more exciting
than I had imagined (having only been across it twice in cloud). Great black
faces and spiky ridges go up to 700 m on the south shoulder of Mount
Pendragon as it slopes down to the 'Green Glen'. Through the day we steam up

and down off this coast, and ten loads are flown in to the 'refuge Hut', and also food and fuel to 'Sailor's Cache' before flying ends in the evening.

14 December   Sitting on my bunk before breakfast, with flying scheduled for 0900, the sun opens through the port and the light swings slowly across the paper as the ship drifts. I read my journal, and wonder why I have been tired. I was tired when we left Britain from lack of sleep during the last frantic preparations, and it is simply that I have not really caught up on that. But over the last couple of weeks I have felt responsibility and care lifting away like morning mist. I know I am still responsible for the physical safety of my team, but all the ifs and buts of preparation have been resolved; we are now committed and we are here. Also, at last, it is no longer largely me driving the expedition: John Highton is now in his element, doing things and persuading others, and the whole team is pulling hard.

Today we kick off with Jem and Chris Hurran going ashore at Walker Point. By lunchtime we finish putting in Dump E there, they come back on board, and the ship steams over to the west coast of Clarence. For the recce flight there, the aircraft will take only one of us, which must be John Highton, as he needs to see the beaches and know where the cache and dump are.

As we steam toward Clarence, the clouds clear from the Ravelin Ridge except the highest step to Mount Irving. It is a truly staggering ridge, 20 km long, rising quickly at the northern end to 1000 m, then half-way along the island stepping up to 1500 m, and reaching 1924 m on the southern plateau. The whole northern half of the ridge, now clear in the sun, is like a white wave about to break; its curling crest is rounded like a foaming head, and the final 300 m is formed of vertical pillared walls of ice: the lower slopes are riven and pitted by icefalls and small avalanches, making a traverse on land extremely dangerous; this was one of our reasons for bringing canoes.

Tomorrow the forecast is for rising wind, and the likelihood that flying will be curtailed at midday, but we hope to get John's party ashore at Cape Bowles. I get the Clarence canoes uncrated and down in the hangar at nine after flying is over. It is worth it, because in the early hours of morning it is difficult to muster the whole team, let alone arouse them to urgent efforts. I sympathise, but this lot are even less punctual than me.

15 December   Flying will start at 0500. I go round to wake the team. There are four blue maggots in the library and I make sure they all know that the smallest one (Len) has to be ready in twenty minutes to go ashore first as planned. 'Yes,' they all four say. When the chopper wants Lennie's rucksack, he isn't there. I rush forward, to meet Nigel and Len carrying a great bulging blue thing with bits falling off it. They load it into the aircraft, but when one rucksack pocket, one hairbrush and one camera fall out, it is sent back into the hangar. I am livid that our first man should be late and unready, but fourteen

The great west wall of Clarence Island drops to the sea from the overhanging mushrooms of Ravelin Ridge at over 1200 m. (CF)

faces grinning away at the whole scene make me see the funny side.

As Len leaves he shakes hands with the Gibbs Islanders in the hangar, and it seems most appropriate. We wish each other good luck, Happy Christmas and Happy New Year, and look forward to meeting again in February. While the stores are being flown into Cape Bowles, everyone gives a hand to get the Gibbs Islanders' food and boxes aft into the hangar.

John is the last to go ashore. He dresses up in his orange 'once only' immersion suit. We shake hands, and away he goes.

Suddenly, they are all ashore,* with just eight of us still on board. As *Endurance* turns to steam west to Gibbs she sounds her siren. It is the seaman's farewell.

It takes the ship five hours to reach Gibbs. The clarity is incredible, the sky clears to blue, and we get our first view of the summit of Mount Irving as we draw away from Clarence. Passing along the south shore of Gibbs in the sun, my party begins to cheer up and grow excited over our own prospects.

A school of Killer Whales south-east of O'Brien scarcely bothers us, as they plough swiftly south. We steam around south of O'Brien Island and then up to the west of Eadie and Aspland. The three islands are superb submerged alpine peaks capped with snow; in the sunshine we can see clearly the banding of green, brown and grey rocks; there seems to be more possibility of moving around the shores than I had expected. We change our plans a bit after this recce and revise our allocations of food and fuel to the various dumps and caches. We are now really keyed up, having seen our own lovely islands; all we want to do is get ashore as soon as possible. The plan is to fly in the Gibbs dumps first thing tomorrow.

16 December   This morning is grey and cloudy. I get dressed nervously for my helicopter recce. We fly into the 'Narrow Island' site first, and the pilot selects a little knob in the sloping bowl as a good landing site for the dump. The ship is standing nearly 3 km off, like a small red toy. A snowstorm is coming, and we rush back to the ship.

The snow is succeeded by low cloud, preventing flying. Frustration. David Deakin, the First Lieutenant, suggests a dump down on the Spit itself, and a recce in the ship's gemini is arranged. I go in with the ship's hydrographer, Peter Banyard, and Sergeant Toft of the Marine detachment. It is 2 km in; then we stop the engine and paddle in towards the shingle beach. Glancing astern I

---

*The Clarence Island team consisted of John Highton, Mike Wimpenny, Dave Monteith, Len Hunt, Chris Hurran, Gordon Turnbull, John Chuter and Nigel Davies.

The Gibbs Island team consisted of Chris Furse, Chris Brown, Andy Simkins, Tim Hallpike, Jem Baylis, Nick Martin, Frank Mogford and Alan Milne.

The Wandering Albatross ranges south of the Antarctic Convergence, but seldom as far as these islands. (CF)

see a black fin cut the surface just behind us. At its second rise I see it is not a dolphin, but a big ugly Leopard Seal. He is 5 m from us with his huge head out of the water and his cold eye looking at us, while his great humped back churns through the surface. He is a great deal bigger than I remember, looking 4 m long. As he swims round us, I hold the boathook like a lance to bang him on the snout, until he disappears. We snub the bows on to the beach, jump out in the small surf, haul the boat out of the water and go up the storm beach which forms this remarkable Spit, like an umbilical cord between 'Narrow Island' on the east and the main part of Gibbs. It is covered with non-breeding penguins and frankly it is a messy, horrible place to put a dump. However, the boxes can be cached safely up the western end among the first penguin nests, which must indicate freedom from waves. Among these Chinstrap Penguins I find two Adelies sitting on eggs. This is an exciting surprise: on Elephant we found no Adelies nesting; the eggs are also surprising, because they are supposed to nest three weeks before the Chinstraps. Peter radios the ship suggesting that the helicopters fly the stores in here, and we launch the gemini. My left boot fills up with very cold water.

Off the beach Sergeant Toft tries to start the engine. There are some nasty noises, and he is left with a metre of cord connecting his hand to the starter. A light breeze drifts the boat out. We make up a knotted cord to use on the flywheel: Peter has a go, because he knows these engines at home. There are a few strenuous pulls and faint hiccups from the back. I sit looking ahead at the little red ship out there. Suddenly the boat leaps forward. I fall back into the stern and one of the paddles falls over the other side. As we scramble up we realise that Peter has been thrown over the stern by the sudden leap. He is 20 m off; his lifejacket is keeping his head well out of the water, and he shouts to put the engine in neutral. Sergeant Toft wrestles with the engine controls and the boat leaps forward then back alarmingly, and round in circles. Finally he stops it. I paddle frantically upwind towards Peter with the only paddle. I am thinking of that big Leopard Seal and hope Peter has forgotten him. After a minute or two we reach him, and haul him in. His immersion suit worked quite well, and he is all right. We get the engine going again just as the seaboat arrives to tow us, and go back to the ship in convoy 5 m apart; penguins porpoise along between the two boats, almost as if playing. The water temperature here is such that a very minor slip can put one in a very dangerous position; we have learnt the lesson without harm! Secretly, I add another point to the canoes *v.* gemini score.

After lunch they fly the stores into the Spit. Andy and Chris Brown go ashore to hump the boxes, and it is all done in an hour. We sail for Aspland and hope to get ashore tonight. Our eight rucksacks are in the hangar. The one remaining

Photographs of Antarctic Prions in flight are rare. These petrels are often called whalebirds. (CF)

dump of stores and five canoes looks quite small, after the enormous heaps of three days ago.

The ship closes our three small islands in the evening and I get into the helicopter for the recce flight. It is cloudy, there are snow showers about. First we fly over the Aspland beach site, which looks adequate. We fly all around Eadie to avoid the narrow turbulent gap between the two islands: the shoulder half-way up Eadie looks too close to the cloud, so instead I choose a flat rock stack for the cache. Rounding the great north-west cape of Aspland we encounter clouds and clouds of Antarctic Fulmars; Chris Lyle, the pilot, vetoes the site entirely, because of bird strike hazard, and turns rapidly around, so tightly that I get an awful sinking feeling. (I must somehow visit this site to census the birds!) We head for O'Brien: the dumpsite is a little corrie cutting back into the island's flat face, with two tongues of glacial ice hanging over it creating dangerous downdraughts. We head back to the ship.

The cache flights are flown to Aspland and Eadie. Flying to O'Brien (to a beach below the corrie) starts desultorily. Nick and Tim are flown in first. Then the pace quickens, as Peter flies in and out with a four-minute cycle time. The deck crew suddenly realise that there is perhaps a chance of getting us all ashore tonight and the pace becomes frenetic. But the light grows dimmer, and the Captain calls a halt at ten, when the stores have been flown in, leaving us with our packs and canoes. It is just as well; the aircraft was icing up on the last run. Peter drops from his little aircraft, spent with nervous energy, and laughing from the success of it.

We six have (another) last drink in the wardroom. Six green bottles. I wonder how Nick and Tim are faring on the island?

Soft-plumaged Petrels patrol Drake Passage around the Antarctic Convergence. (CF)

NICK MARTIN

In we flew, landed on the pebble beach. From just above high water back to the cliff, all the way up the scree (and then beyond) were penguins. Not lovely, clean, adorable ones, but noisy, filthy horrible ones! The beach was wet; the pebbles were treacherously slippery, and stank abominably of penguins. By the time all the boxes had been shifted to a safe nook we were exhausted and had peeled off our jackets and sweaters. Did we mind staying on the island by ourselves for the night? Mind! After twelve months' anticipation! With 30 kg packs on our backs, Tim and I hiked up through the penguins, slipping and slithering everywhere, sweat pouring off us. Thankfully, 120 m up we reached an area in a cwm where it was snow-covered and penguin-free. Choosing a place out of the way of potential avalanches was not easy. Having decided, we dug snow for a level platform. Within the hour we had put up the tent after a fashion and had a hot chocolate. It was after midnight. And so to sleep. We had arrived!

17 December   The 17th is grey again. Among the crowd of fulmars and Cape Pigeons round the ship are five Antarctic Petrels. They fly high and handsome on their narrow wings, often planing along the windward side of the ship at bridge height, unlike the common herd lowdown astern. They really are a sailors' bird. The *Quest* Expedition in 1923 said they saw many at Rowett Island. Now here are these birds, who stay around all forenoon, settling to feed as if at home. Will we find their most northern colony? Could this be their still unknown breeding site near the Weddell Sea?

Through the forenoon the little Wasp flies in the canoes, then us. Suddenly I am standing on the storm beach on O'Brien Island. The helicopter flies away towards *Endurance*, out of sight.

This Cape Pigeon with its checkerboard clown's pattern may meet your ship off Rio or Cape Town; it may have nested almost anywhere in the Antarctic, including our islands. (CF)

2 The Gibbs Islanders

December to February

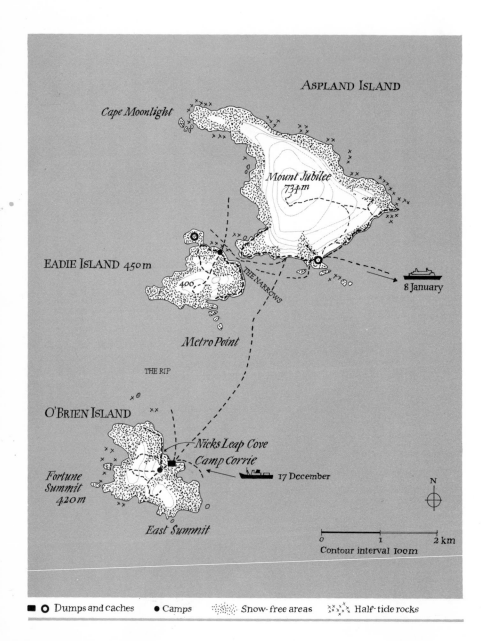

ASPLAND ISLAND

Cape Moonlight

Mount Jubilee
734 m

EADIE ISLAND 450 m

400

THE NARROWS

8 January

Metro Point

THE RIP

O'BRIEN ISLAND

Nicks Leap Cove
Camp Corrie

17 December

Fortune
Summit
420 m

East Summit

N

0   1   2 km
Contour interval 100m

■ O Dumps and caches   ● Camps   ⋰⋰ Snow-free areas   ××× Half-tide rocks

5

Settling in: O'Brien Island

All these interesting animals live continually together in the most copious and rural harmony, nor perhaps in many parts of the world is such perfect and abject happiness to be found.

EDWARD LEAR

17 December Nick and Tim have made a marvellous dump of boxes in one layer, under tarpaulins, on the high storm beach under a rocky point. All over the 10-m-deep, 50-m-long beach are Chinstrap Penguins, cackling like rooks. We gather to set our watches onward one hour, from twelve to one o'clock. This will be our expedition time, two hours behind GMT, one hour ahead of local time (to bamboozle us into getting up earlier).

We lift our packs, and start up to the campsite. We plod through a filthy mire of penguins across the beach, up a dirty snowslope and then a dirty gully full of penguins, each sitting on its nest, fencing, cackling and pecking at our snow gaiters. When you put a glove down for balance it is immediately filthy. As we start to dig out platforms and collect rocks the wind rises quickly to gale force. Chris Brown and I have a hell of a time with our tent. The A-frames and ridge pole keep falling apart, threatening to impale the bits of material flapping frantically in the wind. Three A-frames are too many. Over goes the flysheet: in a minute we will have the valance weighted down with rocks and things will settle down. It is not to be: each time we plonk rocks down, the slippery valance slides from beneath them, the wind finds a hole, and everything collapses into a heap. Below us Alan and Frank's flysheet is flapping madly like a flag, blown horizontal. Jem's tent above is little better; but after an hour the wind subsides a little and we begin to win. Then Nick and Tim arrive down with the remains of their tent; its ridge pole has snapped in two! We have no spare ridge poles at all, and no spare tents at this dump. Nick comes in with us and Tim goes in with Andy and Jem. Three in one of these Vangos is quite possible, but a bit tight.

Standing about our campsite we can take stock of our situation. We are at 100 m with the scree-filled floor of the corrie sloping down first gently and then more steeply to the sea below. Above our right shoulders is the steep broken cliff forming the south side of the corrie. Behind us and to our left are steep snowslopes up to the summit ridge: two great lobes of blue ice dominate the headwall, and rock walls slope to the sea on the other side of the little corrie. Framed between the corrie walls and the penguins on its bed is a U-shaped span of sea with all the islands set out for inspection. Immediately across the sound, Eadie and Aspland rise abruptly from the sea to their spiky snow peaks. To their right we see the south end of Elephant, with Mount Pendragon clear tonight, and the dark spires of little Rowett Island surprisingly distinct. On the right of the frame is Gibbs and peeping round it we sight Clarence 100 km away, its western cliffs shining saffron and pink in the last of the sun.

It is a great prospect, and we are all glad to be here at last. To bed late, replete and content.

18 December   We rise at will. Our first task is to strike and repitch our tents, after the chaos of last night. We are unhappy about the Vangos: the poles are weak; several guys have broken; the valance is very flimsy; the sewn-in groundsheets are tearing at the attachments; the clips for hanging the inner tent to the A-frames are weak. However they are roomy tents once up. Nick splints his ridge pole, and puts the tent up again: Chris and I immediately spread ourselves so that the tent looks just as full again; but it's much easier to get in and out. We each have one side, and half the bell-end at our heads. Our sleeping bags lie on our karrimats, with polybags of clothes crammed against the side walls; cameras, binoculars, books and oddments are in the bell-end. We have the primus on a small box between our heads, and food and cooking utensils

This clean Chinstrap Penguin has come ashore recently. (DM)

down the middle towards the door between our bags. It is very comfortable. We almost look forward to a blow to test our repitched tent.

Today we spend sorting ourselves out. Nick breaks out the stores on the beach: penguins get covered in packing material and we don hats we packed in October. Chris Brown helps me run a check of a hundred Chinstrap Penguin nests, recording the numbers of eggs and chicks; I will do this each day to provide an accurate assessment of hatching dates. Today we find just one chipped egg among this hundred, but elsewhere in the colony I see three tiny chicks, the first of thousands, small, weak and cheeping in clean silvery down, and very attractive. A Leopard Seal patrols close to the beach foot, and the penguins porpoise around the little bay in droves, boiling the water as if in a frenzy, going one way, then the other, and sometimes in several directions at once, like black fish leaping from the water. Tim starts observing the movements of the little bergs in our sound, and also several bigger ones out to the north-east. There are some forceful looking rips of water between our three little islands: working out the best time to canoe becomes an important part of Tim's task, as well as working out the currents. He thinks the rips are tidal: the

Chinstrap Penguins cover the way from the camp down to the canoes on the beach. (FM)

current is easterly in the afternoon; then in the evening a small berg whistles·
through westward at 7 knots!

In the evening Andy gets the radio going. This involves relays of us sitting
and cranking the hand generator around like a hand-operated bicycle. We do
this for ten minutes each. After an hour and a half we are a bit disillusioned with
the batteries. Andy hears nothing from John Chuter this evening, but receives a
message from *Endurance:* 'To Lieutenant Simkins. Lots of love from family
Simkins.' All the crankers jeer and cheer. Andy smiles beatifically. 'Tomorrow
you must all work harder, and for two hours,' he says. This radio and hand
generating may become a major feature of our day if we are not careful. The
main bulk of the matter passed seems to be: 'Signy Island, Signy Island, Signy
Island, this is Elephant Island, Gibbs Island JSE, Do you read me? Over.' If
that takes one and a half hours cranking, we all dread to think what a 200-word
bulletin will require.

19 December, Sunday   We are all late again this morning, but not on
purpose. We struggle out towards ten o'clock (expedition time; nine o'clock
local). It is really my fault starting off the first evening working everyone until
late. Then last night we all started cooking after the radio finished at nine. So
tonight we will meet for our first Sunday service at 1730 and have supper
earlier. I transform my nasty old grey handkerchief into the O'Brien Blue
Maggot flag, tied to a broomstick and rammed into the snow by Jem's tent. He
claims he won the Golden Primus as the first to light up today, but accepts the
Blue Maggot as last pair out of the tent.

This morning there is again only a light breeze and layer cloud. Jem and
Andy are going up the central snow gully to the notch in the·summit ridge,
whence Tim will observe icebergs approaching from Bransfield Strait and the
South Shetlands. I go ahead on my own because I'm not too sure of the fit of my
crampons and want to prove them without holding anyone up. Also I want Jem
and Andy to get to know each other on a rope without the bother of a third man.
They are my only two real climbers in this party and haven't climbed together
before. The first ascent of O'Brien together would be a grand way to start a
climbing partnership. Up the gully I get on to ice with a run out over sloping
rock; suddenly realising I would prefer to have a rope, I grope up with iceaxe
and fingers and (almost) knees. The top is a notch with a hairlip of snow. On
the other side is a Grade IV ice gully, a near vertical chimney to the seashore
250 m below. Over it hang serried ranks of big icicles, vertical at their sturdy
bases, then flaring away because of the wind. In the vertical gullet of sea visible
between the walls of this gully I can see, 70 km off, the dark thumb of
Bridgeman Island, which was steaming and volcanic only a decade ago. Then I
move up left to a perch, and the vertical crack gives me a different peepshow:
the snow-covered hills of King George Island, over 100 km away, stand out
clearly. Sitting there, I look down the gully to watch the three coming·up. There
are some tremendous camera shots. Tim stays for an hour's observations on the
three or four bergs we can see. He will want a fixed rope here for other days
when he comes up alone.

Sleeping bags hang out to dry in camp; Jem and Andy appear on the skyline 300 m above, returning from the first ascent of the island. (CF)

Andy and Jem go back down the gully to a snow traverse, and then work their way out towards the summit. Later from the camp below we can see them climbing through up to the ridge. Later still they reappear, coming down the snowface of the corrie on the right of the two ice lobes. The face is over 300 m, without feature, so they look very exposed. When they reach camp they are elated, having made the first ascent of O'Brien Island 'without really meaning to', as they say. The way down had felt even steeper than it looked, because for the top 200 m it was faintly convex all the way, making them wonder what was to come below. It is for both of them the only first ascent they have ever made. Nowadays few climbers ever bag an unclimbed hill.

Three days ago Alan came to me rather concerned about my Sunday service, as he is an atheist. I am not religious myself but I want to mark Sundays this way here, so I asked him to come, to which he agreed easily. Now he stands with us, in a little circle on the snowslope outside our tents, with all the islands of the Elephant Island group set before us on the sea. We say first 'Our Father', then sing 'For all the Saints'. It is a strange and humbling feeling to hear our puny voices raised in song to no person here in this vast amphitheatre, and all the penguins silent. Then I say my prayer:

'Oh God. In these great places and these far flung islands, we recognise our own insignificance in the face of nature, and our puny weakness. Help us to realise also our strengths as human beings. Help us to realise our full potentials. Help us to help each other to the utmost of our abilities.

Now let us stand silent for half a minute to think together of our people at home, to wish them our love, and to think of all our friends, and particularly those on Clarence Island, to wish them safety and happiness.'

ALAN MILNE
I had thought not to attend, feeling that I would be intruding. Such a personal thing is no place for others who do not hold the same beliefs. But all are welcome, and I'm sure all enjoy and find important this basic, ill-sung, unselfconscious, moving little service. A group of eight raggedly attired men standing in the snow with the greatness of Antarctica around them. We all found ourselves reluctant to return to our tents. We padded about. Snatch of song. Odd snowball. Occasional insult. Prized company. Good.

After supper all crowd into our tent, each bringing his mug and coffee makings. Eight will just fit. We talk over plans. There is a lot here for us to do, on birds, botany, geology and collecting on the foreshore. The tide rips between here and Aspland are not friendly. The beach here is a dumper except at low tide; Aspland looked a little gentler and so offers a better chance of being able to get out when *Lindblad Explorer* arrives on 8 January. That chance we must not miss! Considering all these factors we decide to stay here until just after Christmas, then move over to Aspland. Jem says: 'This place knocks the Alps and Norway and all the rest into a cocked hat.' He is revelling in the snow climbing, botany and sea, all together. He is hooked, like me.

20 December   In the early hours snow patters on the tent, and slithers down in gobbets. But at eight I look out on a calm clouded day and we all emerge at nine (Frank wins the Blue Maggot flag by two minutes).

We go down to the beach, planning to paddle out briefly in the canoes as the sea is calm. First, we set to work to put all the canoes in order, adjusting seats and footrests and fitting rudders and so on. Four take one pair of canoes rafted together; Jem and I each paddle one; Tim and Andy share the fifth boat. We plan to spend an hour out, just to get the feel of canoeing in Antarctic waters, cold, with no help available, and with the thought of the big beasts in the water, the Leopard Seals and Killer Whales. We go out to the first little point, raft up there to check the drift and then head on towards the north-west survey point. Immediately we are in a following swell, screwing us awkwardly about. Jem finds it especially difficult; it is his first time alone in the back cockpit; the great length ahead of him seems to wallow uncontrollably. As soon as we get through into a calm patch beyond, we turn and go back to the beach with little trouble. The raft has simply circled us like a mother hen, with her little 4-hp outboard behaving very well. We talk it over: the little bit of swell was nothing in itself, but its sudden and unexpected presence was a disturbing lesson, and we all admitted that it was a very different feeling from canoeing around Britain. All the danger factors make one tense the whole time; the little swell off the point today

Our canoes share the beach with the Chinstrap Penguins; in the background is Eadie Island. (FM)

seemed far more dangerous than the big waves around Ramsey Island in Pembroke. It was too.

Frank and Alan set to work to make a fish trap out of wire netting and a stores box, hanging a nylon stocking bag of limpets inside. In the afternoon they lay a line of hooks baited with red penguin meat. I visit the little ternery just around the point and get mobbed by the irate parents with their lovely ash grey bodies and white cheeks, swearing at me while invisible on the scree underfoot their chicks freeze, some already away from the little scrapes of chippings which pass for nests. Coming back I see a Leopard Seal half asleep with his head sticking straight up out of the water, penguins in great profusion porpoise around him and he just slowly yawns his huge pink venomous yawn.

Up at the tents, I find Nick hanging up his clothes to dry. He and Tim were trying to get to the north-west around the cliff foot when a piece of rock came away in his hand, Nick pirouetted gracefully, yelled Geronimo, saluted the Queen, and fell 4 m into waist deep water. We call the place 'Nick's Leap Cove'.

Jem is excited because he has found a patch of mosses which looks unspoilt by penguins, and one of the three species looks different from any that Mossy Greene and BAS have shown him. He was collecting algae in the rock pools with Alan this morning, climbed the hill with Andy two days ago and wants a couple of days with a microscope to 'crack the botany' in this corrie. He has found time to browse around and locate three sites with different plant communities. He is proving one of our great strengths now: he does not push himself forward, and does not seem to be hyperactive, but comes out with good observations and advice, and is always alert and doing things.

With today's sunshine and thaw, the gullies overlooking our tents are throwing down rocks and icicles. Our tents are safe, but Frank and Alan's below is in an area of fresh rocks. I should have noticed. An hour ago Jem watched a great table sized chunk of rock career down the rotten gully, leap the little rock ridge, land on the boulders above their tent and shatter: one football sized fragment flew over the tent. One warning is enough. Chris and Jem start digging out a snow platform. I go back to the beach to tell Alan and Frank we will have to move their tent instead of bringing in the set lines. Nothing perturbs Alan, and Frank will never admit distress, so they come up and set about moving, dismantling their shelter wall of snowblocks and all the other trappings of a four-day campsite.

Tim and Andy come back having spent two hours putting a fixed rope up rotten rock under the frowning cliffs of 'Nick's Leap Cove'. While there, a great icicle fell on a group of penguins, killing one and maiming another. It's a tough life being a penguin, everyone is against you. Even us.

As I scrawl my journal late each evening I hear a few thin calls of Black-bellied Storm Petrels through the continual cackling of the Chinstraps. Tonight as I go out for a last pee before bed, I meet one little Black-belly flitting about and landing on the scree. I try to catch him to show Chris, but fail; back at the tent I am glad, Chris is already asleep.

21 December   The morning is cloudy, but hinting sun above. We have got into the swing of being up and out at nine o'clock. Chris and I slipped into an easy routine of one doing supper and the other breakfast. He is much better at cooking than I am. Most people are. This morning he produces breakfast while I lie useless in my bag, hoping that everything will go away.

Four of us go down to fish. Nick comes to film us. A flock of Cape Pigeons starts feeding in the waves breaking on the beach, so I get into a pair of waders and walk to and fro in the surf with Frank, towing a 3-m-long plankton net behind us. Rushing to and from the sea in my waders with my net and bucket feels just like an English seaside holiday, but I don't think the landladies of Eastbourne need fear the competition.

Chris, Frank, Alan and I go out in the raft to drop the trap with its marker buoy, and then to check the line and rebait the hooks. The sun is shining bright and beautiful on all the islands, but there are gusts of wind ruffling the surface from time to time, like a wire scrubber on butter, and from our seats in the water we can see the big waves of the tide rip outside glittering nastily in the sun.

It is a lovely scene with penguins porpoising around a few metres away. Cape Pigeons flutter in a flock all around us and a shag fishes actually between our twin bows. We start hauling up from the windward end. Frank soon gets two fish over 30 cm long, with great lumpy heads and big mouths, Antarctic Cod. He baits up the empty hooks with big fat limpets from the shore. We bring the far end aboard and haul back up to the windward end to take the whole line ashore. Incredibly, there are another six fish on the newly baited hooks: Frank seems to have a magic touch with the fishing. He has a dozen fish with his first

Top: A few non-breeding Adelie Penguins occasionally join the Chinstraps onshore. (FM)

Bottom: Cape Pigeons nest on the cliffs just above the canoes. (CF)

long line. Alan stays with him to examine and preserve the fish. We really need a work tent. Alan tries dissecting one or two fish for parasites, but (a) his hands get desperately cold; (b) the wind blows over a specimen bottle; and (c) a sheathbill attacks the fish, while he is rescuing another bottle from a penguin.

Chris and Nick come with me to try an upper route to the north-western end. There appears to be a reasonable route up a snow gully to 200 m, across a narrow traverse to another gully on to the summit ridge. It will be good for Nick and Chris to get back into the feel of crampons and iceaxe and using a rope. They are not climbers, and are not really keen on it. It will also be good for me to lead a climb for a change, even a Grade I gully like this. It proves to be just a straight gully with lousy snow and we climb together. On a couple of steeper sections we use a deadman and then an iceaxe belay as moral support and for practice.

Beside the little snow pathway of the traverse two fulmars are sitting on their nests. We eat oatmeal blocks standing beside them, they whicker a bit at first but then just sit sleepily: they are plump, soft, lovely birds, with a white velvet head, grey backs and a white belly, all as soft as an owl's feathers, and with the great dark gentle eyes of all the petrels. I think they are becoming my favourite birds here, in place of the Cape Pigeons. These bigger fulmars do not seem to squirt stinking yellow oil on you.

Lovely grey and silver Antarctic Fulmars nest all over the cliffs of O'Brien. (CF)

We come back down the gully to camp. Chris says: 'We have a food problem.'
'What?' I ask, rising to the bait. 'Too much,' he replies. We eat vastly: steak and
onions, mashed potato, peas, fruit pudding and coffee. Outside the Chinstraps
keep up their cackle, and above on the cliffs the fulmars coo like hoarse and
demented Collared Doves. I am at last up to date with my journal. So tonight I
have time to go out to look for the night birds, the storm petrels and the prions.
This evening I saw a prion flitting over the scree, so there is a chance of them,
and there are storm petrels about (I have seen them flitting and heard their calls
from the tent). It is difficult birds' nesting at night: on Elephant six years ago I
used my ears most of all. Here the cacophony of penguins is quite endless,
drowning lesser noises; also the fulmars' hoarse coos resemble the Wilsons
Storm Petrels' grating call, whilst their squeals resemble the piping of
Black-bellied Storm Petrels. At midnight I walk up into the foot of the central
snow gully until the cliff blots out the sound of penguins. There is a lovely
stillness in this placid gully. The occasional fulmar glides ghostlike across; once
or twice a Black-belly switchbacks around the cliffs; but evidently there are few,
if any, nesting up here. So I go down to the beach through the noisome
penguins, and clamber over the rockpoint. Around the corner over the scree flit
the little storm petrels, hither and thither, confusing the eye. One Black-belly
lands near me and enters a hole where piping shows its mate to be. I locate their
particular little chink in the unstable scree and pull out a fat little storm petrel
to prove to myself that it is a Black-belly. When I put him back at the hole he
scrabbles inside. I go back up to the tent well content. It is still light, though
dim. We have only just got to the island, and already it is midsummer's day,
and the days will start drawing in.

22 December   Each evening I wander around the tents, find out what people
are hoping to do next day, and gather a concerted plan which suits the majority.
Last night we agreed that Alan and I would go over the high route to the
northern tip of the island. This morning there is low cloud and little wind, the
barometer has been going slowly down and it has been thawing for two days;
the snow will be wet and sludgy, and there are rockfalls and icefalls down every
gully. Alan and I gather our climbing ironmongery and set off. For me this
consists of a chest harness, several slings and karabiners, crampons, iceaxe, ice
hammer (a new toy for me), a deadman and the rope; Alan brings the same, less
the rope and ice hammer. This is his first snow climb though he has been taught
to use an iceaxe; it is only my second time leading a climb, but Alan doesn't
know that! So for both of us this is exciting. We go up the gully to the same
traverse where the soft fulmars watch us, then into the next gully, which soon
broadens towards the top of the ridge. As it gentles off, I put Alan ahead for the
thrill of seeing over the ridge first. The actual ridge proves further than I
expected; Alan gets desperately tired kicking steps up through the heavy snow.
Finally we gain the crest of the ridge where we sit for a biscuit and a bar of
nutty. The thin cloud around us at last disperses, and we are sitting in a
wonderland, with a soft grey bed of cloud 300 m deep stretching flat over the
seas for kilometres in every direction. Out of this grey bed rise the top halves of

islands: far to the west a faint line of white hills is King George Island; across from us are Eadie and Aspland, then Mount Pendragon on Elephant; Mount Irving on Clarence peeps over the end of Gibbs. We go along the ridge, keeping 5 m back to avoid the cornice but not further: we are on a steeply tilted snowfield; in this weather anything can avalanche. Standing below the top of the northern sawtooth on the ridge we go up one at a time to touch the top of this, Alan's first First Ascent. The ridge of O'Brien, which we now see properly for the first time, is a fantastic ridge. The island lies in one steep slope as the rock beds fall from the south-west crests down to the north-east shores. The whole island resembles a single 50° segment of Dutch cheese cut and laid on its side with the steep rind facing south-west, but some of the beds are broken away and they also lie a little askew, so that at the upper rim the crest is a series of saw teeth. We are standing on one tooth and look past two more to the highest summit, almost separated from the ridge. The west side of the ridge drops sheer into the grey bed of cloud. Alan is as thrilled as I am to have achieved a first ascent, he cannot believe it possible that he, Alan Milne, is the first man ever to touch this lovely snow-covered tooth. As we stand excited, the crack of a rockfall comes muffled in cloud from the corrie below.

We drop back down the ridge; the way to the north-west is barred by great slab cliffs, so we return down to the corrie. For both of us it has been a wonderful day, with the sort of outlooks that one gets but once in a lifetime. As we take the rope off, Alan turns and shakes me by the hand: 'Thank you.'

We get back to camp to find that Andy has been cranking the hand generator since four o'clock with relays of helpers. At half past eight he contacts Signy. A great deal of 'Do you read?' and 'Short tuning call, one, two, three, four . . .' is followed by Signy relaying a telegram: 'To Lieutenant Andrew Simkins, love from family Simkins.' By ten o'clock, all we have got for six hours' cranking is a repeat of one telegram we had already received!

I am having to rethink our plans for Aspland. These last two days I have taken Chris, Nick and Alan up the hill. In my mind I had assumed that they would leap up and down steep snow like ibexes. Alan is as strong as an ox, but today he had to stop and pant every few metres climbing. He thinks it was because he was very tense, his legs rock hard with nerves. The sense of exposure on this island is great: although the slope is not particularly steep, there is no run out at the bottom. From the top at nearly 500 m the snowslope goes relentlessly and directly right down to the sea. This is one of the fascinations of it to me, to be climbing on snow with waves boiling cold over the mountain's feet. Frank is not keen on climbing, which leaves just Andy, Jem, me and Tim (who may be even slower than me). I now aim to cross to Aspland later, cutting down the time, in case only a few of us can climb up the first nasty ridge to reach the glacier bowl above.

I am eating like a horse now. I am not fit yet, and get cramp in my legs in the evenings. However, I am at least level-pegging on fitness with the others; only Andy and Jem seem fitter than me for hills. My boots are sodden, but comfortable, which is marvellous. My hands and fingers are tender, cracked and sore in a number of places but my rope burns from *Endurance* are nearly healed. My face is probably pretty brown by now, but is neither tender nor burnt. In fact all in all I am feeling physically pretty good, and after today's marvellous sunlit and meditative climb above the clouds I am mentally replete and happy. As midnight approaches it grows dim inside the orange tent. I need to light a candle, hoping not to awaken Chris who sleeps from ten each night. The box of matches must be damp, as they keep on going out. Finally I get the candle alight. Then the candle goes out. Slowly it dawns on me: lack of oxygen. I look across at my canary: Chris's bag rises and falls as he breathes. Thank God! I tear open the tent doors to get some ventilation. These Vangos have a waterproof flysheet and no ventilators: when windy they pump enough air, but not when calm. Take care!

ALAN MILNE
Shortly after closing my eyes there was a loud, deep, sharp crack from high up in the crags, followed by an absolute cessation of chatter by all the birds. Complete, expectant, alarming silence. Then the rumble of rockfall, low and distant, louder and closer, thunderous and by us, abating and halting. Scuffing glance of a small stone on the tent. Silence again. The only awareness one of alarm. The only evidence of alarm my heart beat, the force of which almost had me bobbing up and down. Then a new high in noise level from the birds, as always, the two qualities of sound; the cacophony of harsh chatter and screech from the penguins in the rookery around us, and the distant, wavering, high pitched swirl of sound from way up in the crags like a strong wind over far off high tops – vaguely eerie, and caused by the fulmars far above us. Then sleep, with the hope of a cold snap to replace the thaw.

23 December   The woolly hat worked wonders: I enjoyed my best sleep yet, only waking up briefly in the morning hours, whereas hitherto I have woken every hour from three, feeling cold. It is yet another day of low clag and little wind, but today the temperature is below freezing at last. Frank stays to reset his long line. Five of us visit the north-west end of the island. We head down to 'Nick's Leap Cove'. Beyond the fixed rope there is a fringe of rockshelf around the cliff foot. We slip and slide across rounded seaweeded rocks, dodging the waves. In this lovely clean area we meet a Weddell Seal at ease, asleep on the rocks; we cluster around the grey fat creature, its head snaky from the side and broad and doglike from above. Its breathing snuffles and hisses, as its nostrils flare and close. It rolls half on its back, and lifts one flipper, its head watching us warily. Now it humps and ripples its sleek streaked body into one of the rock pools and swims around watching us. We explore the area around the survey point; but we cannot go further round the shore.

Chinstraps here seem further ahead than in our own corrie, and I do a count of nests which confirms this. I am doing this once a day. At each nest I put my boot near the sitting bird's head; when it starts pecking at it, I grasp the bird by the tail and lift (sideways so that it does not shit in my eye) to see what is underneath it. The penguin thus taken by surprise lies still as if stupefied, with its beak in the filth and its flippers resting out on the ground; the position is most indignified but is the approved method to cause minimum disturbance. I sing out: 'First adult ON nest; second adult ABSENT; 1 egg; 1 chick', etc. I am very pleased with the method, which takes half an hour a day and gives a clear picture of the timing of the breeding, but it is a technique particular to penguins over the hatching period. The colony here by the survey point has chicks at 42 per cent of the nests while my study colony back in the corrie has chicks at only 10 per cent of nests. This represents three to four days' difference between the two colonies. It will be interesting to see if there are even bigger differences between O'Brien and colonies on Clarence Island. One penguin sits on her nest faithfully incubating an egg the size of a small thrush's, instead of a normal goose-sized egg. Jem suggests she has been raped by a sheathbill.

We head back to beat the tide. The east-going race is just starting through the straits. At one spot the standing waves come together each minute in a great boil of white water like milk boiling over, or a huge white carnation flower. Even from our clifftop viewpoint it is most impressive under the low roof of grey cloud; it would be no place for a canoe, or any boat.

Back at camp Nick deals out more goodies to eat. Our basic rations are of two kinds. About half are Royal Marine Arctic Rations, an excellent ration of 6500 calories per manday weighing 1.4 kg, mostly dehydrated. The other half are Compo rations, the standard Army field rations in cardboard cartons, containing lots and lots of tins. Each tent has a four-manday Compo box to last for two days. Compo contains about 3500 calories weighing 2.3 kg per manday, not quite enough for a man working hard in this climate. Sir Vivian Fuchs recommended 4100 calories, and the Services consider that 5000 is essential. So we have bulk rations to supplement the Compo: biscuit, eggpowder, flour, tinned fruits and vegetables, meats, herrings in sauces, pickles, chocolates, sugar and breakfast cereals. There is also an extra lot of goodies gathered by Alan Milne, including Dundee whisky cake, Aberdeen honey, peanuts, Fortnum and Mason Christmas puddings, etc. It is these two lots of goodies that Nick is dealing out. Chris and I have a special treat each evening: one piece each from a jar of mixed pickles: the astringent taste cuts like a white knife across our unwashed palates and is utterly delicious.

Andy has had us winding the hand generator since six o'clock. Suddenly at half past eight John Chuter comes on the air from Clarence. It is the first time we have heard him and it's great to hear they are all well. Two of their tents blew down in the 'storm of three days ago', but have been repaired. We did not have that storm, which is amazing just 100 km apart. They have several Pyramid tents; I suspect they may have had just two Vangos pitched and lost both. Having only our four Vangos until we reach Gibbs, we are concerned.

24 December   I have another good night in my woolly hat. Previously I had been taking off my outer trousers when I got into my bag, leaving on both pairs of stockings (to get dry) and longjohns, pants, string vest, shirt and sweater (to keep warm). Last night I just went to bed as I was, leaving my trousers on, using my anorak as a pillow. Chris starts making breakfast just before eight. He really is a good tent partner, no fuss, no bother, no annoying habits. We start with a packet of cereals from the bulk goodies, and powdered milk, then Compo bangers (five each today) and baked beans (½ kg between us). By half past eight we have finished eating and have a mug of coffee in hand. At nine we have a rush to avoid the Blue Maggot flag.

Andy and Jem are trying an icicle gully up from the beach, which offers a possible route to the east summit and the south-east end of the island. They will leave a fixed rope and Tim and I will follow up after helping to fish. This time Frank has seven fish on the hooks and one in the trap. These Antarctic Cod are sluggish fish, fat forward and tapering aft, with big gristly heads and upward-looking eyes. By the time we get back, Andy and Jem are sitting at the foot of the gully with their thumbs down: the icicles were brittle and there was nothing but more above them. It looks as if the only way to the south-east corner is take canoes and look for a beach.

Nick takes a raft with Chris, Tim and Andy. They leave two hours before low tide (when the east-going race will start), puttering away on the outboard, while I get penguin food samples. I choose a clean bird walking uphill from the sea, catch it with a quick scrabble, hold it by the tail with my left hand and hit the back of its neck a heavy blow with the shaft of my iceaxe backhanded with my right: the bird goes limp at the first blow. Then I take it down to the clean tidewashed pebbles on the beach to deal with. I cut up the belly through the tough skin and peel it back. The stomach now lies exposed: I extricate it, shaving away the membranes attaching it to the other viscera. While doing this I am now practised enough to have a quick look behind the kidneys to check whether it has two testes or one ovary: both today's specimens are females. I weigh the full stomach (about 300 g), slice it open, push the pink krill into a plastic bottle, weigh the remaining stomach and throw it to the sheathbills. The krill in the long upper stomach is fresh, pale and easily recognisable; that in the bulbous lower stomach is darker, and digested to look like fishpaste dotted with black eyes of krill. All the krill in these two are about 3 cm long. The bottles will go back to BAS at Cambridge, who will identify, count, and size the contents. I put a pencilled label inside the bottle with my specimen number, then fill it up with 9 per cent formalin. Next I measure the birds' culmen and flipper lengths. From these first two I take samples of muscle, liver and fat, screw them up in silver foil and put them into another smaller bottle with formalin; these samples will be analysed for organochlorines. Long before I have finished, the snow has started gently falling. Although there is little wind, it makes my hands cold sitting here working on the beach in the snow. Frank and Alan are having similar problems cutting up the fish, extracting stomachs and otoliths and measuring and counting fin rays. As Alan says: 'This really is taking science a bit far.' We need a work tent. As a bank of snow cloud pours through the straits between us and Eadie, the canoe party returns around the point, much to my relief. They met a big swell round the next point and were very glad to be rafted. Sitting low in a canoe, waves 2 m high are big ones, and quite frightening when they appear unheralded in empty freezing seas. They sensibly turned back, having found no landing beach. This means that we may be unable to get to the south-east. There is just one chance: Andy thinks he may have seen from the canoes a possible route, up the ridge and across the rockface.

6

Our Small Island: O'Brien

At this point the tides from the Atlantic and the Pacific meet, and in the strait (as on the outer coast) their meeting makes a commotion of whirlpools and combers that in a gale of wind is dangerous to canoes and other frail craft.
JOSHUA SLOCUM

24 December   A festive air is abroad. Someone has stamped out 'JSE, Happy Christmas' on the snowface of the headwall. Nick, Andy and Chris have built a snowman. The gently falling snow brings an olde worlde Christmas air to the whole scene. We even have an iceberg newly grounded opposite our corrie. After supper we gather in Chris's and my tent. It has been a bit frustrating being unable to get all round the island, so we now plan to leave for Aspland on the 29th, if the weather allows. I bring out the map to gather names for the features we have explored. To give names to places never named before is one of the pleasures of exploring. Tonight we are not inspired: 'Camp Corrie', 'Fortune Summit', 'Nick's Leap Cove', 'Long Line Bay' and 'The Rip' go down, but little else.

Tomorrow we will have a holiday, though our 'official Christmas' feast will be in February when we meet the Clarence party. Here Nick plans a sports day, building a toboggan run for polybag races. The penguins are evidently in for a busy day, with sheepdog trials, penguin three-legged races and egg and spoon races.

Frank wistfully talks of his family going to midnight mass. Tonight especially we are all thinking very much of home and family. Faye in Australia will have put Ralf and Paul to bed hours ago. Very soon they will wake up, remember it is Christmas morning, pull up their stockings from the end of the bed and open things one by one, rustling the paper while the grown-ups sleep. At a quarter to midnight six of us gather outside Jem's and Tim's tent and sing carols. The bright light from Andy's Tilley lamp falls on the trodden snow and more flakes drift gently down. The grounded iceberg glimmers wanly in the dusk.

25 December   Last night we gave the Blue Maggot flag to the snowman and now we all oversleep like hibernating bears. As we start cooking breakfast there is a jangling outside and cries of 'Oh, ho, ho, Happy Christmas children; this is Father Christmas with your Christmas goodies.' We look out, eyes screwed against the light on several centimetres of fresh snow. Nick is dressed up in red anorak, with beard and eyebrows of cotton wool stuck on with raspberry jam, jingling a belt load of karabiners and dishing out goodies (a whisky cake, a tin of

herrings-in, a bar of chocolate each and a tin of coffee). Andy is filming him.
Nick goes on to the next tent with his cries of 'Oh, ho, ho' unimpaired, but one
white eyebrow lost in the snow.

All go up to dig a cresta run for the polybag races, while I take the
opportunity to photograph sheathbills hanging in the wind in a display flight
and to catch up on writing. The cresta run is such fun that nobody can possibly
think I am being lazy; so this is a better time to catch up than when we are
sorting out stores, or something tedious like that. I do get a couple of runs
though, following two penguin volunteers.

Today is colder than the previous soft week, with a raw wind blowing below
stratus at 300 m. The straits between us and Aspland are torn with white even
at slack water. This is actually the first day that the temperature has not risen
above freezing at all.

26 December   I wake at four in the morning with the tent rattling and
flapping in the wind, and hear the sifting sound of fine snow on the flysheet. I

The snowman is dimly visible beyond the lower tents. In cold weather there are fewer
rockfalls from the cliffs above. (FM)

am cold, and rather damp. At half past eight, the wind is still blowing and fine cold powder snow is drifting around the tents. It is a day to fester in one's tent, and fester we all do. Forced out at midday by nature I take my camera down to the beach. The sea is white all round the point. The canoes are safe, covered with snow among the penguins. Whether my blizzard photographs will come out is problematical: I have to hold the lens cap on with one gloved hand until the last moment, then whip it off, point the camera without the (misted) viewfinder and press the shutter release wildly. Many penguins are buried in snow on their nests now. Those that are may be better off than those only half drifted up. There must be a lot of chicks dying from wet and cold.

27 December   Today is a cold, claggy day with the odd speckle of snow, but little wind. It is raw. The penguins are cold and wet and miserable; by the end of the day they are very dirty indeed. In these conditions I feel sorry for the messy little brutes. However, walking through a pinky brown slurry of melted snow and shit, penguins splattering ahead and throwing up gobbets of cold wet filth with their flippers, soon cures me of sympathy!

This evening we change round tent partners. Chris has moved up with Nick to get the cine directors together and Andy has moved in with Jem to plot climbing routes on Aspland. Tim has moved in with me: he has already organised everything differently and cooked supper. Once I had rescued my hoard of peanut butter I was happy with the new arrangements!

A young Elephant Seal dozes on the snow. I find them hard to sex, but I think this is a cow. (DM)

Tomorrow we plan to leave for Aspland. We have to leave at 0630, an hour before low water, when the east-going tide race begins. This journey is probably the most dangerous bit of the whole expedition.

28 December   I wake with Jem and Tim saying it is half past four. My bag is fixed round my neck tightly and the string is round the back; with my mind asleep, it takes over a minute to extricate myself and look out. The sea has gone down a little but there is cloud, some snow and an unusual wind coming into the corrie from the east. The weather has an unsettled feel about it. I decide not to go today. Jem goes round telling the other tents. We all relapse into sleep with that strange mixture of sybaritic relief and renewed frustration which always follows such decisions. The weather this forenoon supports the decision. There are many whitecaps on the water; black snow squalls cross the sea, but strangely do not penetrate this secluded little corrie. Still the sun is there in patches and the top of O'Brien is clear, so I decide we will climb O'Brien, in four pairs. As we don our climbing knitting and ironmongery, I find that Chris Brown has a two-hour repair job to do on his snow gaiters, so I resign myself to wait, while the others go off, first Andy and Nick, then Jem and Alan and last Tim and Frank.

Chris finally finishes a craftsman's repair job and we set off up the gully and across the traverse above the corrie headwall. However, by the time we meet Andy and Jem returning it looks as if we will be very late back. I get up to

Older bull Elephant Seals like this smelly couple are quarrelsome but idle. (GT)

within a rope's length of the ridge, when it starts snowing and looking black. As we've passed the steeper bits I feel honour is satisfied and turn back to avoid being caught out in a blow. An hour later we are half-way down, the sun is shining on all the islands, and I wish that I had gone on to that lovely ridge with the foreshortened, snow-plastered teeth.

Today's tromp up the hill confirms that Andy and Jem are our only climbers. Tim turned back quite early, disliking the snow on rock sloping outwards to the corrie below. He was right to turn back when unhappy; nevertheless, it means that I am our third climber, and I am a professional coward on the crag. On the other hand, Nick and Alan tromped up and down happily and look like being good seconds here. Chris was slow but forced himself to do things which frightened him; so the spirit is willing. Frank remains an unknown quantity.

29 December At five o'clock Alan and I wake simultaneously and decide that it is windy, cold, snowy and claggy. So we stay here another day. Andy, Nick, Tim and I try yet another way to the south-east end, up the scree and rock of the ridge beyond the beach. Andy goes happily up the first bits of rock, and Nick follows him well. All the rock on O'Brien slopes downward at a quite gentle angle of $37\frac{1}{2}°$, but it is rotten, like a heap of burnt books. Over the rock on our route lies a layer of earth and small scree fragments. There is nothing trustworthy to step on or hold. We go back down.

If we had to spend another month here, we would get out of our little area one way or another, but it really is hemmed in. The corrie was invisible from *Endurance*, being secluded from the sea. It is also very sheltered from the winds, from all directions. Often we look up to see clouds scudding over, and look down to see white horses everywhere, whilst here we have just a gentle Force 3. It is like a little world of its own, rather a small world, albeit with a fantastic outlook. But we are getting a little bit bored with it. Anyhow I am, and I can at least go on studying penguins. The others have finished their work.

30 December At a quarter past five it is claggy, but I can just see Aspland and the wind is light. I reluctantly admit there is a chance of going, which means I have to get up. Now wearing the shiny garb of leader, I make myself get into boots, grab a bar of chocolate to stiffen my willpower, and go down to overlook the sea. There is some surf on the point, but the beach looks reasonable. So I wake everyone with hearty cries. We will be packed up at seven and take to the water by eight. Shortly thereafter the cloud thickens so that I cannot even see the iceberg half-way to Aspland. Tim has made breakfast in a flash, then we pack up, determined to be on time.

I am first away. The journey down is very slippery, then I paddle through the noisome pink and brown quagmire of the beach colony to arrive at the canoes and drop the pack thankfully on to the dirty pebbles. Tim arrives carrying our flysheet: it is covered with penguin excreta, mud and feathers, very wet and quite disgusting. Apparently it fell off my pack. I wash it in the cold sea. We get the canoes down on to the shingle at low tide. It is five to eight; we still have to load the canoes, and the easterly tide-race is due to start at nine.

Andy joins Jem at a belay on the headwall of the corrie. (FM)

Frank stands looking out to sea. 'There's a lot of white horses just outside the bay,' he says. Nick looks at the sea and at me quizzically and adds: 'It's worse than when we got soaked on that recce.' They are right. The cloud was cleared by wind, and the wind is raising the waves again. I change my mind and say we are not going after all. Everyone looks rather relieved. Nick suggests we load the canoes for practice and everyone sets to with a will. Taking our packs back up to the recently vacated campsite, we pitch the tents again, and finally get in for a brew at one, seven and a half hours after I looked out this morning.

After supper we have a summit brew in Tim's and my tent. We will go for Aspland the first possible day up until and including 5 January, even though that would only give us two days there before *Lindblad Explorer* arrives to mother us to Gibbs on 8 January.

31 December The swell is still there, and the weather looks unsettled with line squalls under clouds. We agree that we cannot go today. Instead Nick and Chris film some climbing sequences on one of the ice lobes on the corrie headwall.

The evening is so brilliantly sunlit that people are stripped to the waist washing the old year off. I am about to join them, when I trip over the side guy of Jem's tent and there is a tearing noise from the flysheet. Suddenly the lovely evening feeling of contentment vanishes. I feel clumsy and guilty; our tents are so important, and so vulnerable. Jem utters not a word of reproof or complaint, but quietly mends it, and makes nothing of it. He is proving to be straight gold.

Tim has had his best day yet observing icebergs, with several marching about in our straits, around Gibbs and up towards Elephant. Tim and I are getting on well in the tent, and I hope this period will make life on the expedition more relaxed for him.

The penguins have nearly all hatched now and the chicks are growing at a tremendous rate. We found the first chick two weeks ago, and already some are so big that their parents cannot really brood them. Their plaintive cheeping calls can be heard amongst the gaggling of the adults as I walk through the colony. Individual adults sound like a duck or a Pink-footed Goose; collectively their noise is like a big rookery or a big flock of geese, or sometimes like the sea's surge on rock (when heard from the tops, hundreds of metres above). In contrast, the Cape Pigeons and fulmars are still incubating eggs. Tonight is Hogmanay. I have a bottle of Highland Cream given to us by Teacher's. We will celebrate at 2200. Alan and Frank have set out small eats down the middle of their tent. There is a pot brewing at the far end, with Alan gleefully dispensing hot water, lemon crystals and Aberdeen honey to make toddies with the whisky.

ALAN MILNE
We were all strangely quiet at first. All with our own thoughts. A story would be told. Laughter. Short silence. Another story. Frank dispensed the whisky, oh! so carefully in the bottle top, while I prepared the toddies.
'May I offer a toast, gentlemen? To those at home whom we would wish to remember kindly.'
Glasses raised.
'To those at home!'

1 January 1977   At seven the day looks hopeful, apart from a light wind: grey, but without white horses. This time everyone is much quicker and by eight most are outside their tents. I go down the scree to overlook the bay, and don't like the wind very much, nor the grey weather. I delay the decision until nine o'clock, then decide: 'not today', cursing myself for not having gone yesterday. With hindsight we could have made it. Our alternative plan is to climb the east summit by the gully. Andy and Jem start out ahead to avoid a queue at the foot of the steep ice pitch. Forty minutes later Nick and I follow them, and then Tim and Chris. Today it is all clag and coldness up there. Nick and I rope up to traverse the snowslope. Twenty m to our right the snow ends; beyond is only cloud. We can hear penguins down there, but can see neither them nor the sea far below. When we reach the foot of the gully, a dim shape far up above shouts down with Jem's voice: 'It's not worth it, all steep brittle ice; you'd best go back.' Looking at the sloping floor of the gully, 2 m wide, with a dark grey veneer of ice overlying uncertain rock, I am almost glad. Nick and I sit in a little snow scoop nest beside the foot of the gully for half an hour drinking tea from his thermos, eating dextrosol from the corners of my pockets, taking a few dim photographs of each other with cloud-shrouded rock and snow behind, and watching the icechips dislodged by Jem and Andy scuttering down the gully and the snowslope to drop into the cloud. Then we go back down. Looking

Top: *O'Brien Island from north-east* (CF). Bottom: *Eadie Island from east* (CF).

'Top: *Camp on Eadie Island* (FM). Bottom: *Summit of O'Brien Island from north-west* (CF).

The grounded iceberg lies half-way across to our planned landfall on Aspland Island. In the distance is Elephant Island. (FM)

up the gully as I sit at its foot belaying Nick, I see the two dim human silhouettes are still on the same steep exit pitch.

Back at camp, we can just see enough sea to make out white horses in the tide rip, before snow arrives and hides the water. I feel vindicated in deciding not to go. We have now decided that we must split into two parties as soon as we get to Aspland. Andy, Jem, Nick and Alan will form a climbing party on Aspland; Chris, Frank and Tim will be in my ology party on Eadie. The snow continues. I relapse into my tent to mend my snow gaiter zip, ending up with eight dainty little white cord bows down the back: I feel I should ring bells or do a Morris dance. I then shave painfully, kneeling over my mess tin in the tent porch. I am the only one who plans to shave: Alan's beard will be grizzled grey; Frank's will be woolly; Andy's will be wispy, like mine; I wonder if Nick's will be smoothly wrinkled, like his hair. Come to think of it, I haven't seen Nick's hair for a fortnight: he keeps his woolly hat on both in and out of bag.

2 January 'Festering' is the traditional word for an expedition's activities when the weather is filthy. And that is what we are doing at midday. We abandoned hope of canoeing after Andy had taken our Sunday service, while the wet snow blew in from the bleak sea.

The snowslope up from the beach with its parallel lines of muddy penguin paths running up like furrows on a field has almost gone now, thawing to reveal the scree. There are always penguins moving up and down this slope, mostly down in the morning, mostly up in the evening, both ways through the middle of the day. Last time on Elephant we counted Chinstraps moving to and fro for all of one twenty-four-hour day, showing that their normal routine was for one of the pair to go to sea in the forenoon to forage, coming back at lunchtime to take over, while the other went down for the afternoon's hunting, returning at night; both adults roosted at the nest. This was unexpectedly short for a foraging trip, as Adelies and Gentoos and other penguins studied are thought to go to sea for two or more days at a time. Here off O'Brien we can always see rafts and crowds and smaller parties of Chinstraps fishing in the tidal eddies, which suggests close-range foraging as at Elephant. As Nick says, the penguin chicks are growing so fast that it looks as if someone is pumping them up with a bicycle pump (actually their parents pumping krill into them). The stomachs of the adults I have taken have been stuffed with over 200 g of pink krill. Feeding that amount twice daily to two chicks (starting at under 100 g) is bound to build them up quickly.

This constant traffic of penguins to and from the sea is difficult to make sense of as a casual watcher, but when you look carefully you can see the clean birds walking purposefully uphill, flippers held back and head forward nodding solemnly with each little stride, while down from their spell on the nest lollop dirty brown penguins. As I walk down again to fetch another day's rations from the beach there is a constant scutter before me of penguins not on their nests, while those on their nests open their beaks and crane their necks towards me to get a peck at my gaitered legs. The fleeing penguins soon accelerate from a purposeful walk to hopping; when they are hard pressed they go down on their bellies, scrabble with their feet on each side and work their flippers alternately like forelegs to toboggan along really very fast. This alternating action with the flippers is interesting because, when swimming, they work both flippers in synchrony. Going down the furrowed snowslope on their besmirched white bellies they work up quite a speed; then they jab their beaks down into the snow, and pirouette around them until they stop, the perfect iceaxe braking action. Gentoo Penguins have a waddling run which is their first stage of acceleration, and they seldom hop; Chinstraps on the other hand never run but instead have a lolloping hop with one leg leading like an interrupted canter.

I doze for an hour in the afternoon. When I wake the sky has cleared and it is my turn to wind the hand generator for half an hour. We are trying to make radio contact with Signy for the first time since Boxing Day. First Andy receives Clarence clearly: they are all well and plan to move to Chinstrap Cove as soon as the weather clears. Andy raises Signy and finally gets across our very first message out, saying we are all safe and well, still at O'Brien and waiting to go to Aspland.

7

The First Antarctic Canoe Voyage: Eadie Island

The dreamers of the day are dangerous men, for they may act their dreams with open eyes, to make it possible.
T. E. LAWRENCE

3 January   At half past seven the weather and sea look good. Soon we are all moving about: first a quick porridge and hot chocolate drink. I collect some of Andy's radio gear and take it down to the beach with my pack. The sea is quite quiet on the beach. I head back up to find Tim has struck our tent and the others are well on their way. I am growing taut inside thinking of the canoeing to come. Andy and I will be paddling Mischief, with the other six divided between the two rafts. In the back of my mind lurks a Leopard Seal nearly as big as the canoe; it suddenly surfaces alongside and inspects me with its cold eye as a prospective meal. The hour's journey is a more dangerous venture than anything we have done hitherto: the first canoe journey ever made in the Antarctic.

We carry the boats down the storm beach to the flatter pebbles exposed now at low tide. It is ten to ten, and we have forty minutes to load and lash down the equipment and man the boats. That dress rehearsal the other day was worth it, for now everyone is doing something useful. We are ready on time. The weather is still good, with no white horses, some sun patches through the stratus cloud, and just a little wind from the east. I am dressed in socks, climbing boots and snow gaiters, longjohns and overtrousers, vest, zipped wetsuit waistcoat, shirt, sweater, buoyancy aid and cagoule, wetsuit helmet and wetsuit mittens. Andy has a towel wrapped round his neck. Three of the raft crews are wearing rubber waders, waterproof up to the waist, which we have found invaluable for landing and putting to sea in the rafts. We put Tarka and Bilbo Baggins' bows into the water and bring down Scaf and the James K. Caird. Then while the raft crews get into their cockpits, Andy and I get into Mischief lying up dry on the beach with her bows pointing down towards the waves.

We do up our spraydecks carefully. We are ready, at last, after six days of waiting, and there is no Leopard Seal in sight. We heave Mischief down the beach, each with a paddle in one hand and the other hand knuckling the beach. A little hesitation in small surf, and we are afloat and heading out through waves, which seem bigger and more loppy than they had done from the shore. The two rafts sort themselves out and start their engines. Now we are off, with Mischief leading an arrowhead. The rafts are close, so we can hear their engines sometimes, and I can just see them by craning my head around precariously.

But as I follow Andy, paddling right, left, right, left, right, left, swinging from the waist and pushing forward with the top arm, it seems as if we are in a world of our own. Mischief rides the swell easily. As we leave the shore the waves get more regular and easy.

We expect the 4 km will take us an hour. First we head for the iceberg aground off the Eadie reef, which is half-way. If we are set towards the rip we will head up eastward of the berg, but if all is well I will go between the berg and Eadie, and then along past Eadie to Aspland. As we get nearer, the clear blue of the berg gets higher and higher. It looked small from O'Brien, but now it looks like a vast white ship as the swell runs along its skirt. We never approached a berg in 1970, but this one looks so peacefully grounded that it must be safe, so we pass it within 100 m, through a crowd of Chinstraps and Cape Pigeons feeding in the eddy behind it. The penguins porpoise around us: it is their world. We have passed the point of no return; if we sight Killers now, we will head for the nearest part of Eadie towering above us a kilometre to port, rather than back to O'Brien far astern.

Now my hands and arms are getting very stiff and aching: the wetsuit mitts slip on the paddle shaft, and their thickness means my fingers are gripping something larger than the ideal 38 mm. I'm glad when Andy admits that he feels the same. I don't want to go through the reef which runs out from the spit because from O'Brien we could usually see breaking water there. We get slowly closer, searching for some way through the rocks ahead, girding the shore. There seems to be just one way in, to a little beach below the snowslope.

I wave my paddle toward this beach. The Tarka/Bilbo raft passes us and heads in to the tiny beach; we follow. As we come in, surf seems to build up from nothing. We hit the beach slope and start to be dragged back, slewing broadside to the next wave, but I jam a paddle into the gravel and Andy jumps out with the bowrope. We are ashore dryshod! It is a marvellous feeling. We have made it! Alan, Frank and Nick are hauling their raft up as we haul out Mischief, all of us laughing and exulting. The Scaf/James K. Caird raft follows us in. As they arrive the swell seems to increase: they hit the beach but the following wave swamps the James K. Caird. Two of us stand with our feet dug into the gravel and our knees braced against the hull, so she does not drag back. Alan brings a bucket, and I start baling furiously, but every wave fills her up again. Meanwhile the others cut the lashings and remove the packs, until at last we can roll Jimmy Caird over to empty the hull, and carry her up the beach. The gear is scattered up the beach, which ends in a 5-m wall of snow at high tide. Above that wall, the snowslope leads up into the sky. It has taken us just over an hour to make the first Antarctic canoe voyage, and another half hour to land. My boots are full of cold water and gravel.

Jem, Chris and I walk along the beach to look at the spit and likely campsites, while the others start sorting out boats and gear. I had thought that the beach was small. Now I find it spacious; there are many parts clean, and free of penguins. On the wide rockshelves Weddell Seals loll around, and a few small Elephant Seals snort defiance as we pass. There is a big beach beyond the spit, and a good place to park the canoes. It really is a nice place, quite different from

Top: Andy and I in Mischief approach the iceberg half-way to Aspland Island. The lens is wet and I am paddling badly, but it is the first Antarctic canoe journey. (FM)

Bottom: Eadie Island (450 m) looks daunting from our landfall on Aspland Island. *Endurance*'s helicopters had found only one beach, to the right through 'The Narrows', where the snow gullies come down from the shoulder. (JB)

the nasty, penguin-trampled, mucky little place I had expected. We could have lived here more happily than on O'Brien.

Jem, Andy, Alan and Nick will pitch camp here tonight and attempt the summit tomorrow. The other four of us are going to canoe over to Eadie in one raft as soon as possible to camp for two nights. First we carry the other three canoes and gear 300 m along the beach to the spit, traipsing to and fro while the Aspland party starts digging out a tent platform on a snowslope just above the beach. Tim has gone along the shore to the narrows between Aspland and Eadie to check the tide. We must shoot these narrows to reach the only beach that *Endurance*'s helicopters could find on Eadie last year. He returns: the gap is 20 m across, with a submerged rock in the middle; there is a swell there now and the east-going stream is pouring through with overfalls. High tide is at eight and Tim expects the current to turn at six; I plan to force our way through against the last of the flood.

At high tide the beach on Eadie disappears as the sea reaches the tent. An iceberg lies grounded off 'Cape Moonlight' as we set off up the gully above camp. (CF)

We stack our gear on to the Tarka/B. Baggins raft. This time I am in the port aft cockpit of the raft, which means I steer and run the engine. We put out at four and approach the gap. As it looks all right I open the engine wide: we shoot through almost before we know it, although Frank and Chris get soaked in the front cockpits, which seem very low in the water, with the carrying handles submerged most of the time. On the other side is a lovely big bay. The cliffs of Aspland stretch away to starboard, and the rocky shores and screes of Eadie to port. We motor slowly along the Eadie shore looking for the beach: it does not look promising so we go on to the stack where the cache is. There is nowhere there to land, so we go back to the recommended place, see a hopeful opening in the rocks and go in. We arrive in a tiny harbour protected by rocks and a little reef. Frank and Tim in waders unload over these rocks.

We pull the raft over the rocks on to a tiny patch of shingle, all pinky white with penguin excrement. There is a little sloping patch of icy snow, which looks good for one tent only. We level it, pitch a tent for the four of us, and have a brew of coffee. Now at seven o'clock we set off clockwise around the shore to see how far we can get. After an hour we find ourselves baulked by sheer cliffs at the icefall on the south-east shore. All round the coast the Chinstraps cackle and peck; I would like to find a Macaroni colony for a change. Arriving back at ten o'clock, we cook up a hoosh supper of Royal Marine Arctic: very welcome indeed at the end of a wonderful day.

A full moon rises over the north-western cape of Aspland as midnight approaches. The snowcap on the cape is invisible against the neutral grey sky, so there appears to be a gap between the black rocks of the cape and the top half of the moon. It is a lovely sight, the peak of Aspland 734 m high across the bay, clear, cool and pale in the night: lovely in itself, but especially to us after waiting to see it for so long.

4 January   The day is fine and the sun is on the tent when we leave to climb Eadie. We clamber up the scree gully. Soon after reaching the snow, the gully suddenly opens to our left, leading up to the summit ridge, a broad highway of snow at about 45° through the desperate rock. We don crampons and slide up right on to the shoulder where I had wanted the cache. It proves to be a lovely flattened shoulder of snow, with a party of fulmars sitting and also some moss. Our altimeters agree it is about 300 m.

We traverse back to the gully across a band of snow. I don't want to rope up now, because it will take much longer to get up, and because I want the psychological benefit of roping up when we start the narrow snow arêtes I fear on the summit ridge. Frank follows along the steep little traverse happily, but Chris and Tim take a great deal longer. Their speed won't matter today: but on longer climbs and glacier crossings on Elephant, it would handicap us. I had been overimpressed by Tim's paper qualifications and the personal climbing clobber jingling round his waist.

Frank leads on up the central gully while I wait for Chris and Tim. Now we follow up Frank's ladder of steps kicked into the snow; it is perfect névé, allowing him to kick firm steps with one swing of the boot, sinking it in so that only the heel stands proud of the slope. The gully goes on for a long time, steepening as we reach its head. The twin lines of Frank's toe-holes extend from him down past Chris, to me and Tim below me, and on down over 150 m to the corner where our little traverse joined the gully: the gully goes straight down to the sea 400 m below us. The slope eases off. We are on the col between the delicate fingered east ridge and a gentle slope up on our right. We walk up this slope to find ourselves on the summit platform! Where is the desperate corniced ridge crest? One by one we clip on and walk on to the summit belayed from below. As we munch our lunchtime nutty, the cloud thins out except on the top 300 m of Aspland above us. We rope up and go down the southern ridge to look down on 'The Rip'; O'Brien's two summits look dead level against the horizon. To the west we can make out the long yellowish white line of King George Island and Chris points out the dim grey cone of Bridgeman Island, faintly visible beyond O'Brien. South of O'Brien and to the westward whole squadrons and flotillas of icebergs proceed. Looking back up, our summit is a high bulge of sugary ice overhanging a cliff we cannot see, but which we know goes down to the sea, where the watery sun glints 450 m below.

We go back over the summit, and down the long gully. Once again Tim comes last, painstakingly searching for each toehold, while the rest of us just kick our own ladders down. Then we traverse across and rest on the shoulder in the faint sun, hoping that Aspland will tear through its thin veil of cloud, and that we will see four tiny dots on its hoary heights far above us. The cloud persists, so we go down a scree slope of stone chips and slivers, soft like bark peelings in a sawmill tip. It goes on down over 100 m to a little gallery of stable rocks hanging above the north-western penguins. This gallery has tiny swathes of green moss carpets between the boulders: it more pleasantly resembles an English garden than anywhere else so far. On the rocky outcrops in the surrouding scree fulmars nest in crowds, squealing their mad cries and nibbling gently at my hand as I lift their soft bodies. They are still brooding eggs. In the middle of this little gallery a pair of skuas quack and fly. They do not dive-bomb in the skuas' spectacular fashion, but hover over our heads and stand on the rocks calling. One of them lands on Chris B's shoulder complaining while their chick walks about calling in a squirrelly whistle.

After filling a polybag with mosses and lichens for Jem, we head on down into a clifftop Chinstrap colony, looking for a way to the cache of food we can see on the flat stack below, in a gap in the penguins. We search for the penguins' ladder up to this clifftop colony and finally find the one trackway up the rocky slope. The track is over a metre wide and nearly as deep in the middle, up a 15-m ramp. It has been worn into the rock by the feet of generations of penguins. As we go down, the evening rush of homecoming commuters is thrown into confusion. This narrow track is the reason the little green gallery has remained untrampled by the Chinstrap hordes. We go back along the shore to the tent, to cook supper and a brew.

What a wonderfully complete and satisfying emotion, to canoe to an unexplored island, to land on the only beach, and then to make the first ascent of a fairytale summit. Let's hope they climbed Aspland too!

We meet our first fierce nesting Brown Skua; defending its chick, it attacks Chris Brown. (FM)

5 January   The day starts grey and fairly calm, hopeful for getting back across to Aspland. Chris goes off for two hours' geology along the shore, while Tim, Frank and I pack up, and load the raft. By eleven we are ready. Chris returns very pleased, with a piece of pinkish rock in his hand: it is a lens of igneous rock in the metamorphic schists. This indicates that the metamorphic rocks are probably of igneous rather than sedimentary origin, which is still a controversial point. It is fun having specialists to breathe meaning and excitement into every chunk of pink rock.

While loading the canoe we have watched a Leopard Seal killing a penguin offshore. This is always a slow, cold process. The Lep's big head appears out of the water, then comes a thrashing splash as the penguin is thrown across the surface. The same cruel performance is repeated deliberately time after time until the skin is flayed off the meat and the seal can crunch the carcase, while

On land the Leopard Seal is remarkably helpless because its flippers are folded palm inward. In the water it is a totally different matter. (FM)

the Kelp Gulls and Cape Pigeons flutter round for the leavings. The Wilsons Storm Petrels also gather round for scraps, but the Antarctic Fulmars pay no attention at all. That is an ordinary death. What makes this particular one so incredible is the shoal of penguins madly porpoising round and round the Leopard as he kills. The water around him is broken by penguins, as sprats fly from mackerel. Why do they do this?

We launch the raft. This time I go in a bow cockpit to inspect the cliffs of Aspland, as we motor towards 'Cape Moonlight'. As we forsake the shelter of Eadie we meet a lumpy swell coming in from the south-west and building up against Aspland. The raft is stable, but the canvas between the two bows fills with water and the weight digs the bows in, so that both are often submerged and the craft feels sluggish as she meets the seas. Frank and I in the front are not too happy, and we signal Tim to turn back for 'The Narrows'. I signal 'rudder orders' to Tim (unsighted behind the deck cargo) by waving an iceaxe. This routine is slow and cumbersome, as we head into 'The Narrows' slewing a bit, but then we straighten, and luckily so, because immediately on the other side we strike through a couple of big waves which drench Frank and me in the front. We realise later that the east-going current must have started sooner than Tim expected, and that we had hit a couple of standing waves or haystacks on the downstream side of the rapids.

Leopard Seals prey on penguins and young Crabeater Seals. (70/71 John Hunt)

I know of a sheltered little beach closer to the spit, with a narrow channel through the 100-m fringe of rocks. As we motor along outside the rocks, the freshening south-west wind is building up a lumpy sea and there are boils of white water between the black teeth. It is very exciting, but somehow not frightening. We wish Nick was on shore to take a cinefilm of us coming in, as it probably looks quite spectacular. We would certainly never have tried this way in without having seen it from the shore. As we near the entrance I can see a 20-m gap looking clear of breaking water or submerged rocks, and wave my iceaxe into it, although I cannot yet see any beach. Once in, there will be no room to turn around. Tim responds perfectly. In no time we are through the gap; there is no great surge of surf up the sluiceway, just a gradual quietening down, until at the far end we arrive gently at a tiny little beach.

We unload the raft and put everything above the high-water level. Then grasping the two tents and our packs we walk around the spit to put the tents up before anything else. The wind is still freshening. Rounding the corner we see the two tents of the Aspland party end to end behind a snow wall. A couple of sleeping bags hang over one tent to dry. It is nearly one o'clock now, but at first no one is in sight. Then, as we get nearer, Jem and Nick hear us and look out. They look tired. 'Did you make it?' we all ask. 'Come in and have a brew,' they say, 'and we'll tell you about it.'

8

'Mount Jubilee': Aspland Island
Jem Baylis

Mad! Mad! Mad!
GLADSTONE

4 January   We hatched out of our sleeping bags that morning with a feeling of confidence and optimism which was really hardly justified. Over the previous three weeks the east summit of O'Brien had repulsed all our attempts, snow conditions had never been ideal and the weather had shown itself to be capricious, averaging between bad and bloody. Nevertheless, with only three and a half days at our disposal, here we were preparing to climb a peak which had looked formidable from O'Brien on the few occasions when it had been visible, and without a thought of failure between us.

As we stumbled around the tents, sorting gear and occasionally dipping a spoon into the communal pot of beans and spam, we had to select an approach route. There appeared to be three possibilities: we could thread our way up through the highly unstable looking seracs immediately above our campsite and thence into the great snowbowl beneath the summit ridge; we could canoe along to the east end of the island and so reach a gently sloping snowfield which gave access (we hoped) to the main ridge; or we could reach this same snowfield by walking along the beach. By the time we were ready to go, the temperature warranted shirt sleeves and knotted hankies: any enthusiasm we might have felt for hide-and-seek amongst the seracs evaporated. The canoes were still full of gravel after our undignified landing the previous day and would have taken time to get ready. So when we finally set out across the small glacier behind the tents, it was with the intention of getting down on to the beach at the first possible opportunity.

We set off in two ropes, Andy and Alan first, followed by Nick and myself. Crossing the glacier snout was no problem, but finding a way down to the beach was not going to be easy, so to avoid wasting time we climbed the rock rib which bounded the glacier to try our luck in the gully beyond. There was no way down, so we crossed the next rib to see what that held in store, another disappointment. By now we were gradually being forced up still further from the beach. As we unwillingly made more height, so the view unfolded in breathtaking beauty: the sea was calm and deep blue, the sky flawless but for a faint darker line away to the south; icebergs and growlers abounded, stark and incredibly white against the blue; and O'Brien soared up from the sea to rake its beautiful saw-toothed ridge against the heavens. It would have been pleasant to sit and enjoy all this in peace but we struggled on across the grain of the slope.

All the gullies bore the scars of recent avalanches, but now we were finding heaps of the debris lying even on the tops of the ridges: we were becoming increasingly conscious of the great line of cornices and icecliffs poised several hundred metres above us. Already small slides of snow and scree slurry were occurring, and occasionally stones bounced past us. Everywhere there was the sound of running water.

Eventually, half-way along the coast, we topped one of the rock ribs and found ourselves on the edge of a huge snowfield which swept right up from the beach to the ridge in an unbroken sweep, completely exposed to everything which dropped off the icecliffs straddling its apex. We were loath to lose height and unwilling to continue much further as we were: so we struck out up the centre of the snowfield for what we hoped was a break in the cliffs above. As the slope steepened the snow improved, and we began to make better progress. With every step nearer the crest of the ridge things looked brighter, but at a point 100 m from the crest we came to a halt. Above us the face steepened sharply, a band of hard ice protruded through the snow above us to our left, and to our right was the headwall of a small gully which dropped vertically away from us. We had never intended tackling this sort of thing: we had only two ice hammers between us, and Alan and Nick were in no way experienced climbers.

Andy led off, first traversing beneath the ice band, then climbing the far end of the ice, then crossing back above it, before finally traversing diagonally across the headwall of the gully and continuing up on to the ridge. Once Andy and Alan had reached the top of the ice band, Nick and I followed. Always the angle was steep and below us the great expanse of white swept smoothly the full 400 m to the sea. In places the ice was rock hard, in others it was soft and rotten, and sometimes it was overlaid with a soft plastering of snow. All the time we were on front points and our muscles told us to hurry; but at the end of each pitch the ice hammers had to be slid back down the rope on krabs to the seconds. After alternate pitches three of us would accumulate on one icescrew, so that the few remaining pegs could be handed forward to Andy. I remember distinctly the mixture of relief and surprise I felt at how well Alan and Nick coped and how, when we finally flopped on the gentle slope above, we all sat and laughed at the expression of profound relief on Alan's face as he burbled enthusiastically over the advantages of level ground; he later confessed that he had never once dared look down during those five pitches!

NICK MARTIN

By the time we had reached 350 m we could look back and see our footprints in the snow far below us, man's first marks here. Above us the icecliffs looked more imposing than ever; and before we could approach the ramp through them, we were faced with an ice wall. The sun disappeared behind the snow shoulder: we were now in shadow, perched on 7-cm wide platforms on a 65° slope with another 100 m to climb. What a prospect! It took Andrew one and a half hours to set up the first two pitches, to reach a stance only 20 m above. During that time I could only shuffle my feet on my little perch. I couldn't even feel my feet. I had to traverse with just my iceaxe, no ice hammer. This meant I had to cut handgrips for my left hand, an exhausting process. My right arm was in agony. Twice poor Jem thought he was

*going to have me swinging from him like a pendulum, when I gasped as handholds broke off
on me. At long last my weary feet took me up over the lip to see the others sitting on a coil of
rope on the snow grinning hugely. We had made it, after three hours on front points!*

*From now on it was like another world as we made our way westward above the snowbowl
towards the summit. Watchful for crevasses, we threaded up past snow hummocks into an
area which looked as though it never saw sunlight. Great organ pipes of frosted and fluted
icicles reached down from cornices above to enveloping carpets of snow. All sounds were
muffled in the amazing stillness. The frosty aspect of the ice gave the icicles a tinge of
turquoise; each hole made by our iceaxes or crampons immediately became bright blue, as if
poured full of brilliant invisible blueness. Every corner we turned brought us some new weird
or spectacular formation of snow or ice. Vast spectres and gargoyles reared up into the sky,
torn apart here and there with great ragged edges, all absolutely motionless, and all
marvellously frosted with wind-whipped glazed snow.*

Inevitably we reached more difficult ground. The line of the ridge continued as
a steep terrace up the south face of the summit 'tit'. We were now at a point
above our campsite and just below the cloud base, so we called a short halt and
had some food. It should have been lunch but we had lost all track of time with
twenty-four hours of daylight. It was then that Alan first complained of bad
cramps in his legs. After we looked at his crampons this was no great surprise:
the front points were virtually useless.

The summit seemed to be composed entirely of huge ice blocks glued together
with frozen snow and 'mushroom' material. This consists of ice crystals
deposited in large masses with the consistency of honeycomb, too hard to accept
the shaft of an iceaxe but crumbling uselessly under front points, iceaxe pick or
hammer. Unfortunately, these mushrooms sat in great rounded, bulging gobs
along the whole crest of the summit ridge, effectively barring progress to all
except dedicated tunnellers. We therefore carried on up the ever-steepening
terrace, hoping that it would run out easily on to the summit. We reached the
end of the terrace without having found a break, and with just sufficient
visibility to see that we were on the edge of nothing. According to our altimeter
and the spotheight on the map we were only about 60 m of serious climbing
from the summit; so, as Alan's cramp would not allow him further, he and I
remained with the sacks and stove whilst Andy and Nick disappeared round the
corner to make a last concerted effort. We had arranged that they would aim to
be back within two hours come what may, and we settled down with a mug of
cocoa to wait as best we could. The deadline came and went. As the minutes
ticked past, so the probability of trouble loomed larger and we began to
consider courses of action. Half an hour after the deadline, we heard a faint
shout. Five minutes later there was another one much nearer. After another ten
minutes we had cocoa brewing and the two were thawing out and telling us
about the first ascent of Aspland.

NICK MARTIN
*Andy and I waved au revoir to the others and crossed a narrow snowbridge over a little saddle
to enter the inner sanctum. Andy led off while I belayed in a tiny enclosed world of complete*

Aspland Island rises out of cloud in a telephoto view from O'Brien beach. Jem and Alan waited in the bowl (behind the upper Cape Pigeon), while Andy and Nick climbed the left side of the summit mushroom. (CF)

whiteness with visibility of 20 m. Five m below my feet was the edge of the snow; below, far below me (700 m) I could hear the roar of the sea and faint penguins. My line connecting me to another living thing gradually slid out into nowhere as Andy climbed. I followed, groping through small ramps and gullies moulded by accumulations of snow. To my consternation I found the rope going up through a small tunnel with the grinning face of Andrew at the top, very pleased with himself at finding it. Up we went, up another pitch on to a very exposed and windy ridge, to be faced with a vertical wall. I sat, gritting my face against the blasting icy wind, and slowly fed out the rope with cold hands. Faint shouts wafted back that the pitch was difficult, and to turn back if I didn't like it. Never! But I saw what he meant. It was a traverse 30 m across a bulging ice wall, with the sea below. At one point the handholds were less than a metre above the footholds. I made it. Andrew went on up: over a bulge, through a little ramp and doorway, and reached the top on one rope's length. On top he tried to undo the rope to look around but it was blowing hard and his glove blew away. Our two hours were past, but our sense of elation was bursting as we raced back down to Jem and Alan, shouting loudly.

It didn't matter that only one of us had reached the top. Andy's jubilation (once he had thawed out) split four ways with plenty to spare. The descent went quickly and smoothly, nagging doubts about having to go back down the difficult rising traverse of the morning were dispelled when we located an easy route which took us down to the east end of the beach. It was as well that it was such an easy angle for, even though it was now ten o'clock in the evening, the snow was still thawing; in our tired condition our progress through the thigh-deep mush was not particularly controlled. We would have fared badly trying to climb up it in the morning had we not been diverted.

We ran out on to the scree above the beach with only one thought in our minds, to get into our sleeping bags as fast as we possibly could. We took off our crampons and set off along the shore at a good pace, each of us in his own little world of blisters and tiredness and thoughts of sleep. We were jolted back into reality when, on rounding an innocent-looking headland, we found our way barred by a small cove where deep cold seawater met steep, unclimbable rock with no intervening beach. Luckily the tide still had a couple of hours to ebb; so we settled down round the stove to convert brash ice, oats and cocoa into porridge, waiting for enough rocks to break surface. After an hour we were able to jump and wade across; then we plodded on in silence over sand, shingle, boulders, miniature glacier snouts and huge quantities of avalanche debris until we reached the glacier which lay next to our tents.

Tired muscles urged us to chance it underneath the snout. We reached a point where the ice projected right over the half tide rockshelf. Andy went first, waiting for a gap between waves, then diving into the narrow slot where the sea had undermined the ice, and wriggling on his stomach to the shingle on the other side. I followed, but the crampons on my rucksack caught the ice, and wriggle as I might there was no avoiding the next wave. I galloped the last couple of hundred metres beneath the tottering ice, pulling off boots and waterproofs and clambering into my sleeping bag to sleep and sleep, and sleep.

We had arrived back at camp at one o'clock in the morning after a seventeen-hour climb, and it seemed no time before we were woken by the voices of the other group returning from Eadie. For a brief moment there was resentment at their return. This was our island, we had climbed it, we four were linked inseparably by our experiences of the previous day; who were these interlopers? But the feeling passed as quickly as it came. We swopped tales and prepared for our departure.

Top: *Eadie and Aspland Islands from O'Brien Island* (CF). Bottom: *Climbing Aspland Island* (NM).

Top: *Camp at Cape Bowles* (ND). Bottom: *Canoes in brash at Chinstrap Cove* (JH).

9
MS *Lindblad Explorer*

They presently paddled within eight or ten yards of the ship and I desired our men to make friendly signs to them in return, conveying a wish for them to come on board . . . they soon commenced shouting and making ludicrous attitudes expressive of joy.
JAMES WEDDELL

5 January   We set to work digging out a tent platform and bringing the rest of the kit round from the canoes. Chris, Tim, Frank and Alan enthusiastically cut out big blocks of snow with the paddles, good shovels in the soft stuff. Gradually a big platform is cut into the snowslope, and on the seaward side a wall of snowblocks grows. We finish with the four tents end to end with a man-high wall to seaward. Chris adds a Union Jack on the battlements, and sticks a few paddle shafts through as gun barrels. Now we are all ready for the Indians, the penguins, and for bad weather.

After supper, Andy gets on to the radio and there is John Chuter clear as a bell from Clarence, and able to receive us for the first time. They have got round to Chinstrap Cove. We wish them a Happy New Year, and tell them our good news. In three days we have achieved a string of firsts – canoeing, climbing and communicating. After the two weeks confined on O'Brien, Aspland seems a new wide world. We can move around, and the living conditions are good.

We build a snow wall to protect the four Vangos. The climbing party got soaked coming back under the glacier snout behind. Gibbs Island is far beyond. (FM)

Later it grows cold, and gusts of wind flurry round the bay. We are in for a westerly blow. Our campsite is ideal, nestled under the steep rock ridge, with our snow walls protecting us from any gusts coming the other way. As the nylon flysheets bang and flap in each gust, we lie snug and content in our bags with mugs of coffee, mulling over the great forward step in our fortunes and achievements these last three days.

6 January   Frank and I will explore along to the eastern point today, and look over the ridge to estimate the bird populations on the north coast. First we go over the snout of the glacier above the camp. Great runways 10 and 20 m wide have been gouged down across the glacier from the gullies above to the icecliff over the sea; it is where the big seracs of the hanging glaciers above have tumbled and roared down into the sea like express trains, with the effect of giant earthmovers. In between these smoothed railway cuttings the surface is covered with more normal looking avalanche debris of snowblocks. We cross quickly without stopping, though today the conditions are much safer than in the thaw when Jem's party crossed.

Beyond the glacier we walk along the shore with occasional detours on snowslopes above. On one triangle of sand above the intertidal rocks eight seals

An agile young Fur Seal comes ashore near camp. The cliffs of O'Brien Island are 4 km beyond, but foreshortened by the camera telephoto. (FM)

lie. Seven are Weddells, but one is dark and bristly like a hog: it is a bull Fur, big but not with the mane of the full-grown breeding bull. He stands up on his front and rear flippers, with his body clear of the ground, and looks at us crossly. I had forgotten how hoglike is their face, in form, expression and texture. This one does not attack or come toward us, as most Furs will. Frank photographs it while I hide behind him brandishing my iceaxe to protect him, and feel more and more redundant as the bull continues its toilet.

After looking around the point we climb up to the ridge, hard going up soft, deep snow, until finally we find a good way to the crest at 250 m and drop down the northern snowslope a little, to scrutinise the precipitous coast. By the time we get back to camp my knees are very tired. I must still be unfit. Chris has had a good day of geology, studying the green and grey schists near the Eadie 'Narrows'.

The wind is blowing up harder and harder now. On the spit itself it is biting cold: in shelter at our camp, Andy registers the gusts at 40 knots (Force 8). The wind is tearing the tops off the waves and O'Brien is blotted from view. We worry about the tents despite the snug wall, but only one guy breaks through the night.

7 January   After breakfast Andy asks me about a strange penguin he has found: 'a funny Macaroni with a crewcut'. It is just 100 m from the tents, and sure enough there is a Rockhopper Penguin standing with a Macaroni at an empty nest site. This is the first record of this Sub-Antarctic species in the Elephant Island group, and I don't know if they have ever been seen before in the South Shetlands. This is really exciting and I take a lot of photographs and then go on beyond 'The Narrows'.

Suddenly a helicopter appears near the spit, and shortly a second helicopter. What excitement! Who can they be? They buzz away together diminishing to insignificance through the straits between O'Brien and Eadie. For a long time afterwards we keep thinking we hear their alien noise again behind our bleak islands. When we get back to the camp, the others are getting the canoes ready for tomorrow. Tim describes what happened:

TIM HALLPIKE
Jem and myself had just returned from collecting mosses and were enjoying a brew when we became aware of an unusual throbbing sound. 'Sounds like a helicopter,' said Jem. 'Don't be daft, Endurance *is miles away, and* Biscoe *doesn't have a helicopter,' I said. 'It's sure as hell not a penguin,' said Jem, and with that scrabbled out of the tent. I followed: what should I see, not one, but two helicopters approaching from the east. One flew close over the camp obviously making a recce. It was a Chilean Naval helicopter. The sovereignty of these islands being such a touchy topic we watched the helicopter circle and approach to land with some trepidation. A safe landing accomplished only 20 m from the tents, an extremely smooth observer with immaculate flying suit and a clipped moustache stepped from the helicopter. Frank, Jem and I were standing like stuffed penguins, hardly believing our eyes. In broken English he asked: 'Do you require any help?' Jem assured him that we were British, were OK, and needed nothing. I offered him a sip of my brew; one look at my encrusted cup was*

Two handsome Macaroni Penguins gossip in the Latin Quarter. (CF)

*obviously enough; he merely shook his head. Ten minutes after our first hearing it the
helicopter was airborne again, a diminishing speck.*

At half past eight we talk to John Chuter on the radio, then listen to him passing
our first bulletin to Signy. After our three weeks of fruitless effort using morse,
he passes it all by voice in three and a half minutes. At last our families back
home will hear how things are going. We also learn that the *Lindblad Explorer*
expects to arrive here at four tomorrow evening, later in the day than I had
hoped: our earliest feasible arrival at Gibbs will be eight tomorrow night, late
and cold.

8 January *The* day dawns calm; the layer of cloud has an air of stability. The
state of weather on this day has been one of the hinges around which this
expedition has been planned. If we cannot get to Gibbs today, our scientific
programme will be badly hit, and we will have to go on to short rations, eating
penguins and fishing to survive. In that case there will be a tremendous urge to
canoe across the deceptive sea to Gibbs without support, if a good day occurs,
though we have not yet had one day good enough for that. I look out of the tent
over the snow wall, and see that the sea is flatter than for many days: my hopes
rise, like a sneeze you fight to hold down.

On the beach a non-breeding Macaroni consorts with a Rockhopper Penguin. This is a very rare record for the South Shetlands. (CF)

We start at nine: bringing the canoes along to the beach below the tents; packing our personal gear; sorting out communal gear (ropes, cine cameras, radios, shovel, sextant, plankton net, doctor's box, etc), and building a cairn with a message in a bottle. Andy has arranged a radio link up, and finally at three o'clock, the Captain of *Lindblad Explorer* comes over. Immediately we can hear that this is a man who knows his business. 'We will be there at half past four local time, which is half past five your expedition time is it not? Yes, good. Then you want us to pick up your eight men with their five canoes and to take them to Gibbs is that right? Yes, correct. Fine, we will do that. You come out, and we will work out how to get everything on board then.' After the whole forenoon, and afternoon, wondering whether *Lindblad* would still be able to help, arriving so late, things are suddenly again good. We strike the tents, load the canoes, dismantle the radio aerials and wait on the beach.

At five Jem shouts: 'Thar she blows.' We all run across to his rock: sure enough a red ship with white topworks is in sight near Gibbs. We get in. The two rafts have some trouble launching in the surf with their heavy loads, so Andy and I get out of Mischief to help heave them into the water. When they are gone we get back into Mischief, put on our spraydecks as she sits on the beach, and hump her down into the water on paddles and hands. As soon as we are paddling we realise that the sea has got up quite a lot in the last few hours, we are swinging up left to lumpy waves coming in, and then screwing down right as their tops brush between Andy in the bow and me aft.

Lindblad Explorer has now hove-to a kilometre off the beach. She has a red high-sided hull, and a white superstructure running the length of the ship. Now we can see she has a gangway down, which will be awkward for our cockleshells. As we get closer we can seen rows of people gathering on three decks, all in red. From two single gantries starboard aft swing a hoisting hook and a bosun's chair: I'm afraid the chair will be impossible to get on to from *Mischief*, so I change our plan for *Mischief* to go alongside first, and wave on the rafts.

Now we are right under the side of *Lindblad Explorer*. She towers up above us. Way up there I can see rows of faces and rows of cameras clicking away. Andy and I lie off, while the rafts try to get alongside the gangway. Here beside the ship the size of the waves is magnified, and her hull disturbs the pattern of the water, so there is an awkward heaving motion. One raft passes a bowline to the men on the gangway, but they do not make it fast. Soon both rafts have slid back on to a rope hanging in the water astern of the gangway. The ship puts on power and swings to port (to avoid the reef?): the two rafts are pushed out and in *Mischief* we suddenly find ourselves clawing our way out from under her stern in the short choppy waves built up by her swing. We paddle round in a circle for the third or fourth time. Tim gets his raft alongside, fending off from the gangway foot grimly as the canoe rises and falls; Chris Brown has got on board, but nothing much is happening yet with the kit. We come alongside Tim's raft. Jem gets out of his cockpit and immediately things start going up the gangway as he gets to work with a knife on the lashings. Soon the raft top is empty, I get out of *Mischief* and we get out the kitbags and tents from inside the hulls, and take off the engine. By this time we are all wet, very wet. The whole procedure is taking too long. Andy goes on board and now at last Chris and he lift *Mischief* out: she has shipped some water and they have a hard haul, but there are many willing helpers. Jem and I are left on the raft and we start baling her out. Twenty minutes later the raft sails into the air hanging from the gantry, bows down but intact. The second one follows soon after: the operation is safely completed.

I meet Captain Kjell Smitterberg. I salute and we shake hands. He says: 'Now first things first. Do you wish first a shower or first a whisky? You are our guests now for two hours.' I stand on the bridge like a Michelin man in all my clobber, dripping water. No one minds. The next two hours on board the *Lindblad Explorer* are like a dream, with friendship, interest, kindness and hospitality heaped upon the eight of us. In clothes we have worn for six weeks, and redolent of penguin colonies, we are incongruous aliens in a high-class tourist world. All we can do is smile our primitive dirty grins at the cameras, which continue to pop and flash as we talk and drink and shower and eat.

NICK MARTIN
We were an extraordinary looking octet surrounded by all the luxuries and trappings of a first-class hotel. It seemed a sacrilege to be stamping around on the deep pile carpets in our

great wet boots. 'Say, would you like a hot toddy?' came wafting over from the entrance to the lounge. The speaker, a lean white-haired Texan with a large cigar, looked at me intently. 'Gosh! I would love one.' I was now being asked whether I would like a hot shower. 'You can use my cabin,' said Sarah, a slight ship's hostess.

Placing my hot rum toddy on the desk in her cabin, I began to peel off the layers of clothing. The inner layers were steaming when I reached them, thanks to the central heating. Then there I was naked for the first time in three and a half weeks. What a sensation! Taking a last gulp of toddy, I went into the bathroom. What bliss: hot water, clean white towels. I revelled in it all, soap suds everywhere, clean hands, clean ears, face and toes.

Immaculately attired stewards helped us into our seats in the dining room and placed grilled grapefruit in front of us with professional deftness. Corks popped and our glasses sparkled with a deep red Burgundy. A little later the Captain came in and assured Chris that all was well and under perfect control. We had just arrived opposite the Spit of Gibbs Island and he would see that all our gear was safely landed. 'Don't worry about anything. Enjoy your supper and we'll call you when all is ready.' I relaxed and contemplated our pudding of bananas, ice cream and chocolate sauce. Mm!

'Say! Commander Furse isn't it?' The speaker was Tom Shartle, our Texan benefactor, cigar still firmly lodged in his mouth. 'Well, how would you like a bottle or two of whisky to take ashore with you? It can get mighty cold at night.' Chris, thinking that we might all get re-addicted to alcohol, laughingly tried to refuse the offer but, seeing our looks, recanted: 'One would be perfect, most generous.' He returned with two bottles 'for good measure'. My heart warmed to him! 'Say! I'd love a photograph of you all. Could you do that? In all the gear, I mean; I want all the gear you know.' 'No problem!' we chorused. Meanwhile, Sarah had beavered away in the galley and triumphantly returned with loaves of bread, oranges, bananas and some of the ship's famed ice cream! We returned to the lounge for coffee then, 'Grab your gear, we're off!' bellowed Chris Furse. Farewell to Lindblad Explorer: *the end of a magical interlude.*

In a few minutes the two rafts and Mischief are together on the water again. As we start paddling towards the island the ship's siren sounds. We stand on our little pebble Spit, looking out at *Lindblad Explorer* as she steams south towards Hope Bay into the aftermath of sunset; it is ten in the evening. Slowly we return to reality. The Spit is a pebbled storm beach 100 m long, between 5 and 10 across and only a couple of metres above the sea. It connects Gibbs Island and 'Narrow Island' like the skin between two sausages. Non-breeding penguins stand about all over it. At the western end is the dump of gear, all safe and sound as Andy and Chris left it a month ago. We lift our packs, tents and snow shovel, plus a bottle of whisky – Nick carries Sarah's huge plastic bag of goodies – and start walking up the penguin track from the north shore of 'Narrow Island' towards the snowbowl where we plan to camp.

We find a reasonable campsite, erect the tents (with the usual maledictions upon the makers) and fall into our bags a little after one o'clock, each with a stiff tot of whisky in his coffee from one of Tom Shartle's bottles.

Tomorrow is Sunday. We have arrived at Gibbs! I told Faye that I would feel confident of success and safety once we arrived on Gibbs Island, and we have made it. I sleep like a babe.

'Narrow Island' from the south-east. Our camp is in line with the distant iceberg. The Spit beyond is masked. The 'Viking's Hat' on the right, the grey spur below it and the foreground beach will prove exciting on 13 and 31 January. (75/76 *Endurance* Flight)

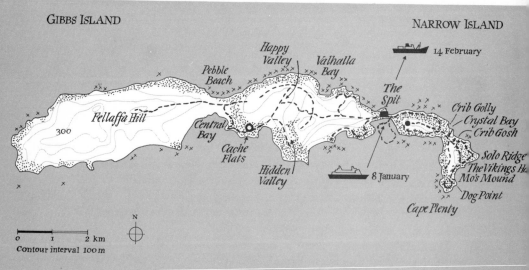

GIBBS ISLAND   NARROW ISLAND

14 February

Happy Valley

Valhalla Bay

Pebble Beach

The Spit

Crib Golly

Crystal Bay

Crib Gosh

Fellaffa Hill

300

Central Bay

Cache Flats

Hidden Valley

8 January

Solo Ridge

The Vikings Ht.

Mo's Mound

Dog Point

Cape Plenty

N

0   1   2 km

Contour interval 100 m

■ ○ Dumps and caches   ● Camps   ⁙ Snow-free areas   ⤬⤬⤬ Half-tide rocks

10
Gibbs Island

And now there came both mist and snow
And it grew wondrous cold.
And ice, mast high, came floating by,
As green as emerald.
SAMUEL TAYLOR COLERIDGE

10 January   The four Vango and one Arctic Pyramid tents are on the gentle top of a snowslope which runs down to a bowl or flat above the southern cliffs. The knobbly yellow dunite rocks form a broken crest to the ridge just above us and are also scattered about in frost shattered outcrops and moraine heaps in the snow of the bowl. Going up to the ridge crest I look down over slopes of snow and snow-covered scree to the northern sea, green over the inshore rocks. Ten bergs lie in a confused fleet between us and Elephant, which is dimly visible under the same pall of cloud. A Snow Petrel flying along over the northern cliffs gives promise of new birds here. In the bowl below our tents is a scattered colony of Antarctic Terns, they fly querulously around me. The snow must have buried many of their nests, and I can see tracks centring around sad little trampled patches of snow. I do not see any chicks, but find six nests with eggs: this is a very much later hatching than at O'Brien, perhaps two or even three weeks. I wonder what is the cause?

11 January   I do a nest check in the Macaroni colony to get actual figures for the numbers of adults at the nest, and the number of addled eggs still being brooded. Today I smash the few eggs I see, and every one is either addled or contains a dead chick; some of these explode with a loud 'pop', emitting the nastiest acrid stench I have ever smelt. Suddenly I see a strange Macaroni standing huddled over an empty nest site. It has white eyebrows in front of its eyes and below its eartufts. Then I notice that it has white from the eye down, instead of the Macaroni's black chin. It must be a Royal Penguin; they breed at Macquarie Island in the New Zealand sector of the Sub-Antarctic, so it is an exciting vagrant, the seventh penguin species I have seen in these islands.

Meanwhile two trammel nets have been set; Tim's tide gauge is in the water; and Jem and Chris have walked along the ridge eastward and come back saying there seems to be a lot of promise for the botany and geology. A good day.

12 January   Frank is delighted to have caught two grey, scaleless, slimy fish, which are all mouth and tail, like sea anchors, and are some sort of Ice Fish.

Tim has spent the whole day with his tide gauge, as the ink refuses to run when cold. If he can get one good series of records over fourteen days, it will provide the first decent tidal observations from the whole Antarctic Peninsula area. This is incredible, when the Drake Passage constriction is a major factor in all studies of water circulation on a global scale.

Today the Cape Pigeon chicks have started hatching.

Top: The Antarctic Tern has a smoky grey body. (CF)

Bottom: Beyond the drying Polywarm bags are dunite stonefields. 'Mo's Mound' peers from cloud. (CF)

13 January   I am to have a day on my own, birds-nesting and mapping. I am going to the eastern end, and will look for a route along the shore to the southernmost point.

The rocks here on 'Narrow Island' are mostly serpentinised dunite. Geologically this is very interesting as it is material from the upper mantle below the earth's crustal plates, and this is the only upper mantle outcrop known in the whole of this half of Antarctica. Aesthetically it is rather ugly rock, bordering on the grotesque: an ochrous yellow, sooty black in parts. The bedrock weathers not by fracturing along planes of weakness but by eroding away in a abstracted pattern. Great hunks of rock gradually wither and perish like an old man's face collapsing on itself in wrinkles, unlike the shattered heaps of schist with hewn plane surfaces. Yet when hunks of it fall off a face, the newly exposed surfaces are the lovely variegated green of serpentine, as if Utrillo had been playing, brushing white into a viridian canvas.

I go down the rock ridge south of the camp, then east along the clifftop below the snowbowl. Here the dunite has been reduced to stone fields with lumps from the size of tennis balls to that of footballs. Because their shapes have no regularity these lumps do not sort themselves into patterns like schistose scree; as you walk upon them they move a little, grinding their teeth dully. In some areas, the last stages of weathering have been reached: there is just a pulp of granules. On such flat areas little thumbs of moss and algae grow like worm casts on the beach, and in specially sheltered stable patches the mosses may coalesce to form a green carpet. At the foot of our bowl I find several little moss carpets almost as big as a tablecloth: here I find a skua with a downy buff chick. The Antarctic Terns scattered over the rest of the bowl attack the skuas whenever they fly upward from their mossy flat. In the skuas' parish I also find tufts of the pallid green lichen *Usnea antarctica* 10 cm high like it grows on Elephant, whilst on O'Brien we found only a few scrawny miniatures.

Jem prospects each island before selecting a few representative sites, where he collects samples and makes quantitative observations, casting down quadrats, mapping the vegetation in the 20-cm squares, so that objective comparisons can be drawn between sites on different islands, at different heights, on different soils, facing different directions and in wet and dry areas. Apart from his own prospecting, he uses us as scouts, bringing back polybags of mosses like schoolchildren, thus casting his net wide before he chooses the most representative sites for careful study. Today I collect a big bagful.

Crossing a huge, filthy penguin colony, I see a leucistic Chinstrap. It is a lovely bird; the plumage pattern is exactly as in a normal bird, but instead of black it is a faint burnt umber, the colour of a Barn Owl. I start to climb up towards the ridge. Here there are masses of Cape Pigeons, and I lift a sample as I pass: thirteen have chicks and six eggs, of which five are chipping. It is obviously near the end of a spread of hatching covering perhaps only five days. I must get follow-up counts on the fulmars to see how they compare in time and in spread. I am finding the siting of the fulmars' and Cape Pigeons' nests very difficult to compare: the fulmars seem to have a more catholic taste, varying from ledges on the steepest faces like kittiwakes at home, to open sites on quite gentle scree slopes; the Cape Pigeons seem to prefer broken rock with some debris and usually with more overhead protection (against skuas or rockfalls?). Yet here the Capes are on quite open sites. The only consistent difference seems to be that the Cape Pigeons have a ceiling above which they do not nest: on Elephant the ceiling was about 170 m, on O'Brien and Eadie about 50 m, on this ridge they extend up to about 130 m (level with the top penguin). The fulmars extend up to the top here at 250 m and on Eadie reached over 300 m.

The wind is rising; low clouds drive eastwards over the grey sea now streaked with white. I reach the next ridge and look over a rotten cornice to find that the back of 'Mo's Mound' is cloven steeply into the sea 200 m below me. My ridge is very exposed, mostly cliff on the left, and on the right deep steep snow waiting to follow the recent big slab avalanche beyond. I would like to be roped, and to have my crampons, but laziness directs me up the crest to the top 100 m, where three great boulders form a crown or 'Viking's Hat'. Over the first corniced shoulder it eases off and the final part looks better with lumpy dunite boulders between narrow tongues of ice running up to the big block poised at the top of my ridge. The glazed rock proves worse than it looks, with ice disappearing towards the cliff: I drag myself up on multiple pressure holds, including forearms, knees, once even my chin, then I chop steps up ice to a tiny saddle. In front of me now is only one little traverse left up under the overhang of the big boulder, one of the 'Viking's' horns. As soon as I move out on to this snowslope I realise it is nasty: underneath my left boot it gets steeper and disappears 5 m below over the precipice to the sea 300 m below. Meltwater is splattering down the eave of the big boulder in the wind. I distrust my footholds. The iceaxe in my left hand shows me how rotten the snow is; the axe brushes it aside to hit first thawing ice, then rock. I ram my right arm down between the snow and the rock at each move, but it is only a psychological hold, as the iceaxe breaks out each time. I carefully stamp enormous steps into the slushy snow, hoping that they have some sort of key with the ice below. One step at a time I cross the little traverse, not too slow lest I lose my nerve, not too fast lest I trust a step before it is compacted. At last I feel my iceaxe go all the way home into firm snow on the breast above. I am safely up! Over this last half hour I have been more frightened than I have ever been in the hills before.* Now as I stand on the 'Viking's' pate my world unfurls before me: along the ridge I can see our tiny tents perched high above the snowy bowl; looking past the whole length of snowy Gibbs I see clouded O'Brien on the horizon.

Returning along the ridge I find a sheltered cranny above the eastern cliffs. I sit to eat my biscuit, listening to the faint cackle of penguins occasionally wafting up from far below. Nearby is a skua's nest and their calls reach me, but over and above all is the blast of wind on the rock. A big tabular berg below has a faintly red top, perhaps snow algae; the red sets off the pure green and blue shadows of its white walls, which float between grey sea and grey cloud without horizon. Just an hour's clamber and walk away is our camp, but no one knows I am here: not even the wind can find me in my sheltered sconce. As I get up, a

*Or since.

great dark bird sails up over the head of the gully and veers out past the next
ridge toward the sea. Its effortless play, its thin black wings and the
wedge-shaped ash grey mantle proclaim it the master of winds, the
Light-mantled Sooty Albatross. It seems a fitting climax to a day of mapping
birds, to see this fabled bird on its fleeting visit. Was its last landfall Macquarie
Island? Will its next be South Georgia?

16 January   After two days of rain and winds that have carried off Tim's tide
gauge, the rain has stopped. Our cloud is now just part of the cap of Gibbs: at
200 m the camp is simply immersed in the cloud. Down on the shore it is clear.
Much of my way is below cloud as I walk east along the ridge to the white
fulmar colony. I lift over a hundred fulmars quickly. There are four chicks,
thirty-one chipped eggs, fifty-seven unchipped eggs and eleven empty nests: like
the Cape Pigeons it seems they have a very concentrated hatching period. Soon
I will have to bump three of these lovely soft creatures with their nibbling bills
and mad laughing cries; I am not looking forward to it. At last on a cliff rim
below 'Mo's Mound' I find our first colony of Blue-eyed Shags. The young are
big and querulously nagging their parents for food; in fact a few are well
feathered and move around in a teenage gang. The colony is mingled with
Chinstraps and with Macaronis. Some of the penguins are nesting in shags'
nests: I wonder if they are slowly ousting them? On Elephant, the shags usually
fled on our close approach; here they crouch spread-eagled over their young,
saying their quiet determined little 'garr' noises at me. One adult crouches flat

A heraldic Blue-eyed Shag crouches on its nest. Half the south coast of Gibbs can
be seen beyond. (CF)

A Wilsons Storm Petrel flits over the screes. Little bigger than House Martins, they nest underground in the gentler parts of all our islands, and wander as far north as Britain. (DM)

on the nest while its two chicks stand over it! Is it hiding from me? I take several photos of these strange, primitive, heraldic and beautiful birds and then meander back, reaching camp at seven to find Nick preparing a great pot of Royal Marine Arctic mutton and peas with delicious tinned potatoes and spices from his goodies.

By midnight it has turned wonderfully crisp and cold: tonight I will go out looking for the night birds, the storm petrels and prions. The night is almost light enough to read; the wind is silent. Northwards over the ridge, stars tingle in a sky of darkest blue; southwards over the sea the sky is white, turning to watery red and gold just above the line of low cloud on the horizon. The sun must be just below there. I take three little dayglo flags and walk down into the bowl toward the cliffs; my boots crunch into the snow, now hardening beautifully in the snap of cold.

Almost at once I can hear the Black-bellied Storm Petrels calling from their nests in the scree: there are the thin whistles, the 'wheeee' advertising calls, which are so strangely ventriloquial, and there are the excited 'pip-pip-peep-pip-peep' calls of greeting and fighting. Following the latter sound is the easiest way of finding a nest. As I get to the clifftop I arrive in a little thicket of Black-bellies, flying fast and wild around the rock outcrops and down the steep scree gullies, the white of their bodies just visible as they pelt past. These are my Elephant Island special birds, the ones that the experts thought we would not see. They seem to have their centre of world population

Tim observes the movements of icebergs from above the camp. Beyond is the route west.
(CF)

here in our islands, as they flit past to their nests to relieve their mates, who
have been brooding their single white eggs for two days or so. Like the Wilsons
Storm Petrels their laying is staggered from mid-December right through until
mid-January. The first chicks will not hatch until the end of January and the
latest a month later. The chicks will not leave the nests until April, and many of
them will be entombed by winter snowfalls before they fledge. Snowfalls are a
major hazard for these little underground nesters; their staggered breeding
season is a mechanism which prevents the whole population being wiped out by
any bad week of snowdrifts during the breeding season. Most nests contain
remains of chicks which have been snowed in, or eggs, which the parents desert
to save themselves when the drifts pile up. Chicks and even eggs can survive two
or three days without the parent, but not much longer. A day or two after the
chick is hatched the parents leave it, only returning briefly at night to
regurgitate food into the tiny ball of fluff, at first the size of a matchbox.

I have company watching. Silhouetted against the southern sky is a skua,
standing on a big rock. He is hunting the Black-bellies as they come in,
preferring their fat 100-g bodies to the little 50-g Wilsons Storm Petrels. On the
scree above I creep toward a chorus of 'pips and peeps' and find one Black-belly
sitting outside a cranny under a big boulder. Another faces it at the entrance.
The visitor scrabbles away and flies off as I shine my torch on its soft ashy grey
head. There is no egg in the nest. I follow another flurry of calls and find two
birds in a nest, one brooding an egg: I put up a flag, so that I can revisit the nest

later. After wandering happily in the impersonal night for an hour and a half, I go back to the tent, climb into my bag and sleep.

17 January   This evening I decide to try some penguin meat. I have never tasted it, and feel that I ought to, so that when people ask me I know how fishy it is. Nick advises frying it in margarine. The red meat darkens like liver. Finally I try a little piece, feeling a bit squeamish. It is not fishy at all, but has a flavour which is vaguely familiar: is it liver? I try a bigger bit, and Nick tries some. It tastes and feels like a slightly tough sirloin steak, surprisingly good. Then Frank offers us a couple of fillets off today's fish catch: we fry them in margarine, sprinkled with parsley flakes. The white flesh is absolutely delicious, tender and friable, with a faint but decidedly pleasant flavour of clean, sweet fish like turbot. We have totted up our food: we have almost enough to last us on full rations until *Endurance* arrives. Now we know that penguin and fish would be good supplements if we need them.

18 January   Walking along the spit, Alan notices a large Leopard Seal lying on the cobbles surrounded by penguins. One Chinstrap is actually standing on the seal's back as it sleeps! In sleep, it shudders, as if dreaming. Still sleeping it yawns its hideous pink yawn, and then shuts its mouth back to the obscene smile its curling lip suggests. A Leopard is very awkward on land and the penguins are oblivious of it, and it of them. Its huge flippers are folded back with the 'palms' against its stomach, making them totally useless for any sort of progression on land. Even the blubbery Weddell can put its flippers out sideways with the palms upon the ground. In the water it is another matter. Yesterday evening we watched a horrid sight. In the middle of the bay a Leopard had wounded a Chinstrap. The penguin could not use its flippers to fly under water, only managing a pitiful dog-paddle on the surface, using its feet, with its beak stretched up in terrified endeavour. The Leopard swam slowly behind it, and beside it, so as to keep the penguin circling frantically in the centre of the bay seeking the land, which grew more hopeless each moment. It was like a cat with a mouse, but somehow more chilling and cruel in that icy sea. Finally after several minutes of horror, and several mutilating half bites, the seal grabbed the poor Chinstrap and began that last bestial act of thrashing it out of its skin against the cold sea surface.

It is remarkable how we have got over our initial revulsion at the filth and noise of a penguin colony. Now we look at these odd birds more carefully, beginning to admire them for their dedication to life and family, and even to like them for their similarity to little people. The sight of the traffic going up and down the penguin ladder is most affecting. The clean ones shuffle and hop

A chinstrap Penguin regurgitates krill into the throat of one of its chicks. The other adult may have already left for its turn at sea. Each brings in 250–880 g of food at a time. (DM)

Above: A sheathbill hangs in the updraughts above the penguins. They peck peck noisily at our equipment. Most of us dislike these 'Gollum birds'. Elephant Island is the sheathbills' last staging post before Drake Passage on their autumn migration. (CF)

Left: A Chinstrap Penguin dozes over its two chicks, while its mate forages at sea. (DM)

upward, heads down and flippers back, their tummies round with krill; the dirty ones hop and stagger down, head up to avoid somersaulting, trousered legs prominent each side of flat emptied stomachs. Seemingly endlessly the traffic goes, each individual serious, preoccupied and single minded.

On the other hand, everyone has developed a loathing for the sheathbills or paddies. These white birds, like pigeons, hop about the penguin rookeries licking up the soft waste, pecking holes in eggs and finishing off the softer parts of dead chicks and adults; they have some grotesquely nauseating habits, like licking the snot from the noses of sleeping seals. I admire them, the only land birds living in the Antarctic: they even migrate across Drake Passage to winter in Magallanes, crossing the roughest stretch of ocean in the world. Their snowy plumage contradicts their habits, but their scaly beaks and calculating eyes are in character. Only in flight do they look beautiful, false white doves of peace against the grey sea, black rock and rich pink penguin scree.

11
Accidents and Recoveries

Fear death? to feel the fog in my throat
The mist in my face
When the snows begin, and the blasts denote
I am nearing the place
ROBERT BROWNING

21 January   Leaving Alan as leader of the five at base camp, Jem, Nick and I
set off westwards for a few days. The cloud has settled to a low stratus when we
leave, but I am looking forward so much to our first journey overland to a new
camp that it scarcely matters.

Beyond the rockfall we put on crampons, rope up, wave farewell to the
fishermen in the canoes out in the bay and walk up into the cloud. It is fairly
steep, soft, wet, sludgy snow which collapses exhaustingly backwards at each
step. Finally the slope eases off when my altimeter reads 1250 ft. Visibility is
only about 20 m, but there is a faint light in the cloud on our right as if the sun is
there, and sometimes a dim line on my left suggests a cornice as we feel our way
along the ridge. Continuing west by compass we start climbing higher, and stop
in a windscoop for lunch. As we rope up again, it starts to rain in the cloud –
raining, at 400 m, in Antarctica! With the rain comes a wind. We plough up
through knee-deep snow, enveloped in blank whiteness, until shadows on each
side gradually form a narrowing snow ridge at nearly 500 m.

The other side falls into the unknown. After descending a little I come to a
steep little drop: below it I can see nothing but cloud. Is there an icefall down
there? Or a steepening ice lobe? Or a cliff? Or the snow headwall of a corrie
waiting to avalanche? We need to get down soon before the wind and rain turn
into a blizzard, so I decide to try it, with a little pinch of fear of what steep lies
below. One leg breaks through and I pull Nick from his iceaxe belay. I land
head down on a drift. When I get up, a schrund wall stretches right and left
above me into clag but now I can see below; there is a snowslope, at least for the
first 5 m of the enveloping whiteness. We go on down into a windscoop, then
left, but it peters out on to a shadowy rockface. So I plod back up the windscoop
into the teeth of the strengthening wind, then unwillingly make myself move out
on to the very rim where the wind comes blasting up out of the steep blankness
below. Soon a snowslope becomes visible 10 m below my feet. Telling Nick to
walk with a tight rope, I gingerly edge down off the crest. Miraculously the
slope goes on down, getting no steeper despite a few crevasses. Soon I hear
penguins faintly cackling below to the left, but keep dropping northwards

towards the compression at the axis of the valley. Now grey patches of ice show in the white-out. At last we drop out of the cloud at 200 m and walk easily down a lovely glacier with grey crunchy ice and crevasses filled with firm white snow. It is a long, narrow, valley glacier, almost alpine, except that on the sea below us is a perfect glittering iceberg.

My shoulders feel as if they have been steadily pulled apart for five hours by my 25-kg pack and my legs are exhausted from pushing and struggling in the heavy snow. But we reach the flat area of the cache, dig out a platform in the snow, and by eight have the tent up. We are all tired and weary and our clothes are sodden from wet snow, sweat and rain; but we are content and fall asleep after a big supper and many brews.

24 January After one day exploring round the cache and another holed up in a blizzard, we decide to go along the ridge to the west end of the island.

Beyond the moraines we stop to put on crampons and tie on to the rope. Jem leads and I go in the middle with a prussik each side and two ropes dangling to trip me up. We plod up lovely crisp firm névé, our crampons forking into the surface with a delicious cold crunching noise (Nick likens it to eating iced celery). They leave scarcely a mark, just twelve narrow slots for each footprint from the 3-cm tapered steep spikes. Up and up the ridge we go. We skirt round the left of the summit mushrooms to a spur where tilting ice blocks are overlaid and softened by snow. A snowfilled schrund beyond leads like a cliff path up to a steep ramp cased in ice. At the top of the ramp is an awkward belay stance, where the wind barges and buffets me, while Jem leads over the bulge above.

As we walk up the gentle summit ridge to the top the cloud descends on us and the wind increases. It will take the value and the pleasure out of the walk so we decide to abandon it and go back down to two snow-free bluffs on the south coast to do a bird census.

Jem goes first, back down our crampons' spike-marks in the névé to the bulge above the glazed ramp. I give him an iceaxe belay over the bulge, then follow him down and give Nick an iceaxe belay as he climbs down. Jem goes on down the ramp. When Nick reaches me I follow Jem down, kicking through the thick, hard ice coating into snow. At first I go slowly, driving my iceaxe in deeply, taking two steps down and repeating the process. Then as the gradient eases I speed up a little, walking down with the iceaxe across in the braking position, plonking the pick into the ice in front of my chest and keeping on stepping down until the axe is in front of my face, then taking it out and plonking it in again opposite my chest and keeping on stepping down without losing the rhythm and . . . 'HOLD!'

Suddenly the rope below snaps me off the ramp and I am shooting down the ice slope with a weight on my chest harness dragging me down. Instinct drives the point of my pick on to the iron-hard ice, but it goes on flying past my nose, or am I slowing? There is a jerk from above, and I stop, almost. Lifting my eyes from their desperate concentration on the head of my axe, I see Nick 20 m above, still on the steep bit at the belay; the top half of him seems to be plucked backwards off the ice. Now both ropes are slack on me. I stop quite soon. Jem must have stopped also. I look up again. Ten m above me comes Nick's body, iceaxe vainly clawing at the glazed ramp as mine had before. He is hurtling straight down on to me. My eye photographs the bottoms of his two boots: twenty-four crampon spikes coming straight for my face at 30 km an hour. I am stopped. When he hits me he should stop too. He hits me. We go on down the ramp together. I don't know what I feel, just hit, and unable to drive my iceaxe in again as our bodies are all mixed up. We slide past Jem. Five m down we stop in a heap, seemingly on the lip of the ramp above the steep snowslope. I can see! I can hear Jem: 'Are you all right?' Miraculously I am all right, only one hell of a bruise on my left wrist. 'Are you all right, Nick?' I ask. There is no answer. Suddenly fear hits me a second blow. 'Nick's hurt,' I say to Jem, struggling to untangle myself from underneath his inert body, handicapped by our packs, the rope, my iceaxe, my prussiks. 'Christ,' says Jem. At that moment I free myself from Nick to see blood spattered down the snow and rich blood around his eye. I bend over him with the layman's nausea at the thought of severe injury. The blood seems to come from a cut on his eyebrow. Oh, thank God. 'It's OK, Nick,' I say. 'Your eye's OK, just a boxer's cut above it.' 'It's not my eye I'm worried about,' he says. 'It's my balls.' Oh wonderful! He's conscious, and sensible.

The wind is pouring ice particles over us now, so I help Nick to stand and support him into the schrund where there is some shelter. Jem quickly secures the loose gear and comes down with a first aid kit to attend to Nick. It looks as though both his grazed groin and his cut eye will be all right, but he has had the hell of a fright, being thrown down 50 m of ice, further than either Jem or I. He is obviously shocked and groggy, quite apart from looking like a horror film, with blood all over his face. He will be able to walk back rather than be carried, which makes all the difference. Cheered by this, my left wrist really begins to hurt and I look at it. It is not just a bruise. One crampon spike must have buried itself in the hollow between the two big tendons to my thumb. That hollow is now a bloody wound 3 cm long and I can only assume that deep. It makes me feel a little sick. Jem wraps it up efficiently in a bandage to staunch any bleeding, and I put my bloody dachstein mitt back on.

Nick recovers with coffee. First he comments on the icy spatters descending on him from the icicles far above on the cornice; then he remembers his camera and calls for a photograph. My camera has stopped winding, so I use Nick's after wiping blood and ice off the lens. 'Bloody hell, it's black and white film,' says Nick. It takes us under an hour to get back down, Nick still shaken, and my left hand pretty useless. Once at the tent Jem brews for us, cleans up the blood, squeezes on lashings of white antiseptic cream and bandages us up. He then goes off to finish collecting mosses and lichens at a series of sites across the island, from the south shore to the northern cliffs. Left on our own, Nick and I soon relapse into sleep.

We have decided to go back tomorrow if the weather is reasonable, so that Alan can stitch us up and fill us with antibiotics. Nick thinks his crampons are clean, but they went through my dachsteins, which have absorbed a great deal of penguin colony, so this seems prudent.

25 January   We have a big, leisurely breakfast then prepare to go back. The weather is reasonable, cloud at 200 m and a high wind outside our little sheltered patch, but looking steady. We strike the tent, but leave it cached here with the primus to save humping to and fro. Instead we are taking back full bottles of paraffin and RM Arctic rations, to help our shortages back at base camp.

We put on crampons right beside the tent platform and set off the way we came four days ago. This time the snow is firm and crisp, so the going is easy, although all three of us are soon sweating hard as we trudge up the glacier. This time we know that the way is safe as we go up into the cloud. In places we can even follow our own footprints, driven deep into the soft snow that day, and now filled with white sprindrift whilst the rest of the surface is hoary and darker. We stop for lunch in the little cradle below the schrund at the top, comfortably out of the wind, knowing that most of the uphill plod is behind us. From there it takes only an hour and a half before we are taking our crampons off before scrambling round the scree to the Spit. We are all pleased to have got here without trouble.

When we finally arrive on the scree above the Spit, we see Andy and Chris B carrying the big medical chest away towards the camp. Good grief; what can have happened here? We shout and they finally turn to wait. The box is for Alan, who has fallen on the scree and badly hurt his leg. They have carried him back up to the camp. As we round the corner we see the vacant space where tents and dump boxes had been. Two days ago the winds here were appalling. At the camp it went off the scale of the anemometer and Andy estimated about 80 knots steady.

We descend toward the Spit; thence we will walk up the pale grey penguin ladder on the left of the ridge to the camp on snow above. The 'Viking's Hat' just breaks the horizon. (CF)

ANDY SIMKINS

23 January   At midnight I decided to check the conditions on the Spit. Through the driving spindrift I could see a foaming, angry sea breaking clean over it. Our first concern was the canoes, which would be exposed directly to the force of the wind. We headed down the rockfall. Alan was the first to round the corner at the bottom, and found that the canoes were fine, just as we left them and riding the storm beautifully. We agreed to deal with them after we had sorted out the boxes and tent on the other side. But how were we to cross over to the other side?

In the bay to the south the waves were rearing up 3 to 4 m, topped with creamy foam which roared towards the Spit, smashing a path through it, tossing boulders aside as if they were mere pebbles. The shape of the Spit had changed completely, the sea had removed over a metre from its surface.

Eventually, in waders and with linked arms, the water swirling round us waist deep, we reached our stores. One pile of boxes had been pushed en masse into the side of the tent; the apex had ripped with the strain, but the boxes had met sufficient resistance to be halted. The other pile, receiving less force from the waves, had nevertheless been knocked sideways: two boxes had broken free and been tossed into the sea. While Tim started to sort out his hydrographic boxes Alan and I went along the north shore to look for kit. Items were floating everywhere but luckily most seemed to be trapped amongst the rocks. We clambered amongst the slippery rocks collecting items, occasionally going into the water up to our waists. We found two sleeping bags, camera and climbing equipment, and a host of smaller things. We also saw some items being blown out to sea towards Elephant, and it was impossible to say how much had already been lost.

Frank stared in horror at his fishing kit, in particular a long line which I had sorted out with freezing cold bare fingers for two hours the previous day: it now resembled unravelled knitting buried in the stones. While Frank sorted out his fishing gear, Alan dived into the tent to save his specimens, microscope and dissecting equipment. Tim and I started to move the boxes to higher ground, lifting them over the slippery, penguin-ridden rocks up on to the west ridge. It was hard, sweaty work as the boxes weighed 30 to 70 kg and some were smashed. When that was complete we decided to drop the sick-looking tent. Rocks as well as boxes had been pushed on to the valance, which took time to clear, but once collapsed we shoved it into its bag and carried it high amongst the rocks. The three of us made easy meat of the remaining boxes, putting them higgledy-piggledy amongst the penguins.

At last the danger had passed and we could assess the result of the storm. We appeared luckily to have lost very little: only two boxes had been swept into the sea and we had subsequently found most of that kit. One jerrican of kerosene was a severe loss and would mean immediate rationing for cooking. Tim's 'transit' box (painted dayglo orange and brimful of rocks) had disappeared altogether. Chris Brown's geological specimens had either been buried or carried out to sea. At 0200 we fought our way back to camp.

25 January again   When we reach the camp, Alan is not too downhearted: he is going to knock himself out with a muscle relaxant and hopes that his cartilage will find its own way back tonight. Failing that, one of us will have to manipulate it back. Now who's squeamish? He looks at our cuts, says Dr Jem has done a fine clean job, and gives me a dozen antibiotic bombs to swallow.

26 January   It blows all night. With neither snow nor rain it blasts up from the south. As gusts hit the camp we can hear a tent rattle, then sometimes there is an inexplicable pause before our tent tries to take off, drowning all external noise with the crack of flapping, flailing nylon. Sleep is difficult because of the noise. Andy is the one who has to get up twice a day come fester or foul weather, to take his met readings: he shouts messages, rude and otherwise, over the roar of the wind. Now his anemometer is swinging between 45 and about 70 knots: maximum. Andy tells us that Gale Force 8 is 34-40 knots, Storm Force 10 is 48-55 knots and Hurricane Force 12 is 64 knots or more. So we are experiencing Storm Force 10 gusting to Hurricane Force 12. All the tents are still standing, which is quite a marvel. I visit Alan to check my wrist: his knee has unlocked, so now it will be a matter of time and gentle exercise.

27 January   There are only two Adelie chicks left out of three. They are not guarded by adults now, though Frank saw two adults feeding them recently. Although they did not hatch before the Chinstraps they are already well feathered (as far as we can see through the mud). As we eat lunch, one Adelie adult comes ashore to feed the chicks. Each time some krill is gobbled out of its

One adult Adelie Penguin comes ashore. The black Adelie chicks look like mud puddings; they are given a hard time by the neighbouring Chinstraps. (CF, photo taken earlier)

throat by one of the chicks I leap forward hoping to make them drop a few for me: each time the pink krill vanishes instantaneously down two pink throats. The penguin's tongue and the roof of its mouth are lined with rows of backward-pointing cartilaginous spikes half a centimetre long: once trapped there, a krill is on a one-way ratchet system to the stomach. Within an hour the Adelie adult has fed the chicks and departed. How different this is from the Chinstraps, most of whose nests are still guarded by one adult, with the chicks still downy.

When I get up to the camp Jem is starting to dry his moss specimens. He is a hot stone fanatic. The stone sits on the primus heating up; on the stone sits a cardboard ration box containing a whole lot of brown envelopes of botanical specimens. When he turns off the primus, the heat in the stone continues drying out the specimens. It is very neat.

Before supper I walk to see how the terns are getting on in the moraine colony. Antarctic Terns nest spaced out at 10 to 15 m or more, but all families rise and attack their traditional enemy, the skua (or any others, like me). As you walk through the colonised area there is a rolling carpet of crying, swearing birds darting in at your head. Their lovely pearl grey bodies set off the whites of their underwings, tail and eye slash, and in turn are set off by the two red paddles of their feet cushioned into the soft coverts. The chicks leave the nests after two or three days and freeze at any disturbance. Both eggs and chicks are cryptically coloured and very difficult to see. The best way to find them is to retire and wait for the adults to settle. This time I am lucky: on the first patch of stone chips and moss, I find a cold cracked egg, then a single warm egg. This is unbelievably late: most of the colony at O'Brien had hatched by the end of December, with some chicks already well feathered then. This could be an addled egg, but these terns are very temperamental and don't sit long when hatching is overdue. The next nest resolves my doubt: it holds one egg and one tiny, damp chick breathing deeply. Retiring quickly to allow the parents to return, I almost step on two chicks crouched immobile by my feet, nearly full feathered, about a month old. The range of hatching seems to be from mid-December (earliest O'Brien) to late January (latest here). This is a wide spread for the Antarctic, where most species seem pushed to cram their breeding cycles into the short season. Apart from the storm petrels the only ones that have wide scatter are the fish-eaters: Gentoo Penguins and Blue-eyed Shags. Perhaps the terns spread their breeding for both reasons: because they are fish-eaters, and also because they are prone to failure due to snowdrifting.

Top: Antarctic Terns nest on moraines, or scree slopes or even ledges on quite steep cliffs. They exercise communal defence of the colonial territory against their arch-enemy the Brown Skua. They have no defence against their other enemy, the snowdrift, except their varied breeding dates. (CF)

Bottom: The big bold Brown Skua is the eagle of the Antarctic. To be dive-bombed by a fierce pair is an exhilarating experience. One once carried off my glove as I protected myself. (DM)

29 January   At midday the sun breaks through the cloud a little. I go east past 'Crib Gosh' and find a pair of skuas still brooding their egg. I love these great brown bombers, hovering a metre away yelling their long calls. After a little while I leave them in peace with their olive egg and go up to the 'col' to look at the route to the southern cape. On the sea, 250 m below, is a mass of birds feeding, presumably where an eastward current eddies around the southern cape bringing food to the surface. A great raft of over 1000 Cape Pigeons swims in a sharply defined triangle, others flutter over the waves elsewhere. Fulmars are there in smaller numbers, with several Giant Petrels, and there is one Black-browed Albatross. One sees an albatross so seldom near the coast that it is always exciting. Here obviously is a great mixing of waters; I will call this southernmost tip of Gibbs Island 'Cape Plenty', if I can get there.

Kelp Gulls frequent the cliff points near 'Cape Plenty' but I did not find their nests. They are perhaps the shyest of all the species here. (CF)

31 January   My wrist is now usable though still swollen and aching, so I go with Chris Brown to 'Cape Plenty' – over the 'Viking's Hat', roping down 'Solo Ridge', then down a steep spur (100 m of snow and 100 m of earthy scree) to the shingle beach. We walk along it below rotten cliffs which drop down from 'Mo's Mound' out of low gloomy cloud. Half-way along, a cliff spur stopped Nick and Andy last week: we have brought waders, but skirt it dryshod at eleven o'clock, today's low low tide.

We come to a band of beautiful rock running down the beach into the sea from a snow gully. It is level with the shingle, but is actually one solid sheet of strikingly lovely conglomerate rock with scoops and bumps and hollows on the surface. It is a mosaic of smooth pebbles, soft greens, blues and greys 10–20 cm across set into a material like concrete. The pebbles are scattered, each one surrounded and set off by the creamy white matrix. Chris says the matrix is due to the calcite in the rocks which dissolves in the meltwater and is deposited when the ph value changes below the high tide mark.

We split for our work. I clamber up a big scree slope. Dark chocolate Cape Pigeon chicks spit red liquid at me, smelling sickly sweet like ancient sardines. In my sample 22 of them are alone and 17 guarded by an adult, yet only one of 60 fulmar chicks above is alone. On top I find an unexpected plateau with moss carpets and great swathes of *Usnea* covering the rocks in tufts almost like miniature bushes; it is common on Elephant but we have seen very little hitherto on these islands. The raw wind now driving the cloud across from the west, deposits glistening dew on the pallid green lichen. I go back to join Chris.

At six we head back but can't get past the cliff point even with waders. Both tide and swell have risen, so we resign ourselves to waiting until tonight's high low tide at eleven. We sit on our packs against the cliff; Chris chats away entertainingly in face of my usual repartee ('Yes', 'No', or 'Grunt'). By eight o'clock it is getting colder; the surf is heavier and the tide higher. Waves hit the cliff with a bang, repeatedly sending great sprays of water 10 m high, sometimes with large fronds of seaweed flying up like black fireworks into the grey sky. The iceberg 400 m offshore sometimes disappears in the cloud: a group of black specks on it are penguins; others are trying to leap out of the water on to the sloping ice. They repeatedly shoot up out of the water, pause suspended for an instant and then fall back; occasionally one catches a good wave to a higher position; that speck then walks up to join the roosting group.

At a quarter to eleven we return to the ford. Chris gets into our one pair of waders in the gloom. Everything else is in his rucksack so he will have both hands free. We tie on to the rope so that I can hold him if he gets caught in the undertow. We tie a figure of eight half-way along the rope: when he has got over he will get to a dry place, take off the waders, tie them to the figure of eight and shout for me to haul them back. Chris wades out below the cliff overhang. He stands waiting for a series of smaller waves then makes a run for it, in the thigh-deep backwash of a wave. He reaches the rounded rock and gets half-way up it, then seems to be stuck. One, two, three, four waves sweep in, crashing against the rock and covering him. At last he moves again, and disappears round the cliff. In the gathering darkness ten minutes pass, then fifteen. At last there is a faint shout above the roar of the waves and I haul the waders back and put them on. In the shadow of the overhang the undertow sweeps me off my feet and a wave goes over me. Reaching the rock I fumble with soft rubber feet on slippery rock until Chris heaves on the rope. How he got up without it I don't know. We exchange experiences. Chris is ebullient, for him this is 'the most exciting moment of the expedition so far'.

CHRIS BROWN

Tied on to the rope I pressed forward slowly. The sea became louder and higher as I approached. A gap in the waves came and I slithered past the overhang as fast as my load allowed and turned left. I was confronted with a slippery wall 2 m high with one or two minute handholds, and then a seemingly vast expanse of sloping slippery rock with no handholds at all. I heard an increasing roar and looked over my shoulder: a large roller was sweeping in majestically. Near panic. Risk going higher and losing my handholds? I stood my ground. The wave swept around and over me; my hands (gloveless and very cold) clawed at the handholds; my nails broke off as I held myself against the backwash. Another wave swept over. Then I climbed or rather crawled up on to the sloping rock, and at last scrabbled out to safety. I reached the rope's limit within range of the waves, but taking off the waders with painful hands, all I recollect was a great sense of urgency to get the waders tied on to the rope and returned to Chris. This took some time in virtual darkness.

We are both streaming freezing water, so quickly move off to get warm. At the foot of the gully we put on crampons. The earthy scree is desperate going, just like porridge. At last we both reach the snow. It is half past twelve, and completely dark. My legs feel like bits of string.

We climb up the snowslope. Gradually the snow gets more and more icy. We are on front points, and tired: so we finally rope up. On the next pitch I am glad of it, as my crampons suddenly skid away from me on rock. But being roped slows us up and we get cold. By the time we unrope on the ridge beyond the 'Viking's Hat' it is two o'clock. We fumble along the ridge in pitch blackness among rotten pinnacles. Some big loose rocks go crashing down the gullies on our right, the sounds fading into the night towards the penguins far below.

Suddenly I notice that the Wilsons Storm Petrel calls have been replaced by the nest calls of Black-bellies. We have strayed on to the cliffs! We can hear penguins below and there are fulmar chicks all around. We have to claw our way back up. At last we reach 'Crib Gosh' and cross it on all fours. Now, past all the tricky bits, we sit in a little rockfall area and split our last packet of Rolos. I have made a good transect of the storm petrels and it is very clear how the Black-bellies predominate on the cliffs and the Wilsons on the flatter areas. All the fulmar chicks we passed tonight were alone, and this must mean that the adults are at sea feeding nocturnally.

It is half past three and beginning to grow perceptibly lighter. Now that the dangers are behind us tiredness sweeps over me. We trudge on up endless moraines, stopping once to sit and pant and once to drink at a meltpool. At last at four o'clock we stagger into camp: 'Goodnight Chris, see you tomorrow evening.' Now I take my time, slowly lowering my sack of rocks, undoing my boots. Jem has woken up and lights the primus while I struggle out of my snow gaiters, sodden anorak, sodden trousers and outer socks and now (oh joy!) into my lovely Polywarm. Hot chocolate threads a path of warmth down to my stomach. I blow out the candle and snuggle down into the deep warmth of my bag. It is five o'clock, dawn. I am going to sleep until the day after tomorrow.

1 February   Frank comes in for a brew, bringing a little bottle in which swims a red and white fish about 3 cm long, opening and shutting its square mouth just like a big fierce fish. It is only the fourth species he has caught here, and it's the Plunder Fish, *Harpagifer bispinis*, which the BM especially asked him to collect. It is a lovely, colourful little thing, with relations in Chile and South Georgia and even up in northern temperate waters.

3 February   A tiny Fur Seal a metre long is on the Spit, separate from the usual group of four bulls. It is probably a one-year-old male, and is comparatively tame. Frank photographs it. It just wants to sleep. I put my boot close by: it half-heartedly growls and taps the toe with its teeth then flops down again, shuffling its flippers underneath it as if to keep warm, and looking up at us with eyes that appear much larger than the older ones'.

We climb up from the Spit and go north a little to overlook 'Valhalla Bay', a dark Wagnerian bay carved out of vertical 200-m cliffs, overhung in turn by thick icecliffs. As I start down the scree a mixed flock of petrels flies into the cliffs below. Some of them are fulmars but about fifteen are Antarctic Petrels. This is potentially the most exciting ornithological discovery of the expedition. Until a colony was recently found down the Antarctic Peninsula, the only known breeding sites of this lovely petrel were far to the south on the continent, as much as 250 km inland. I go down the loose scree slope towards the clifftop below, but it gradually steepens. Long before I reach the edge the slabs I dislodge are sliding unpleasantly far towards the unseen drop. Every few minutes one, two, three or as many as twenty Antarctic Petrels are in sight flying below me. They seem to concentrate on this length of cliff just east of the bay. One small colony of Antarctic Petrels would be very exciting indeed, far north of the most northerly known colony, but we will go on now to the cache. After we return to the Spit I will come here on a day-trip to rope down the unstable cliffs, but first Andy, Nick and I spend three days around the cache.

7 February   We slide down to the screes overlooking 'Valhalla Bay' to prove that Antarctic Petrels breed there. Andy and Nick start lunch, while I go to find the best way down. I wander along the clifftop, and there they aren't. I sit waiting for them for half an hour. Plenty of fulmars sail by and plenty of Cape Pigeons. Out at sea several Giant Petrels, a flock of about a hundred Cape Pigeons, two Kelp Gulls and a scattering of Wilsons Storm Petrels cluster about a bull Fur Seal, who is lazing about in the water and presumably has killed something, providing scraps. Still there are no Antarctic Petrels; gradually I accept that the birds three days ago were chance visitors, perhaps drifted north from the Weddell by the weather system which brought the storm next day. As if to cheer me up, a Light-mantled Sooty Albatross sails majestically along the clifftop below me, its wings drooping motionless, its dark eye comprehending all without curiosity. These superb albatrosses seldom come close to land. It is as if Gibbs Island is part of the sea, a big ship rather than an island.

After supper Andy gets on to the radio. There is still no word from Clarence, but Signy passes a message from *Endurance:* she will be off Clarence pm 7 February, today! I hope they are ready!

8 February   Today *Endurance* talks, but is not very clear, and cannot hear us. She is just off Clarence Island. Signy has to relay her message to us bit by bit. There are four of us in the Arctic Pyramid, Andy on the radio, Alan winding the generator with his pipe out of the corner of his mouth, Jem and I hunched in the other two corners. The military language is difficult to comprehend.

A. Sitrep 082230 Zulu. From Sugar Loaf Cache A2. Alpha Mike today in fine spirits.
B. Am presently recovering gear from Cape Bowles. All persons and gear will be recovered by close of play tonight.
C. Intentions for Wednesday. Alpha Mike land 3 persons on Cornwallis if possible. Land 4 persons and gear at Walker Point. Cdr Highton to remain on board for Gibbs recovery. Papa Mike on completion to be off Gibbs Island to recover Cdr Furse to discuss remaining recovery. If time permits will attempt recovery of outlying dumps. Do not propose recovery of main camp till Alpha Mike Thursday. Suggest R/T schedule if your equipment allows 0100Z tonight and 1500Z tomorrow.

There is a marvellous sense of relief through the whole camp: the Clarence party is all safe; mail should arrive tomorrow afternoon; and *Endurance* will pick up our outlying caches, with our scientific specimens.

As I sit looking out over the sea three birds fly from the west: Antarctic Petrels. Things begin to suggest a pattern. Perhaps the non-breeders and failed breeders are beginning to disperse from the breeding grounds like the Fur Seals and these waters are favourite feeding grounds.

Towards midnight I potter down to my fulmars. This afternoon eleven chicks were on their own, while seven were still being guarded. Tonight I find eighteen chicks alone, with not a single adult there. The chicks sit very erect but soft and floppy in their white down as I shine the bright torch upon them each in turn. Their black eyes seem to start from the sides of their heads. Here is more evidence that these lovely creatures are nocturnal feeders.

An Antarctic Fulmar prepares to defend its chick. They sit tight so that you can lift them off. These lovely petrels do not spit so often as either their Arctic descendants, or the Cape Pigeons. (ND)

12
Suspense

Howbeit, we shall be cast upon a certain island.
ACTS 27: v, 26

9 February *Endurance* seems to have brought beautiful sunlit weather with
her. Down at the Spit I chase off nine bull Fur Seals who lollop down the beach
into the water. Most of the team get down too and we stand around watching.
Now I see an insect approaching from the south. The Wasp comes over, casting
a smoke canister down to gauge the wind; he sweeps back southward, then
comes in and lands. Chris Lyle, the pilot, smiles and waves, as we do. The
observer hops out with an orange immersion suit, and a bag: the mail! I throw
that to Jem, clamber into the suit, and lifejacket, clumsily looking for
disremembered toggles, and grab my pack. Now I am sitting in the helicopter,
facing aft. Within seconds I am looking back at Gibbs Island almost as a
strange island. I cannot grasp scale from a helicopter. There, near the top of
that snowslope, must be our tents, my home for most of a month: I can't even
see them. We are close over *Endurance*. We thump down neatly. I get out,
awkward in my orange womble suit. Bearded faces smile at me and I shuffle
towards the hangar with my pack, with the lifejacket strapping my neck to my
crutch.

There is John Highton, grinning hugely and indestructibly, his beard almost
white, in expedition gear, but bootless and clean. 'Happy New Year', they all
cry, shaking hands. All needs saying at once, but there is to be no time. I must
go up to the Captain to plan today's recovery. We drop off my pack in the cabin,
which John and I will share tonight.

'How's it been?' I ask.

'Fantastic. Tremendous. Incredible. Superb. What an island. Bloody
marvellous: I've never had such a wonderful time in all my life!' is John's
answer.

By this time we are on the bridge. The Captain asks: 'Would it suit you for us
to recover the outlying dumps first, while you strike camp, then to come back to
pick you up with the dump? You will spend the night on board, ready to fly into
Elephant tomorrow.' That is marvellous: it gains us half a day. I will now be
flown back to organise the shore end, where everyone will be cosily reading their

A pair of Macaroni Penguins guard the filthy track down to the Spit. At the far end of the
Spit two big boulders shelter a patch of storm beach. (FM)

mail, expecting the pickup tomorrow morning. I leave my pack and my camera as I should be here tonight. We get to the hangar. John shows me Bosscat and Tigger, one split and splintered across the bow cockpit, the aft end of the other broken upwards. 'These are the better two,' he says. 'We can use them for spares on Elephant. The other two are up on the forecastle ready to be buried at sea.' Three minutes later we are flying into the Spit. I get out and the Wasp lifts away. Frank is half-way down the penguin ladder. I make tent-collapsing and running-fast signs at him. As I reach the top I shout the news of the new plan and get people striking tents and packing up. As we descend the wind rises, rushing up the screes to twist me as it wishes. Going down the penguin ladder there are rocks and stones going down as usual, and gravel flying upwards on the wind. We get the biggest boxes out on to the cargo nets in the middle of the Spit and stack the smaller stuff nearby.

By the time we have carried all the boxes out it is six o'clock: there is a hiatus. At last I can get at my mail. Now I realise that the others have not read theirs either. Jem delves into the bag, pulls out a thick swatch of letters, and hands them out. They have been sorted by name, so come out in batches first for one man, then another. Jem gets to the end of one swatch. Now another. Frank has still not got one. I can feel his desperate hope: this will be the first letter from Chris after her miscarriage on the eve of our departure. A fourth swatch comes out; still there is no letter for Frank. At last, most of the fifth bundle is for Frank! A penguin on the rock above squirts white liquid over Alan's neck: he is too intent on letters to heed it. Most lean against the same rock, but each is separate in his own world at home, where the mind's eye rests. Faye tells of the boys in Australia. The boys tell of the beaches there. Polly, my mother, tells of the boys' safe arrival back. She writes the loveliest letters, full to the brim with afterthoughts crammed into odd corners. Paul, my father, writes cursing his failing memory, but managing to send his love, pride and best wishes around the world's rim. I also get my appointment to my next job. Now, I go back to two letters from Faye. As I start to read about Sydney and Bondi Beach, the writing blurs. Looking up from my trance of golden sunshine and brown family swimming, I see snow falling, gently but decidedly. We sit on reading, but now I begin to wonder: will *Endurance* recover us this evening after all?

It is getting late, so we put up the three Arctic Pyramids in a rush. Two naked inners and one with a torn outer are soon standing on the little area of cobbles at the west end of the Spit. By nine it is clear *Endurance* will not pick us up tonight, though it has now stopped snowing. We all go into our tents. Because I have no sleeping bag I commandeer the centre berth between Nick and Chris in the best tent. We have a plywood floor with a cargo net and karrimats on top. The spare sleeping bag is hard to find and probably still sodden from the storm, so we do not bother for this one night. I have no spoon, no cup! Sleeping bag is bad enough: spoon and cup are really serious. Nick and Chris let me use theirs in turn. Greater mateship hath no man.

10 February   We heft the boxes and nets back on to the Spit in case they start flying at ship's eight o'clock (our nine) but we leave the tents until the last

A bull Elephant Seal lies on the Spit. Beyond in the rockfall are penguins, and a cave. (FM)

minute. There is thin cloud at sea level on the north side of the Spit, but southward it is clear. We hang about waiting, but *Endurance* does not appear. What has kept her today? Perhaps she has to finish off the outlying dumps this morning? Later in the forenoon the wind gets up; the cloud closes down, so we can only see the two small icebergs close in. It starts to rain and visibility diminishes. We retreat to our tents, each knowing his task if we hear the buzz of a helicopter. It rains harder. The two naked tents are cold and wet.

Nick unwittingly walks into a big grey Weddell bull camouflaged on grey cobbles. It suddenly lunges toward him with a snap snap of snakelike jaws, so quick that Nick is completely surprised. Later I find the big Weddell in front of our tent: as I approach it snaps again. It would be dangerous outside the door, so we try to shoo it away. It just snaps at us. We throw big pebbles. After a little more snapping it rolls back on to its stomach and humps away. I throw a few more pebbles to keep it moving. One hits it on the head. It suddenly stops lumbering along and subsides like a piece of pastry on a board. I can't have killed it surely? Its flippers quiver and sag loosely; its jaw hangs loose and tremulous; but it is still breathing. I must have knocked it out. Soon it recovers and dozes.

Endurance has hove into view, heading west-south-west and well offshore. Out there she seems to be pitching a lot, although here it is a pleasant evening.

Slowly she passes on her way and disappears into clouded gloom in the south-west. It does not look as if we will be picked up today. We haul the boxes back again, the fourth move now.

11 February   Once again from half past three I get little sleep. After breakfast we yet again put out two cargo nets and some of the heavier boxes. Through the forenoon *Endurance* steams up and down offshore. The wind is very gusty. Once we can see the helicopter brought out on deck; then at ten it is taken back inside. Frank breaks out his handline to catch some fresh fish for the skipper.

Four Fur Seals play in the surf, corkscrewing, somersaulting and seemingly playing tag: one by one they catch waves and surf on to the beach. Three of them walk over the Spit (frightening the little Crabeater into a panic), shuffle and march on down into the surf on the south side, while the biggest bull stays to rest his injured flipper. They really are lovely and lively animals. They are the only seals which sound like real fierce wild animals with their grunting barks and their little sniffy 'nff-nffs' (like circus sealions). One comes out of the southern surf, sees us, hesitates, barks, and then advances angrily towards us. There are four of us big men standing there, with cobbles in hand and all ready to run. Before we prove our cowardice one cobble frightens him and he lollops back into the sea.

Living here on the beach we are a part of the Chinstraps' daily life. Parties of moulting birds wend their way through the encampment in crocodiles, each in turn crashing into a guy. Couples of chicks pursue reluctant adults past our door, squeaking and tumbling over each other to nibble at the parents' throat and cheeks until finally it stands at bay, 'chews the cud' briefly and allows the chick to ram his head down its throat to gobble krill. A fully feathered chick struts around the beach among the loiterers, wet from his first swim; others like muddy grey woolly toys lie about dozing in the muck. The moulting birds stand sleepily, their fronts tattered and dirty, their backs showing white stars where some of the dull black feathers have gone; occasionally they spar with their neighbours or with passing birds.

Andy shouts that waves are breaking on to the boxes. We fetch them up on to a higher bit of the beach. By 1 pm the waves are washing up to this too. We watch anxiously. On the north shore the sight of the sea's majesty is awesome. Protected from the west at the tents I had not realised the full measure of this storm. Great seas are running in from the north-west and smashing on to the shore here in a welter of white. Through this mad foam incredibly some penguins are coming and going. They are swept 20 m out and then seconds later come pouring back the same distance over and between the boulders. If the wind shifts to the east the camp will become untenable. The surf is now threatening it even as it is. I set watches for the night, and we build a rampart of cobbles like a seawall round the tents.

Watches organised, I go into the tent, where Nick is cooking a huge pot of curried chicken. Andy shouts from outside: 'Chris, we ought to move the boxes up on to the scree; they are getting washed by waves.' We finish the curry and go out to help Tim and Andy. Tim has had a brainwave: he is intent on building a platform of boxes at the back of the storm beach, on which a Pyramid can be pitched like a stilt house. It is a great idea, just the sort of complicated civil engineering construction that Tim loves most. The waves are now gnawing at the cobble slope below the wigwam. These scouring seas will obviously carry off the stones before long, so we put the one empty box on the beach immediately in front of the tent and fill it completely with rocks as a breakwater. The Ultimate is on the edge of the southern scarp of the beach, but it only gets the seas through a 5-m gap between the western shore and the greenhouse-sized boulder in front of the wigwam. The wigwam is in the front line, getting the main waves on the Spit bending around this boulder. Our torn complete tent is 2 m north of the wigwam: although lower, it is protected from the north by a cottage-sized boulder and only gets second hand waves as they sluice past the wigwam and pour down the north side.

I go back to our tent. It is three hours to high tide and I aim to get as much sleep as possible before our watch begins. As I doze off, the roar of the waves and the deep rattle of the dragged cobbles seems to fade a little, as if the surf is reducing or being deflected further away. Lying fully clothed and booted, ready to leap out, I don't really sleep, yet when Alan shakes me at eleven with some message I must be asleep; I mumble that I will be out at a quarter past, and doze off again.

The wigwam and the Ulimate on the right and the cottage-sized boulder on the left protect our one complete Arctic Pyramid tent. The canoes nestle under the far cliff. (AS)

I wake sharply five minutes later as the import of his message sinks home: 'Chris, it looks as if we will have to abandon the wigwam; the waves are now washing up on to the tarpaulin.' I find the others outside, spellbound by the power and glory of the scene. The sky overhead is largely clear, with clouds scudding over towards the north-east. The blue is still too faded and wan to show stars, and there is light enough to see the great waves thundering in from both sides to hang like dark walls before tumbling upon the white of their predecessors. Now almost every wave is crossing the Spit, like two white armies pouring across No-man's Land to clash and then retreat. Both horizons are dark, vicious purple, with the white crests of big combers glimmering, almost shining, as they move across.

But there are more urgent things to do than gaze at this rumbling, thundering sea. As it rages over the Spit it threatens to wash us away, and particularly the wigwam. We put Tim's idea into action. First we complete the square platform of nine boxes at the back of our little patch of storm beach next to the Ultimate. Next we lash two cargo nets over the platform to bind it together. Now we bring over the other naked Arctic Pyramid, and erect it on top of the box platform; it just fits. It looks a reasonable emergency tent for all eight of us sitting up.

It is nearly midnight. We decide to take forty minutes each. At twenty past one I go out. Chris is standing between the wigwam and the Ultimate, looking at the ramparts. At every wave white pours around the greenhouse boulder tearing at the glacis. Every so often a bigger wave comes over the ramparts and pours past the tents. It starts to rain and sleet. I stand watching the waves, occasionally going out to add a stone. In the wigwam I can hear a primus; a candle inside cheers the darkness outside and I guess at the contorted shadows on the white tent walls. Slowly it seems that the tide is falling a little. Finally at three it is an hour since a wave last girdled the tents and I go back, leaving the camp unguarded.

12 February It is light, and it is the morning of our fourth day of waiting, since I came back from the ship for two hours to strike camp. There is no chance of flying in this wind and sea. Overnight the barometer has risen from 982 to 1004 millebars, a staggering leap. Today we do not take any boxes out on to the Spit, so instead have a leisurely breakfast and then sit about. Suddenly there is a crash of solid water on the tent, out of nowhere. I have my boots on, so scramble out, past a Weddell Seal asleep a metre from the door.

Frank and Jem are outside their tent. 'We've been smashed; we are moving up to the cave Jem found.' The two seaward poles have been bent inward like hoops. They were hit by the solid wave. Alan was the only one inside and is still there gathering bits. Frank was half in and got soaked, water travelling from knees to neck both inside and outside his waterproofs. The box of rocks has disappeared from the ramparts.

They have everything in hand, and need little help. They are going up to a sort of cave which they will roof over with one tarpaulin with the other as flooring. When the wigwam's sad little patch of pebbles is vacated, Nick, Chris and I set to work to build new ramparts. We then fill the pots up with snow again and go inside for a brew. As we do so Frank comes to the door. 'Alan has been stunned by a rock falling through the roof of the cave, he is bleeding from a gash on his skull, and is only partially conscious, though it seems like a temporary stunning.' I go up to sit with Alan. He is lying on his back in the cave, shivering, with his head resting on his rolled sleeping bag. He doesn't know what's going on. Frank hands in his sleeping bag: I wrestle to get it up the length of Alan. With the warmth he seems to relax and keeps dozing. Later Jem dresses Alan's head and finds two gashes 2 cm long on his crown, which have bled a lot but are not too deep, and look clean. Alan is now sleeping and they have put on his duvet and put him back in his bag. Now at last Frank and Jem can rest themselves after the filthy struggle to set up house in their bleak cave. But they are cold. I do not envy them, and feel guilty as I go back to our lovely tent.

At four Tim asks for help taking down the Ultimate. It has taken some solid water and one pole is broken. I curse myself for sheer laziness in not taking it down earlier. After a look at the raging surf at low tide, it seems that we will

A group of sodden, filthy, moulting Chinstraps stand miserably above the two remaining tents. After three nights here we feel like they look. (AS)

have to evacuate this evening, strike our tents, put the boxes higher in the dirty scree and go up to Jem and Frank's cave. In the meantime we build up the ramparts further.

When I am shaken awake for my two o'clock watch, however, Chris says the waves are only reaching the ramparts very occasionally. It is calm for my watch and the surf seems to decrease. By three, with high tide past, we are clearly safe for the night so I turn in.

13 February   At half past six I am awake, cold and unlikely to get back to sleep as I lie shivering, so I put the primus on. Thawed out, I go to get snow for breakfast. In the cave Alan is awake, which is a good sign. He says they have had a reasonable night in their bags, cold but without the threat of waves curling over them. When I get back it is snowing lightly. The barometer is a little higher than yesterday. The sea is now quite calm and I am hopeful *Endurance* will be able to fly. I cannot see her anywhere, but we are ready. The ramparts stand lonely, cold, wet and proud as they were laid yesterday. In the end the sea will destroy them, but not yet. I drag two nets on to the Spit, bring down the small boxes and kitbags from the penguin colony and wipe off the pink slime. It starts to snow more. There looks little chance of a helicopter. I am exhausted by this waiting, go into the tent and curl up in the middle of the tent floorboard with my boots against the tent door. I will sleep to catch up on these miserable nights. With the primus on I am warm and drowsy.

'Chopper!' Nick is wriggling out of his bag. There is the roar of engines overhead. I scramble out into grey mid-forenoon, grab two boxes and go out on the Spit. There are signs of feverish activity from both surviving tents.

The helicopter lands. The crewman jumps out and comes towards me, waiting outside the rotor arc, buffeted by its wind. He has a sandy beard. In one hand he holds a plastic bucket with 'Message' written on it. In the other he holds my camera and snow goggles which I left on board *Endurance*.

'We'll have the first load out in two minutes,' I shout in his ear over the engine roar.

'You'd better read the message,' he shouts back in my ear, 'you may not be coming off.'

This is unbelievable. I wrestle with the clamp lid of the bucket, clasping camera and goggles against the rotor downwash. Inside are all the philatelic letters! I rip off my mittens and stuff them into my mouth to stop them blowing away and scrabble through the wet papers until I find an official envelope. I tear it open.

Yesterday evening we lifted the three from Cornwallis Is. and put them into Walker Point with Cdr Highton. His team is now complete. The stores collected from O'Brien, Eadie and Aspland Islands are still on board. Present weather makes it unlikely that I can lift you and your team from Gibbs Island today. Even if this is achieved, present forecast makes it improbable that I could land you on Elephant Island by 141200 (P), when I have to leave. The ship is required in the Falklands to provide transport and hotel accommodation for the Minister of State. I propose to:

1. Remain here for twenty-four hours in case a magic change occurs.
2. Provide you with food and fuel to last you until March.
3. Try and return to implement lift 22/23 Feb. This may not be approved because of my
reduced time for hydrographic work.
I have discussed this with John Highton and would be grateful for your immediate comments
— and food and fuel requirements. Request you set watch on 4103. Sorry this tale is gloomy.
I know you will be disappointed.

Disappointed! I simply cannot comprehend it. Surely they cannot just leave us?

Spend another month on this heap of wet scree and penguins with breakers washing around our sodden tents?

The crewman comes back from the helicopter carrying my rucksack. Andy carries it off to the tents. The other three are standing in the snow on the beach, watching blankly. Up in the penguin colony I can see Jem outside the cave.

The crewman says: 'What do you need?'

My brain races. It is 13 February today. Pickup perhaps 19 March. Say forty days. $8 \times 40 =$ '320 mandays of food I think.' He writes it down. With winter nights approaching: 'Ten jerricans of paraffin.' He writes that down. 'Oh and two tents please.' He writes that down, and turns to go.

'Our doctor has concussion,' I bellow in his ear, grabbing him by the shoulders. 'My doctor must be flown off,' I yell. He understands, nods and gets back into the helicopter. It leaves, diminishing toward a miserable grey ship.

I stumble back along the Spit to the camp, unable to think of anything I can say to cheer the four standing there. At this moment I should rise above bitter disappointment, and lift their morale. I cannot. I hand the letter to Chris, and go up through the penguins to the cave. Jem and Frank have got Alan outside, standing, looking groggy. He is still concussed. I tell him that I think he must go off to the ship now. I take his pack and he follows me shakily down the scree, copying my footholds and handholds. We put him inside our tent. His boots stick outside the door toes up, as if he were poleaxed inside. Nick sits with Alan, the rest of us stand hunched in the light rain in a miserable row sheltering behind a rock.

The helicopter does not come back.

I suggest that the rest go back into their tents for a brew. Jem produces the first flash of humour in this bitter half hour: 'Please sir, may I stay to see the helicopter?' We all stay there hunched. As the rain and cold goes down our necks, so does the horrid enormity of it begin to sink into our souls. Gibbs is a small island. We are sick of walking up and down that muddy scree track through stonefalls and dead penguins. We have done the scientific work, and do not have enough equipment to occupy another month.

I get everyone to prepare their packs, ready to leave for Elephant with nothing but a pack each. This involves a bit of sorting out, as some of us have put things into boxes for Elephant. It keeps us occupied in our misery.

The helicopter reappears and lands. We get Alan out and Jem and Frank start putting on his womble suit. I give him messages until I realise he is finding it hard enough to keep his balance, let alone remember messages. I get out my

sodden notebook, and frantically write. My ballpen slips and misses as the
drizzle soaks the paper. 'I have to agree of course. But we want to go to
Elephant. We are prepared to risk not being landed there. We would prefer to
be recovered with only our packs and landed at Elephant, which would only be
seven helicopter flights. If we are marooned we require 320 mandays food, 10
jerricans paraffin and 2 tents.' Alan goes, clutching the message, too confused to
realise that he may not see us again.

The helicopter returns soon with a cargo of food slung below it. It drops the
net on the Spit. As it flies away we walk out disconsolately and carry the boxes
back to the penguin scree. It starts ferrying more. Each load is another nail in
our coffin. I have a radio schedule at 1300 to talk to the Captain, but he may be
committed by then. We all think of arguments for taking us off. Frank brings the
Captain's four fish he caught two days ago. We put them in a polybag. I add
messages reiterating that we desperately want to get off with just our packs, to
be landed anywhere on Elephant, giving a map of Elephant with good
helicopter landings and another showing the few landing beaches; asking for
candles; sending signals and letters to be despatched. Each time the chopper
approaches I walk out holding aloft the bag of fish and messages. Not until
midday do they take it. They give me a message from the Captain: 'Dear Chris,
I am truly sorry but I see virtually no hope of landing you at Elephant.' The
helicopter has now flown in nine loads. The crewman puts up one finger. Ten
minutes later it flies in the tenth load of rations. We could all have been on
board, with a whole day to land on Elephant. The engine noise vanishes. The
penguin cackle is again the background noise. We are deserted.

Jem and Frank move down from the cave, now thick with ooze from penguins
in the rain. Chris and I move out so they can have a decent tent at last. We
flatten the ramparts to make space for the third Arctic Pyramid where it was
smashed yesterday. I join Tim in the Pyramid on the boxes. Frank has run out
of tobacco.

At one I talk to the Captain. He has now had all my damp, tattered messages.
The opportunity to recover us has been lost; the wind is again rising. The ship
will hang around until tomorrow hoping to pick us up. I ask myself 'Why not
this morning?' but I do not ask him. The last thing I must do now is antagonise
the ship. He sounds more helpful over the radio than in the letter, and I feel a
shade less downcast.

The rain increases. We have lunch crammed into a Pyramid, in soaking
clothes, with boots on. We will all go over to the cache, to get a change of air,
exploring westward, hoping the ship will collect us on 22nd. Today we will eat
as much as we want. Tomorrow we will move off the Spit, giving ourselves a
day to get dry and human again. The wind is rising. We are keeping half-hour
watches as the ship will fire flares if she decides to recover us. It is soaking
standing outside. Chris and I raft the canoes close to the cliffs, lash them and
load them with rocks. I go into the stilt tent as Tim relieves me on watch. It is
not as wet as I expected. The primus keeps it warm. Some water sprays off the
walls as the wind shakes it but I am already sodden from the waist down and
damp above. I unpack my sack. Tonight I will sleep in my lovely Polywarm, use

a spoon, my own mug! I look for a message from John Highton: there is none.

At six I talk to the Captain again by radio. The ship will stay offshore hoping for better weather tomorrow. Their 'dropdead' time to desert us is 1200. Alan has improved a bit after a relapse.

14 February   The radio link is at 0600. The weather is quiet, a grey veil of clag over the sea to the north, but clear to the south. The wind is light and the surf is not too bad, though some waves still reach the crest of the Spit. I tell the Captain it looks good for flying, not quite good enough yet for boats. He says that they will decide whether or not it is good enough.

We loiter about the camp. On the ramparts a few penguins stand like survivors of a siege. One lies dead, hanging half over the glacis, a soldier killed at his post.

Endurance steams west well offshore in the grey south, pitching a bit. Closer in the sea is calmer. Then she steams back eastward closer in. Still she has no helicopter on deck. It looks perfect flying conditions. She disappears around 'Cape Plenty'. We are all out in such good weather. We have our packs ready, and can strike the tents in a flash. Everything else is secured; most things stacked in the rockfall among the penguins; the boxes under our tent held by two cargo nets and rope; the canoes at the far end of the Spit. *Endurance* does not reappear. We wait. Slowly we begin to lose hope once more. Seven o'clock passes. Then eight.

Now she reappears off 'Cape Plenty'. Her aldis flashes us. There is a helicopter on deck, they are going to fly us off! At nine o'clock they radio. They will recover not only us, but also gear. We start taking boxes from the scree on to the Spit. One helicopter takes off! We strike the tents.

We will go off in alphabetical order. Jem stands out on the Spit with his pack. The helicopter lands. The crewman delivers a bag of womble suits. He stays on the beach to help load stores: Jem gets into one suit, and Chris B another. Jem leaves. We unlash boxes, and start humping them out on to the Spit. It is the seventh time we have stumbled across these cobbles with these big boxes. The helicopter flies in again, takes off Chris and lands another aircrewman. Now everything is a rush.

The second chopper starts shuttling to and fro. The forenoon passes in a joyous haze of effort. The food boxes come down from the filthy scree. Gradually the loads go. Then Tim, then Nick fly out. Now surely we all must go! We bring everything on to the Spit. Before Andy packs up the radio he makes a last call: it sounds as if the weather is clamping down; we may not get everything off. Frank, Andy and I carry food back to the camp plus canoe gear. The aircrewman says next trip they will take a canoe. Everything is topsy-turvy. We rush to get Mischief, taking out stores and stones. We unraft Tarka and B. Baggins. On the Spit all is chaos; internal loads, external loads, vice versa, nets, canoes. The crewman says the Captain wants me next. I promise Frank and Andy that I won't let the ship leave them. Frank says that he will come off last: brave lad.

Now I am in the helicopter, flying over the sea, away to *Endurance*. I cannot stop smiling. Perhaps it was all just a nightmare? Andy and Frank arrive. All safe!

Alan caused them much concern yesterday. Once on board he really went to pieces. The ship's doctor X-rayed his skull, suspected it was fractured and had his trepanning tools in the steriliser in case Alan haemorrhaged. This morning Paul opened up the gashes to look: there was penguin shit embedded in the bone, but it was not fractured. There could be complications in the next forty-eight hours. I am certain that he should stay on board, not run any risk ashore on Elephant, but can the ship land him next week? I feel sure they will try and the Captain promises anyhow to bring him south.

I am just beginning to smell myself. The bandage on my wrist is six days old, impregnated with penguin. Every time I lift a delicious sharp gin to my mouth, my nose gets a waft of Chinstrap. The officers say we smell better (not less) than the Clarence Islanders. I agree to save time by only dropping some food and paraffin at Cache F2 rather than a whole fishing camp with canoes. We will canoe down there from the Hut. Now we lie hove-to off the 'Refuge Hut'. The sun has come out. After these last five days, it is as if we have arrived at the threshold of a new world. Indeed it is a new and very different island. Cloud shadows waft across the undulating surface of Endurance Glacier, a creased white plain as wide as Gibbs was long. Isolated rocky bluffs prop up a great piled, snowy hinterland. The choppers ply to and fro, diminishing to minute dots towards the 'Refuge Hut'. Soon all is ashore; flying stops for an hour while the ship steams east for Walker Point.

Now it is six o'clock. We are about to fly into Walker Point. I drop out last on to mossed flat scree. John Highton grabs my pack. We have arrived. Oh joy!

We have landed just by the campsite, on the crest of a moraine at 200 m. Three Vango tents and an Arctic Guinea huddle in a square, inside a palisade of boxes. Everyone is out. We go round shaking hands, wishing each other a Happy New Year. Frank as first ashore has brought word that the tent change would happen this evening, each tent shared by one Gibbs and one Clarence man paired to suit their sciences and other tasks.

It is two months since I last saw the Clarence Islanders. They are looking cheerful, in rude health, and as ribald as before. Lennie has grown hair like a pop singer, and sports an Indian-style band tied round his head. Gordon is looking much fitter and sharper. Chris Hurran is much as before, but more assured; he bounces up cheerfully as if he has worn well, like his clothes. Dave Monteith has grown a buccaneering scoundrel's black beard and now rejoices in the name Bwana D. Mike Wimpenny looks much better for a gingery full set which has transformed his lugubrious walrus moustache and suits his confident smile; the tic which troubled one eyelid at home has vanished. John Chuter looks like a big blue ball on stick-legs as he peers out from his duvet jacket, clean shaven like me with a pink nose. I fail to recognise Nigel Davies as he hides behind a Pentax; yet I think he has changed least of all despite the beard.

The helicopter is going. The ship turns north-east: she fires two green flares. We loose off two red miniflares in reply. We are again alone on our islands.

The sun is shining. We stand on a gentle ridge of shattered rocks bedded in

The little Wasp helicopter drops a last load before leaving. Behind lies the Stadium Glacier with 'The Mask' and 'The Emblem'. (ND)

moss and smothered with pale green bushy *Usnea* lichens. It is a pleasant country compared to Gibbs. I cannot hear a penguin. Skuas rush through the air above. North of us stretches the broad, gentle surface of the Stadium Glacier, splitting into great blocks as it reaches the eastern sea, where stands Cornwallis, clean, grey and white. And beyond the glacier stands proud Pardo Ridge. To the east rise the three unclimbed hills, not 800 m, but very impressive with their mushroom ridges, tumbled icefalls and bare black rockfaces. Beckoning above is the crooked snowfinger, the summit of 'The Emblem'. Due north the little thumb of 'The Necklace' stands in a gap. West of it the wall of 'High Peak' ridge rises sheer to over 900 m from the low plain of the glacier.

They are digging platforms for the extra tents. These will form a regimental block, two rows of four, all opening on the centre corridor, except John Chuter's little Arctic Guinea, which faces outwards to the hills. After supper John Highton and I lie in our bags, resting on one elbow, clutching great mugs of brew. John lights one of his long cigars and begins to tell the tales of Clarence. He is a great raconteur. The stories of adventures come bit by bit, as one event reminds him of another. They will continue over the next days here. Just when I think there is no more to tell, Lennie or someone will scratch his head and say, 'Long John, do you remember that time when . . .', and away goes John on another tale.

North of Cape Bowles a shelf at 300 m is dominated by the cliffs of Mount Irving.
(75/76 *Endurance* Flight)

3   The Clarence Islanders

December to February

John Highton

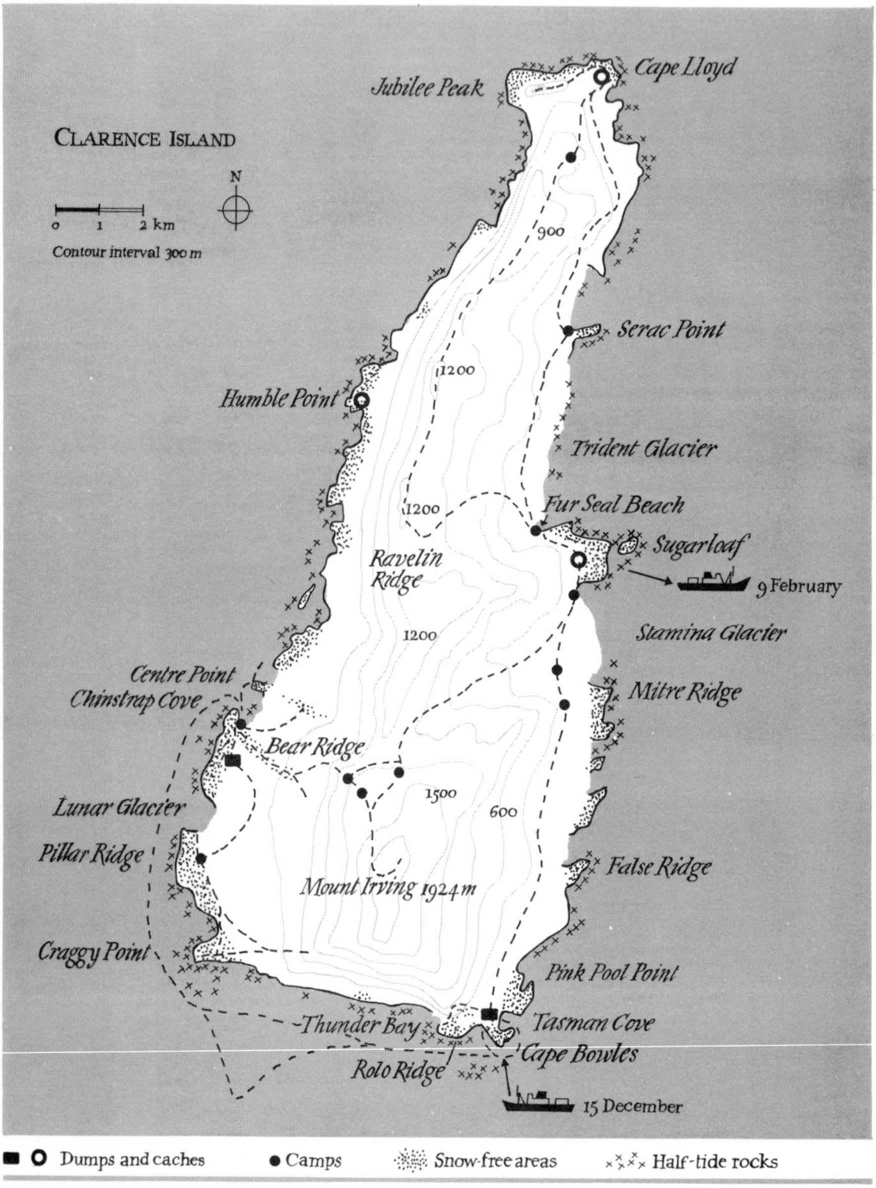

CLARENCE ISLAND

N

0 1 2 km

Contour interval 300 m

Jubilee Peak

Cape Lloyd

900

Serac Point

1200

Humble Point

Trident Glacier

1200

Fur Seal Beach

Ravelin Ridge

Sugarloaf

9 February

Stamina Glacier

1200

Centre Point

Mitre Ridge

Chinstrap Cove

Bear Ridge

1500

600

Lunar Glacier

Pillar Ridge

False Ridge

Craggy Point

Mount Irving 1924 m

Pink Pool Point

Thunder Bay

Tasman Cove

Cape Bowles

Rolo Ridge

15 December

■ O Dumps and caches   ● Camps   Snow-free areas   ×ˣ×ˣ× Half-tide rocks

13
Clarence: Cape Bowles and the West

Round the cape of a sudden came the sea,
And the sun looked over the mountain's rim:
Straight was a path of gold for him,
And the need of a world of men for me.
ROBERT BROWNING

15 December   This is it! We landed at Cape Bowles by 1200; a siren burst from a tiny *Endurance* and we were on our own. A campsite was selected and we moved most of the stores up to the site and put up the tents. Chris F's Ultimate Pyramids are an abortion; we broke the first one as they seem to be designed for the beach at St Tropez. So we put up two Arctic Pyramids and the Vangos. By 7 pm we were settled, not a little overwhelmed by our surroundings.

16 December   We explored 'Pink Pool Point' (our first naming here) and got back to camp having found one or two small crevasses. Our walk helped to get people accustomed to the surroundings. We established that to get north from here we would have to go at least 300 m higher. Later we launched the canoes and canoed round to 'Tasman Cove', a magnificent and very protected bay.

19 December   The canoes set sail under power around 'Tasman Bay'; the tidemeter worked; birds were counted (26,000 penguin nests on Cape Bowles alone). An iceberg was tracked: it passed going more or less due north at 1.125 kph (less than it looked). Len and I put up the second Ultimate Pyramid on the beach. It proved to be a much better tent than I originally thought, and will become our camp-out tent for up to three persons.

We celebrated Gordon's birthday with a communal dinner outside! – a great success. We were all in good spirits and after congratulatory speeches and a song, we washed up and assembled on the point for our evening meeting.

20 December
CHRIS HURRAN
The Chinstrap nests are very dense on 'Pink Pool Point'. I use a slow, accurate method of estimating nests, dividing the area up into rectangles, counting penguins along the sides and multiplying. At the point I have to stop, I have reached a staggering 33,550 nests. There are many penguin carcases. One penguin had died on its nest; its mate was roosting on top of it, presumably still trying to hatch out the eggs. I am getting quite used to the smell, and noise, and being pecked at; but I am still irritated by getting guano all over my gloves.

North of Cape Bowles lay 'Pink Pool Point', named after the wallows among these Chinstrap Penguins. Try to estimate the numbers by halving and quartering the area and counting along the sides of sample rectangles. Over the whole point there were nearly 30,000 nests! (DM)

By late afternoon the wind was gusting over 60 knots. We battened down, but not enough to prevent two Vangos collapsing, both with broken poles to windward. By this time the wind must have been gusting up to 80 knots and Nigel, Len, Gordon and I moved into Arctic Pyramids to weather out the storm.

21 December After a quick check round I discovered that a canoe raft was adrift in 'Tasman Cove'. Nigel, Len and I shot off to rescue it. The Ultimate flysheet was recovered from the bay and other stores found at the bottom of the cliff – three empty boxes and one box containing wetsuits. Our misfortunes were not so bad, though it looks as though we might be one Vango down. The remainder stayed up top to sort out the chaos. I decided to double secure our site by building dry-stone walls, which took four hours' work.

22 December It was a beautiful day, with fine views to the summit ridges of Clarence, mostly spent repairing damage and completing the dry-stone wall. All tents were bedded down with shale, which is much better than individual rocks – which shift in the wind and tear the valances. I think, had we been dug in as we are now, we would have had no problems the other night.

24 December   Dave, Len and I set off towards Sugar Loaf on a five day recce of the island. On crampons we made good progress over 'Petrel Glacier' up to the ridge around which I thought lay 'Stamina Glacier' (later named). However, after an hour's struggle up a 245-m ice slope, we realised that 'False Ridge' was all too false: ahead of us across a steep bowl lay another ridge. The going got worse and worse and by 4 pm we were pretty tired and still had only got half-way across the snowfield after 'False Ridge'. By 6.30 we reached the ridge ready to camp, and saw the glacier with Sugar Loaf apparently only a short distance away. Refreshed by the thought that a couple of hours would get us there, we set off down the snowslope to the glacier just west of a rocky outcrop. The bottom of the slope was very sludgy indeed and I worried about the state of the glacier. We progressed one step at a time up to our knees in sugary snow, and about 10 pm we arrived at 'Weddell Cove' too tired to consider going up the final slope to Sugar Loaf. After setting up our camp on the beach, only a metre above the waves, and a welcome curry cooked by David, we fell asleep absolutely exhausted – thirteen hours to cover about 11 km!

25 December   Christmas! We awoke refreshed at about 10.30, slightly surprised not to have been washed away! We set out for Sugar Loaf and quickly found a penguin ladder up. Four ladders give access to the beach, one of which is snow from top to bottom and is great fun to glissade down. This one also leads to the best landing place for canoes.

We got back at about 6 pm, cold and a little damp. After a snack and wet we played Scrabble. Then supper, cocoa, diary, and now bed. An unusual Christmas Day. Tomorrow we return to Cape Bowles. Movement is too much like hard work and to get to the top would take several days, certainly more than two.

26 December   I was alarmed to find that the brash ice had been swept away from our bit of beach and that a heavy sea was running. As we were only a metre above high water, this was of some concern. The icecliff at the end of 'Stamina Glacier' was also being badly eroded by the heavy seas: enormous chunks of ice were falling off, causing mini tidal waves about 6 m high. Dave and I went up to get food and fuel from the cache. This proved an exciting exercise, as the tide was too far in for us to reach the penguin ladders. So we scaled in appalling conditions a 45° slope which ended up in a rocky gully at about 55° with loose slab all sloping down and out. The adrenalin pumped round and it took us nearly two hours to get to the dump only 650 m away. We got back to find Lennie all prepared for evening Scrabble. As the game progressed the tide got higher, and the crashes and bangs of falling ice became more deafening. I was getting quite agitated and at about 19.30 decided that we could stay no longer. By 2100 we were packed up and left, hoping to get across 'Stamina Glacier' at least. The going was very bad and three hours later, with a white-out imminent, I called a halt some two-thirds of the way across. We were warm but very wet and after supper we turned in at about 0300. This flogging through snow up to one's knees, one step at a time and falling into occasional crevasses, is exhausting.

27 December   White-out! We had breakfast at leisure listening to the wind and snow. Scrabble. The day continued white-out until gone midnight by which time the light had gone – just flat white everywhere. So we turned in at about 2300 for 0600 start.

28 December   We got away booted and spurred in low cloud at 0800. It quickly became apparent that our return was going to be pretty slow. Apart from the snow conditions, which were bloody (one foot in up to knees, and struggle to get next one forward) the visibility was worsening, with cloud lowering, and frequent heavy gusts of wind with accompanying spindrift. There were in the end enough brief glimpses to see us on to the rock outcrop in the middle of 'Abandon Hope'; from there on for a couple of hours we had bright sunshine and made famous progress. We negotiated the steep slope around the bottom of 'False Ridge' without any great problem and set off on the home leg along the glacial step above the icecliffs. Once again the weather closed in and it took some time to find our way down to the campsite. We arrived just after 7 pm, some eleven hours after setting out. We were all very tired but pleased with our adventure.

30 December   I decided to go exploring over 'Rolo Ridge' to a bay I had seen. We crossed the ridge at 180 m and dropped southwards into a snow basin. The climb up is steep but without crevasses, as one goes close to rock all the way.

Weddell Seals roll over on their sides like this when alarmed on land.
(70/71 George Bruce)

The other side looks as though it should clear of snow quite quickly. The conditions were good. No more one-step-up-and-slither-back! And what a great place it turned out to be: a wide bay, ended by a glacier and a beach, part pebbles and part sand, popular with penguin and seal. There were seventeen seals (sixteen Weddell, one Leopard) of both sexes with three pups on the stretches not overhung by icecliffs. An estimated 20,000 penguins use the place, including three pairs of Macaronis with chicks. It is a dumper beach, but protected from all but southerly winds, and would be a fine place to camp with the strip of sand behind the shingle beach. We called it 'Thunder Bay' because of the avalanches.

31 December   Our New Year's Eve dinner included Penguin Strogonoff, very tasty and tender. New Year was celebrated with Teacher's Whisky at 2200 to coincide with home. A very pleasant evening and we all managed to stand three and a half hours in the Arctic Pyramid together.

3 January   At midday we finally decided the moment had come to move west. The visibility had worsened considerably and there were frequent snow showers, but the wind was minimal. I felt the small seas we were getting in 'Tasman Cove' would disappear when we got round the south side of the island. So, up sticks and away. It took us from 1400 to 1645 to clear into the canoes (I'm sure we'll get better at this) and a further hour or so to get on the move just

A curious Weddell Seal inspects the photographer. (DM)

before 6 pm. We made excellent progress in two cats, and with me in Happy Haggis hanging on to one catamaran.

NIGEL DAVIES

Both rafts managed to get out OK. We were very impressed with our raft as she rode the waves out: there was obviously going to be no problem. The sea was very confused as we rounded Cape Bowles, but as we moved along the south coast of the island the wind came from astern and the water got calmer. The clouds were very low around Mount Irving and it started to snow as we were abreast 'Thunder Bay'. It continued snowing until we got to within a kilometre of Craggy Point rocks. Here the vista really opened up, and we were able to see Elephant Island 40 km away to the west and Cornwallis to the north-west. The weather looked dark and snow-laden to the north but the sea in our area was calm. We pressed on. We had about 12 km to complete from point to point. The engines ran perfectly and we refuelled them every hour, kneeling across the cockpit and tipping the petrol from a gallon can into the tank with the engine running. There were many grounded bergs off the west coast, and we had to slow down and paddle when we ran into thick brash ice off the glacier snout. I didn't want to risk breaking a propeller shearpin. We got through without much trouble and started the engines when we had paddled clear. I kept pretty warm during the trip except for my hands, which I had to nurse a little as I had accidentally soaked my gloves. We even had tea and biscuits on the way round, which we passed around to Gordon and Mike in the front. It was all very gentlemanly and highly successful. We eventually nosed carefully into Chinstrap Cove at about 2000, frightened off penguins by the score, and drove up on to the beach. It had taken us only two hours.

The beach is about 30 m across and beautifully protected by a 20-m cliff to seaward and a number of rocks and grounded icebergs to stop the seas coming in. The dump is on a lovely moss-covered bluff with a skua's nest some 220 m above the sea. We set up camp slowly and well on our platform. A very good day.

8 January By 1000 it was beautifully sunny, and the attempt on Mount Irving was on. Mike, Dave and I prepared as quickly as we could and left at 1145. By this time it was very hot indeed, and sun beating down unmercifully and hardly a breath of wind. We made good time up on to the saddle under 'Mummy Bear', where we rested scarcely one hour after starting, having made 400 m in about 3 km. We now had to drop down on to 'Right Glacier' and this proved to be our first excitement as we hit a steep slope (60° in places) and had to abandon ourselves to gravity. All went well until cloud descended on us as we got on to the upper part of the steeply crevassed slope leading on to Ravelin Ridge. Just below the top of the slope at 1400 m we got into a crevasse. With the light fading we couldn't find an obvious way out, so I decided to camp in the crevasse. We hacked out a good flat platform – the shovel is very useful and well worth carrying – and by midnight we were in our tent brewing and cooking.

9 January With sunshine our hopes were reborn, but by the time we had breakfasted and decamped, the sun was only just visible through the mist. Half

Len and Chris Hurran rope up above Chinstrap Cove. Icebergs litter the sea off Humble Point, 8 km beyond. (ND)

an hour later we clambered out on to the plateau some 70 m above our campsite. Visibility was down to a few metres but I was pretty sure of my directions, so we set out for the summit across the plateau at 120° magnetic. After about twenty minutes we hit the ice wall flanking the summit ridge at about 1560 m. I turned almost due south and keeping as high as possible under the icecliff climbed steadily upwards. By the time we were at 1750 m the snow, which had begun to fall quite heavily in the wind which had sprung up from the north, was quickly obliterating our tracks. We found a way up through the ice wall and cut back north of east at 1730. I have little doubt that we had reached the summit at 1924 m. It is very exposed and the snow uneven due to the wind. We spent very little time there. My camera shutter froze open, so Dave took a token shot and we started down.

All went very well until we got on to the plateau. With no landmarks, we crossed it until we came to the top of the slopes leading down to 'Right Glacier'. Apart from one enormous crevasse and the ground dipping away sharply none

The west wall of Mount Irving is so uncomplicated that it looks deceptively small here. In reality its 1924 m dominates this campsite. (ND)

of us could see anything and time was getting on. So I found a fairly level spot (in a crevasse again) and decided to camp. We were in by 2130 and decided not to have the evening meal in case we should be stuck for another night out. So we had two cups of soup and our snack. I am very pleased to have made the first ascent of Mount Irving, but am a little alarmed that I don't know exactly where we are.

10 January   After checks at 0500 and 0700 (still white-out) it cleared a bit at 0800, and we saw where we were. We had strayed on to the north end of the mountain, and were amazed to see the Ravelin Ridge on our left! So we decamped as quickly as we could – it was very windy and there had been much new snow – and set off in intermittent visibility for the plateau and the steep slope down to 'Right Glacier'. It was magnificent there in the sunshine and howling wind with spindrift coursing across the plateau. We hit the top of the snowslope perfectly and with reasonable visibility. Though we could not ski quickly down it, we made pretty good progress, apart from my disappearing into a large crevasse suspended only by my elbows.

We arrived at the bottom hot, and ready for a wet. So we brewed up in bright sunshine, the only patch around. It was a good moment, and only then did I feel the importance of our achievement – not only a first ascent, but on ski also, up and down!

We got back after a trudge over the col between 'Daddy' and 'Mummy Bear' to find John C and Len at 'Skua Camp'. Two out of three Vangos had blown down with little damage.

11 January

CHRIS HURRAN

We go out to sea on a falling tide with John C filming. Just as we reach the mouth of the cove and are negotiating the iceberg, there is a loud rumble from the glacier as a big section falls into the sea. It sets up an enormous wave but by the time it reaches us we turn our bows to face it and ride it with comfort. Out of the cove we find that the sea is like a millpond and in quick succession we see our first Fur Seal of the expedition and, miracle of miracles, the buoy for the missing fish trap (it contains nothing but the bait and a couple of starfish). We continue south to the area where the trammel net was lost and spend a fruitless hour trawling for it. It is incredible how quickly it shelves in this area – it seems to go suddenly from about 30 m deep to over 80, in one place in a channel only about 100 m wide. The calm weather is too good to waste, so after a quick snack back in the cove we rig the raft for plankton and hydrographic work. We move south to a point about 300 m off the centre of 'Lunar Glacier' to start a transect of five or six stations as far north as 'Centre Point'. The idea is to haul two different sized plankton nets, and take associated readings of depth, clarity and temperature with samples of water for analysis of oxygen, salinity and silicate contents. At each station we first lower the lead line and Secchi disc, then the two plankton nets in turn and finally the Nansen bottle goes down twice. The whole procedure takes about forty-five minutes each time: it is hard work for Gordon and me, but pretty cold for Nigel. After our third station we remain anchored and have a bite to eat. Eventually after five stations and five hours at sea, we return to the cove at 2000 feeling cold.

12 January   By midday we were basking in warm sunshine. Dave, Chris, Mike and I left to climb 'Mummy Bear' and try 'Daddy Bear', At 1545 we were on top of 'Mummy Bear' at 700 m, having gone the whole way on ski. The last bit, up a steep sided ridge corniced at the top, was exhilarating. There is only room for one at a time and the ridge on the other side is virtually impassable without treading cornice. I was prepared to have a go at 'Daddy Bear', but the others were bothered by its appearance. As we came down 'Mummy Bear' on crampons (the ridge was far too narrow to ski down) the wind sprang up, the sun rapidly disappeared and we found ourselves cold and damp.

14 January   Today the wind blew harder and harder from the north. At midday I went out to see how all was going. This coincided with the collapse of Nigel and Len's Vango, so I helped get it down and installed them in our Ultimate. A few minutes later John C and Dave's Vango blew down, so we got them into Chris and Mike's tent, which was being sheltered a bit by our Ultimate. The wind continued to increase and by 1880 it was blowing a steady 60 knots with gusts of very much more than that. It also started to rain heavily.

15 January

CHRIS HURRAN

The day is devoted to drying out and patching up after yesterday's storm. Once again from the two wrecked Vangos we are able to salvage one reasonable one. As the cove comes into sight there is a horrific moment when it seems that everything has gone; but as we move lower we see that the canoes have been washed up on to the rocks. The tent has disappeared and one of the canoes is completely broken in two. Once on the beach we begin to sort through the wreckage, all the time surrounded by the most concentrated number of penguins yet seen. The high seas have obviously driven them off the rocks. Bunny has been completely wrecked, Bosscat has a split seam and a couple of holes, Tigger and Happy Haggis have minor damage and Bear Pooh has escaped unhurt. Both engines have been immersed, but Nigel gets them working. The tent is found on the opposite side of the cove, tangled round the fish trap and with a rather tired penguin inside. The cine camera is found half buried in the beach, probably ruined. The main losses seem to be the Nansen bottle, and Gordon's surgical instruments and drugs. Havoc has also been wrought amongst the penguins. All the nests near the tent have been washed out and there are dead chicks everywhere. This seems to indicate that it was an exceptional storm, as they usually nest away from natural hazards, such as rockfalls and avalanche slopes. We return to 'Skua Camp' as the clag comes down and arrive at 2030 as it begins to rain, in time for a radio contact with Gibbs.

16 January   Nigel, John C, Dave and Mike set off towards Craggy Point after a quick Sunday service. The weather looks fairly promising but there is rather too much clarity in the atmosphere for the improvement to last very long.

17 January   The weather has now held us up for four full days, a pity as our time to return east approaches fast. If the seas continue, we may not get to Humble Point for the twenty-four hours we need there. One thing is certain – we must take the first opportunity from Saturday to take the canoes round to Sugar Loaf.

18 January   Today we hoped to get off Humble Point. When we got to the cove it appeared that our chances might be very good even if the tide was far too far out and there was a lot of brash from a large collapse at the end of 'Right Glacier'. So we rafted Happy Haggis and Bear Pooh together and I took Tigger. After a couple of hours the tide was far enough in to set out. The waves seemed to have got up a bit, even going through the brash, which was very thick. All went fairly well until Lennie lost his paddle. The raft broached and was carried

Chinstrap Penguins pour past the tent and canoes at the back of the little cove. (ND)

broadside, so I shot past in case I speared them and waited outside the first line of brash. It was pretty rough and the way back in was getting worse and worse. It shortly became plain that the others were not coming out so I waited for several wave repeats before I decided to make my entrance. I got about two-thirds of the way in before being chuffed by a wave which was breaking even in the brash. An exciting moment which was repeated a moment later without any real problem and I ground my way in.

LEN HUNT
The narrow cove was chock-full of large lumps of brash ice. Half-way out of the cove, a large wave came rolling in and squashed the canoes between ice and rock. The rock was on my side; I heard a loud crack. We had to keep paddling as there were some whacking big waves

Bear Pooh and Bosscat lie in 'Leopard Cove' at low tide. (ND)

coming in. Near the entrance we broached and a big wave came in from my side and washed right over, landing lumps of ice on the canoe, on me and on my spraydeck, which collapsed. I never had time to refit it: we had to get the raft facing into the waves. We managed this after being hit a few times. Just at the entrance a huge wave hit us so hard I had my paddle ripped out of my hands by some brash. It lifted the raft up so that it was nearly on its side! I was right down in the water, while Gordon and Chris H were up in the air. It smashed us on to the rocks and this time I was certain that it had holed Happy Haggis. The backwash dragged us off into a sort of stopper and it dragged the front of the raft down under the water. We had to get back to the beach before my canoe filled up and sank. They were all paddling like blazes. We were hit time after time by huge waves, it was almost as if they had been waiting for us to move and then started coming in. The canoe was holed quite badly and the rudder was smashed and bent. Eventually we managed to get back in, where Happy Haggis sank. We all jumped out into the water, dragged the raft up the beach and had a look. Happy Haggis' aft end, from just behind my cockpit, was nearly broken in two. We repaired the damage as best we could, and came round to pitch our tent in 'Leopard Cove'. I think that we were bloody lucky that we weren't turned over, but (as usual) somebody was watching over us, and we got through it with minor damage. All our kit is soaked. I'll be sleeping in a wet

Two Ultimate Pyramids nestle above Craggy Point. These were good tents for mobile parties, our only good ones. (DM)

bag tonight but it doesn't worry me, I'll be warm enough. I'm beginning to wonder if we will ever get to Humble Point. We will just have to try again.

19 January   We left 'Leopard Cove' at midday, having spent a comfortable night, and Lennie was just about dry. We set off up the corner of the glacier, crossed the lower part of 'Right Glacier' and moved quite quickly diagonally to the left across the glacier, gaining 200 m in the process. We arrived at the southern base of 'The Horn', and fairly quickly got to the top. I fell into quite a big crevasse, and got a bit of a shock when I heard the snow bridge hit the bottom some seconds later. 'The Horn' is a very noticeable peak of 400 m and it deserves a name as a good landmark. Afterwards we tramped up 'Centre Ridge' in very bad conditions before I decided to head back. We crossed 'Right Glacier', and went over 'Baby Bear Ridge'. Reaching 'Skua Camp' at 1800, we found Nigel, John C, Dave and Mike already back from their expedition to Craggy Point. They have had a good four days, travelling mainly on skis to explore the south-west point of the island and climb 'The Ramp', a snow peak we had already named from 'Skua Camp'.

14

'Nibelheim' and Ravelin Ridge

Ah, but a man's reach should exceed his grasp,
Or what's a heaven for?
ROBERT BROWNING

20 January   Set up radio and spoke to Gibbs. We will be picked up from Cape
Bowles 8-10 February. Chris, John C, Gordon and I are going back over the top
to Sugar Loaf. The others will take the canoes.

21 January   At 1315 we set off up 'Midnight Glacier', at a slow pace since
Gordon has had little experience and is not very fit. We had to have two rests in
the first half hour, struggled up to the pass by 'Daddy Bear' in two hours and
had lunch. By this time the weather was improving and we had occasional
views to 1000 m. We crossed 'Right Glacier' without problem, and at the base of
the steep slope up to the Ridge I decided to camp (at 600 m). By this time
Gordon really was feeling the pace and the weight, and it would have taken
until long after dark to get to the next suitable campsite at the top. We had a lot
of digging to do to get space for two tents but this was fairly quickly achieved
and we settled in at 1900. After supper we had a long discussion on the conflicts
between the scientific and adventurous aims of the expedition. Barometer is
steady at 29.4 inches.

22 January   We made very good progress for the first 200 m before losing all
visibility. I ended up on a pretty steep slope. Within minutes Gordon was in
trouble with the skis and it took an hour to get him into crampons. Then we
made reasonable progress up the slope through the ice avalanche, before it
became obvious that the rest of us weren't going to maintain much progress on
skis. So off skis and into crampons. The snow was wet and cloggy and balled up
in the crampons, and we made slow progress. As we got higher, the wind got up,
and visibility disappeared, so I decided to go for my old crevasse campsite.
Gordon was getting pretty disillusioned and fed-up and wanted to stop every
four or five paces despite my slow pace.

23 January   Awoke to no wind and steady barometer (29.0 at sea level). We
packed up and set out in warm sunshine, and got on to the plateau in time to see
Irving fairly clearly, though the visibility was beginning to go and the wind was
getting up from the east. I decided to have a go at Irving, so we donned ski and
set out. An hour later at 1700 m I felt forced to turn back as visibility was down

to the end of my skis, and the wind was howling with a mass of spindrift. I tried to get down the way we came up but soon got on to some very steep slopes and ended up taking off skis and putting on crampons. I then tried again – and promptly stepped on to quite a steep slope (about 50°) and set off a wind slab avalanche. Fortunately I got my axe in very quickly and stopped before putting much weight on Gordon.

It is not a nice situation, not being able to see anything except other climbers on the rope, and then only the one behind. The avalanche disturbed me quite a bit. After a little more probing around when the sun appeared over the spindrift (one could still see absolutely nothing), I decided that we must stop, at least until we could see where we were. I felt that we had wandered on to the top of the lower icecliff. The weather was very squally and I couldn't put much trust in the altimeter. So we dug a small hole to wait in and watch, while I started digging a snowhole on a 40° slope. Time was about 1530. The spindrift and wind got worse, and we were thankful when we had progressed far enough to get all four working inside. With four axes and one shovel we were in by 2200, wet but warm. Digging a snowhole certainly prevents chill and depression.

CHRIS HURRAN
The basic design is a simple long T-shaped tunnel, high enough to stand up in, with two two-man sleeping shelves off the end of it at waist height. The snow is not bad for digging. The final move is to bring in the packs. We block ourselves in with skis, a flysheet and rucksacks and quite quickly the sprindrift seals the entrance. I am absolutely soaking, and

Flashlight catches Chris Hurran and John Highton settling down in their half of the snowhole on the plateau. Polywarm bags, Travel Scrabble and curried porridge all help survival. (CH)

cold, with the odd spasm of cramp. The other three are all in the same state. Inside the snowhole it is silent and still, while the hooligan continues outside.

24 January   Outside spindrift was still howling about with nil visibility. So we sorted out and checked food, paraffin and hexamine. We have enough to keep us going for three days. We are quite comfortable. The hole is pretty dry, and inside it is absolutely calm, despite the hooligan outside.

GORDON TURNBULL
It is strange and a little frightening to find oneself in such a situation but things could be a lot worse. A pipe is a real friend. I am desperately trying to remember all the guidelines to survival I learnt for this expedition. We are warm and in good health and spirits. Lying on a polythene survival bag and a karrimat the body is shielded from cold ice below. It is not cold to write but when my hat is removed my ears feel the sudden chill. The temperature is about minus 5°C.

CHRIS HURRAN
I call the snowhole 'Nibelheim', as holes in the roof are thawing through to give the whole place a distinctly Wagnerian appearance.

25 January   Awoke at 0430 refreshed, to find it much colder in the snowhole. We had all slept very well, being both warm and dry. Outside there were blue skies and cloud and I decided that today we would move. The plateau was beautiful, carved into great waves of drift by the heavy winds. I had not seen it like this before. I also had quite good views of the saddle above 'Stamina Glacier'. I doubt whether a climbing party could make it, past an enormous ice pyramid, and another very steep slope beyond, back on to the Ravelin Ridge. So that way is out and I won't try it. We were a crowd of beginners on skis really. I had to lead us as none of the others could control their direction downhill and there was much falling, making slow progress. But the weather was nice even if a bit windy, and we were all quite comfortable. The snow was varied, from powdered to crust, until we got to about 500 m when it turned into absolute slush with a thin ice crust on top. It took a long time to get down to 'Weddell Cove'. There we found much brash, and a heavy sea running in, washing over our Christmas campsite. One Weddell, one Fur Seal and a few Chinstraps all looked very battered. We took off skis and scrambled through jumbled loose brash ice to the penguin ladder, beating the tide narrowly.

By the time we got up to the food cache it was 1800 and the wind was howling. We picked a spot nearby and levelled a platform. By 2100 we were in. After a meeting we turned in replete, to the howl of blustering winds and flapping of our tents. The first traverse of Clarence has been completed – an epic 9 to 10 km in five days!

26 January   A bad night. The wind must have been gusting well over 60 knots and it was noisy, cramped and wet. There was no sign of a lessening of the wind, so we were resigned to another day in tent. We have eaten, sewed, written,

An Ultimate Pyramid stands on a snow platform at Sugar Loaf. Here the Chinstrap Penguins nest up to 300 m high: what a daily climb on their little legs! (GT)

chatted all day. I hope that this wind is not permanent, otherwise we will do little here. To the hills tomorrow.

27 January   Lo and behold, the sun appeared though it was very cold. I decided that Chris and I should nip over to the north to have a look. Fifteen minutes of great going and we were there: a haven on this side of the island! A beautiful beach 150 m by 40 is covered with forty Fur Seals, one Elephant (male), one Weddell (male) and countless birds. I decided that the Sugar Loaf area was good for more than gale-force winds. Time is running out now. Tomorrow John C and I will go to Bowles to collect oddments and leave messages for the canoeists and return here the day after.

On our way back from 'Fur Seal Beach', I climbed up Sugar Loaf Ridge to spy out the lie of the land down to 'Stamina Glacier'. By this time the weather was absolutely brilliant and the atmosphere frigidly transparent. The colours of the ice were electric and it is a pity that my camera froze up. The temperature must have been about minus 10°C at 300 m, with a wind chill factor of another 20°C.

28 January   John C and I got away by 1115, making tremendous progress on good crampon snow all the way to 'False Ridge' (three hours). There John fell on steep ice, hurting his left leg a bit. I had to chase half his kit down the hill to stop it rolling and blowing into the sea.

We eventually arrived at Cape Bowles at 1730 to find Nigel installed. He had quite a story to tell. On 22 January, though the weather was far from perfect, he had a curiously strong conviction that they must leave. In the battered canoes they set off on a desperate journey round Craggy Point to Cape Bowles, baling the whole way. They had taken to the sea just in time: a storm raged at the Cape for the next five days.

29 January   I decided to leave John C at Cape Bowles with Nigel and Dave because of his leg and Mike, Lennie and I set off on crampons at 1115. We made pretty good progress up to 'False Ridge', where we had a slow but exhilarating ice climb up to the ridge. There lunch in the sun and off across 'Abandon Hope' to 'Mitre Ridge' – again quite good going – and on to 'Stamina'. The problem came getting up on to Sugar Loaf Ridge. The wind had given us a bit of a battering across 'Stamina' and we were all pretty tired. It took all my determination to stagger up through this 40° crevassed slope on to the ridge. We made it, and got down to 'Fur Seal Beach' after nine hours. I was very glad to get there. The wind was blowing in heavy gusts, but we got a Vango up all right.

LEN HUNT

The going was fantastic: the snow was hard but for a few patches of soft, deep powder and we went like crazy. The sun was beating down and we all got tanned by the late afternoon when it disappeared behind the ever-present clag. The only dodgy bit we had was on 'Mitre Ridge'. We had to cross an avalanche slope that was just ready to go. It took us about twenty minutes to get down it and every minute was spent in a cold sweat. We crossed 'Stamina

Brown Skuas and Fur Seals loaf on 'Fur Seal Beach'. Ice falling from the glacier beyond sends waves up the beach carrying these bits of brash ice. (LH)

Glacier' in an hour flat and arrived at 'Fur Seal Beach' at 2030. We pitched our tent next to Chris and Gordon's. The wind hit us again through the night and broke a pole, but we repaired it by lashing a ski stick to it. There was an icefall off the glacier into the sea directly across the bay from us and the wave came foaming across the bay and up the beach, scattering penguins as it came.

30 January   The glacier is disintegrating in the most incredible crashes and bangs. Two very big tidal waves hit the beach but did not get as far as us. The others have not arrived and I don't really expect them in these conditions. So Mike, Chris and I will head off to Cape Lloyd by the low level route tomorrow as we must try to get there and I think that is the most likely way to succeed, the weather being what it is.

2 February   Two excellent days had brought us to Cape Lloyd. Much to my surprise we found there a gas operated light beacon that wasn't there when our cache was flown in. It had been placed there by AP *Piloto Pardo* on 18 December (we saw them passing southwards that afternoon). I left a message in a magic marker on the beacon:

This place was visited on the 2nd February 1977 by members of a British Expedition which has occupied the island from the 15th December 1976 to 8th February 1977. J. Highton, C. Hurran, M. Wimpenny.

Shortly after 1500 we set off into the murk for 'Jubilee Peak', a most spectacular peak, rising narrowly up on the extreme north end of the island with only one apparent route up, along the east ridge. The average slope of the ridge is not great but there is quite a long section of 200 m at over 45° and one large mushroom completely blocking the ridge. This fortunately had split, leaving a steep but not too difficult climb of about 60 m on to the summit ridge. There were several places where belays were necessary because of the immense exposure: the ridge narrows down to less than 30 cm in places, with overhanging mushrooms to cross as well. It would have been worse if it had been very clear, though more exhilarating! We reached the top at about 1730 and got glimpses of the ridge we had come up, and down to the west. We also saw the cliffs on the west side of the island. Most spectacular. I recorded the height of 'Jubilee' as nearly 700 m.

   Snow conditions deteriorated and the wind got up. If this continues I will have to stay off the Ravelin Ridge tomorrow.

3 February   We decided to have a go at Ravelin Ridge. We set out at 1410 and made good ground up to 500 m when we encountered hard ice. I persevered on ski up to 750 m when it became too difficult so we cramponed up in the clag – just as well as the slope increased to about 45° for 100 m. After three hours we were on the ridge. Though we got occasional glimpses of ridge (and one iceberg) the going was slow and mushrooms began to crop up everywhere. So I decided to camp on the ridge at 950 m.

4 February   What a ridge it was! As we moved along we got occasional glimpses of where we had been – it was hard to believe that we had managed. The ridge is extremely narrow in places (less than 3 m) with a 1000-m drop on the west. It must be one of the most memorable days I have ever spent in the mountains. A combination of grandeur, and sheer physical exertion pitted against the mountain. Below us was a layer of clag, which prevented all but fleeting glimpses of Sugar Loaf and the rest of Clarence, but we had stupendous views back along the ridge towards Cornwallis and Elephant. We reached a maximum of 1300 m on Ravelin Ridge before dropping down to the southerly arm of 'Trident Glacier', which was in poor condition and much more crevassed than I thought. So it took time to get down; we had to put on skis because the sugar got up to my crutch and in that one cannot move.

We eventually got to 'Fur Seal Beach' and the others. Three of them came a kilometre or two in the gloom to greet us. It was good to be all together again and to catch up on news. The day we left Cape Bowles a huge icefall had landed on the canoes. Nigel could not get down to the beach for fear of further falls until the following day, but his worst fears were realised: the canoes were badly smashed and only one engine had survived. Bad weather trapped them at the Cape for two more days, but eventually he, John C (despite his bad ankle) and Dave made it over Sugar Loaf Ridge to join Lennie and Gordon.

I have decided that John C and Gordon should stay here to be picked up on Tuesday (8 February), while the rest of us set off south to arrive at Cape Bowles the day after tomorrow.

The four canoes lie among the debris of an ice avalanche below Cape Bowles. Many penguins are also buried – nowhere is safe on Clarence Island. (ND)

15
Farewell to Long John's Kingdom

The average wind force (over the South Shetlands) is considerably higher than indicated in the climatic tables.
THE ANTARCTIC PILOT

7 February   The weather yesterday and today has made it impossible to get back to Cape Bowles. We will simply move up to Sugar Loaf, build a fire as a beacon, and assume that *Endurance* will look for us there.

At 2000 we foregathered in the alcove overlooking the beach and 'Trident Glacier' for a dinner to celebrate the Queen's Jubilee and our own sadness at leaving Clarence. An excellent dinner prepared by John C and Gordon.

8 February   After watching all morning, we eventually saw *Endurance* steaming north from Bowles at midday. We were helicoptered off and had lunch on board before going to Bowles for a rushed pack-up of stores which was completed by 1800. In the meantime Dump B had been collected from 'Skua Camp'.

9 February   We sailed round to Prince Charles Strait and dropped off John C, Chris, Dave and Gordon at Walker Point on Elephant Island. I remained on board to greet Chris Furse, while Nigel, Mike and Len were dropped on Cornwallis Island for a two-day visit.

NIGEL DAVIES
'Flying Stations' was at 0900. After an initial recce flight Lennie and I were lifted off and landed on a point of rock below the big snow couloir on the south-west side of Cornwallis. The helicopter was only able to put two wheels down and we had to jump out into a load of penguin mire! Whilst we were climbing out of our survival suits the helo went back to Endurance *and returned. Mike took his turn at jumping boot-deep into penguin shit and away they went. We were on our own again.*

Behind us Cornwallis rose in a steep snow couloir topped by a rock ridge and the summit point. It looked very impressive. There were signs of avalanches in the couloir and gullies. We had a quick recce and decided to erect the tent on a snow platform. There didn't seem to be anywhere else we could put it. To get there involved a treacherous walk up the penguin colony amongst rounded granite boulders covered in filth.

Mike went off with a big hammer to chip granite. He seems very pleased to have a change in rock scenery. Lennie and I got on with digging the snow platform, which proved more difficult than expected, because there was hard ice only half a metre or so down, and we had to hack much of this away to get an adequate platform. It was not until 1430 that we had the

Ultimate up. We retired inside for a brew and a snack and by 1600 we were ready to attempt the summit.

The weather had been very calm with strato cumulus at about 1000 m and the sun had almost broken through but by the time we left camp a disturbing little breeze had started. We went off up the snowslope behind the tent, eventually gained a rock ridge at about 180 m, and moved over this to cut across the top of a rocky cwm to yet another ridge! But here our troubles began. The ridge ran up steeply towards an ice mushroom and we had to traverse along the top of the steep snowslope towards it. The snow was soft in places and Lennie didn't like it much. I decided to drop down to the snowfield again and cross to a rock ridge further north. After an hour we reached the summit of the ice mushroom via an ice wall, a steep snowslope and an interesting traverse along a corniced ridge. The summit we called 'White Tor', but the other summit (some 400 m further along a very steep ridge), was about 100 m higher than our ice mushroom. To reach it we would have to drop down again and traverse across a large ice field to climb up from the other side. As the weather appeared to be closing in from the north with a cold wind, we put Lennie on the mushroom top, took photographs and returned whence we had come. By the time we reached our tent at 2000 there was thick sea mist falling, snow and a cold wind!

Len felt quite chuffed that we had got to one of the summits but I was a little disappointed we hadn't made the proper summit, as I think Mike was too.

10 February   *Woke to find Mike starting the primus. It was a dismal morning with thick mist, light sleet and a chill, wet wind. By 1130 Mike and I decided we must make a move or we would be in the tent all day. We put on waterproofs and (leaving Lennie still in his sleeping bag reading) visited the ternery we had spotted yesterday. While Mike wandered off chipping rocks and counting nests I took some photos of a tern feeding its young on a small sprat. The chick was the size of a small hen's egg and very fluffy. The Antarctic Terns are pretty birds with black cap, creamy grey plumage and bright red beaks and feet. They put up an awful racket when we went through the colony but eventually settled down.*

We climbed up to the ridge, before dropping down into the stone couloir, for a look at the penguin colony: Mike estimated that there were 2000 nesting pairs, all Chinstraps as far as we could see. We made our way back to the tent where Lennie had a brew on, and settled down as best we could. There was wet gear everywhere from the heavy rain and the condensation inside. We spent the rest of the evening brewing, cooking and chatting about the expedition.

11 February   *The weather has been so warm over the last thirty-six hours that most of the snow has melted from the face we camped on. We all got out and lugged granodiorite boulders up from the penguin colony below us, and Mike set to work with the snow shovel to prop up the sagging platform. It is shrinking by the hour.*

We have plenty of food but very little paraffin and have started to conserve fuel to make sure that we last through. At the latest we should be picked up on Monday night (14 February). We discussed the possibilities of penguin steaks and black pudding, and the state of play of the helicopter.

At 1550 Endurance *sounded her siren and we trooped out to see her steaming up and down off the island. I expect she has the Gibbs party on board and is waiting for a break to lift us off. A helicopter made an attempt to land on 'Dolphin Point' at 1630. The wind started to get up, and just before the helo arrived a violent gust from the snowslopes above had broken one of the Ultimate poles. Mike went down to the pick-up point, whilst Len hovered around outside the tent watching. I was busy trying to hold up the tent pole. The helo was unable to land, and the wind was too strong for winching. Len said that the Wasp had very nearly gone into the sea after moving off from its first attempted hover over 'Dolphin Point'. About fifteen minutes later the helo returned to drop off another few days' supplies of food, fuel and a spare cooker, then returned to* Endurance, *which disappeared into the mist in the direction of Gibbs Island.*

Our troubles now increased with the little Pyramid tent. Millions of litres of water were pouring off the ice slope around us and our flimsy little snow platform was rapidly melting. The wind was coming from the north-west. I spent a long cold time outside the tent positioning icescrews for the guys and putting a guy on the broken pole. Mike was meantime wrestling manfully with the broken apex of the Pyramid over the top of the tent and secured it from both sides with the climbing rope, but the next gust knocked the offside pole right through the snow platform. Mike went out this time: he wedged my piton hammer into the snow platform at an angle and rested the end of the pole on the head of the hammer and things returned almost to normal. However, about 2200 the pole must have slipped off and the apex of the tent started to slide down towards us. By now it was getting dark and we were wet and cold; even if the tent collapsed we decided to stay inside it in our sleeping bags. At least we would have a waterproof and a windproof cover over us. It was very damp sleeping against the soggy, limp folds of the collapsed wall and I woke up several times with the wet nylon clinging around my head. I looked out of the tent at 0115 and was relieved to find that it had started to freeze, so the possibility of the snow platform collapsing was now lessened. I slept better after that. Mike Wimpenny had the best night as he was sandwiched between Len and myself with a metre of space above his head. The wind kept up its incessant tattoo for the rest of the night.

12 February   *We survived the night quite well and 0830 found us ready for a good breakfast. The sky was much clearer with patches of blue. Clarence and Elephant Island were visible across the sea. The sea was a carpet of grey and white for the wind was still blowing gale force: it had backed to the west, and was now blowing directly on to the ice face. However by some quirk of rock formation or cliff profile we seemed to be in a dead spot, with only the occasional blow shaking the tent.*

At 1400 we sighted Endurance *on the horizon making towards us. The Wasp flew over and tried a few runs. Mike was down there: they lowered a mail bag with survival gear down to him and indicated that he put it on. I was watching from the tent door. While Mike got the yellow suit on the Wasp hovered over to the tent and the observer made hand signals to pack up camp. So they intended to lift us off, although the wind was still very strong. They returned to winch Mike off the point, whilst Len and I packed up our personal gear. We were so busy inside the tent that we didn't notice Mike winched up and dropped down again: the wind was too strong. Mike eventually appeared from 'Dolphin Point' and told us it was off.*

Next the Wasp returned and dropped off forty manday rations and half a jerrican of fuel! We now presumed that we would be left alone for some considerable time, so we started to unpack. The helicopter returned to Endurance *and Mike wandered down to the drop point carrying his rock samples.*

It was now that the tent was avalanched with five or six Chinstrap Penguins. The noise and wind from the helicopter had alarmed them and they had all hopped off up to the top of the colony and started to climb the ice wall. Most had successfully negotiated this by digging in their toes and beaks and slowly winning a way up. However, one penguin (having a quick peck at another who was treading on his head to get higher) lost his hold and started to slide down the ice slope tail first. In the course of this 20-m slide the unfortunate Chinstrap collected five of its companions from the ice wall. The end result was a scrabbling cartwheeling feathered thump as six penguins came to a sudden stop against the uphill tent wall. It sounded as though an avalanche had hit us and Lennie shot out of the tent like a hare on the run! The penguins recovered their dignity, shook their ruffled feathers, gave the tent a jaundiced stare and hopped off diagonally up the slope.

To our amazement the helicopter battered its way back against the wind at 1730 and dropped a message attached to a chipping hammer near the tent: they wanted to pick us up after all, one at a time with kit. With muttered curses we set to and repacked. I had just settled into the tent again and blown up my lilo! This time they lifted Mike off to the ship, leaving us to pack his kit. It was 1815 before we were ready to move down to the penguin colony. I was last to be picked up at about 1845. It was pretty ghastly down in the penguin colony. My clothes were covered in filth after hurrying down from the campsite, through slippery rocks, and every time the helo hovered overhead a fine spray of penguin shit hit me. I was winched up from the point following Mike's rucksack and positioned in the starboard doorway behind the pilot. My legs were hanging outside and I looked down over the foaming sea as we whirled off in the direction of Elephant Island. I had thought that we were going to the ship but half-way across Prince Charles Strait the observer lifted my earmuffs and shouted that we were going to Walker Point direct. So I sat there slowly getting colder and colder for the 14-km trip. The wind was pretty violent as we came in over Walker Point but I could see the four red anoraked figures coming from the dump to greet us. I was dropped off with Mike's kit and over the next half hour Mike, Lennie and John Highton all arrived.

The four days on Elephant have clearly been even less comfortable for Gordon, Dave, John C and Chris than for the trio on Cornwallis, and we arrived to find John C's Arctic Guinea buried in a pit half a metre deep to keep it out of the wind. Both Vangos had blown down in the storm and they had all spent a night in polythene survival bags under the tattered remnants. As John C said, the island has so far been an exercise in survival. The constant battering of the wind has made it impossible to do any but the simplest tasks outside. Outside is another world: howling, blasting, cold and wet. Communication is almost impossible and one has to shout to make oneself heard.

13 February   I awoke to a beautiful sunrise over Clarence – all the colours of the rainbow in the sky. But by 0800 it was blowing a hooligan and snow was coming horizontally out of the mist down Stadium Glacier. I checked round at about 1000 and all was well. Plainly we won't see the Gibbs Islanders today! Nothing we could do except sit tight. It was too bad to go out and get stuff from boxes. We reconnected guys on five occasions and repaired one pole; otherwise an uneventful day.

14 February   They arrived!

4 Elephant Island

February and March

The camp at Walker Point. (ND)

16
Christmas Together at Walker Point

Question: Who took a party of children to the Never Never Land?
Answer: Peter Pan (2 points) or Commander Furse (1 point).
HMS ENDURANCE QUIZ PROGRAMME

14 February   We have been separated for two months. For two months we have each shared the adventure of our lives in a close group of eight friends. From experience in 1970-71, I warned the whole team that we may find it difficult to readjust now as we all meet together. We have developed different attitudes, habits, jokes and catchphrases; each group feels in some ways superior. We may also have slight but very real prejudices, jealousies, suspicions, even unreasoning resentments.

To break this down very quickly now, I have shuffled the two parties in the tents at Walker Point. Each tent is shared by a Gibbs Islander and a Clarence Islander. After 'Christmas' we will be splitting into small parties exploring: I will ensure that each rope has both Clarence and Gibbs Islanders. After this first week of enforced mixing, it should be as if we have never been apart. No. It will never quite be that. We cannot share these last two months with anyone who has not been with us. Nevertheless in a week or two it should be unnecessary to stipulate particular mixes.

Lying in the Ultimate at Walker Point, warm in our maggots on the moss, bellies full, hot mugs in hand, John Highton puffing his pipe contentedly and the tent flapping half-heartedly, we discuss the personalities of our two teams. In general, the Clarence Islanders are more extrovert, cheerfully loud, blasphemous and rough. John remarks that the Gibbs Islanders seem 'more serious'. That is apt. It is partly because the last five days on Gibbs Spit have scarred us, but it is also a function of our personalities. It was the quality of patience which dominated my selections last year, with the possibility of our being marooned on Aspland. John and I have each been very happy with our teams. I, with no failures, tell John the strengths and weaknesses of the individuals. John does likewise.

I'm a listener, not a talker, which fits well with John in a tent as he is the opposite. It is great to have met again after two months and to find we still like each other! This is the classic situation for rivalry when a second-in-command, himself an excellent leader, 'returns to headquarters' after a period of independent command. With John and his team rested and I and mine tired after five nights on Gibbs Spit, this meeting could have been difficult. It's great to find John so loyal. He doesn't even complain about my snores, much!

We have lost time in the last five days. John and I must work out a programme for the next four weeks. This first night I am too exhausted to work out details, but a general framework emerges. It centres around getting Frank's fishing party established down by Rowett Island, and John's ambition to climb all the hills along Pardo Ridge. The other things we have to do include surveys of Walker Point and Stinker Point in the west; coring and levelling work on Endurance Glacier; and a geological recce on the north coast. I also want to make the canoe journey from Cape Valentine to Point Wild, and to visit 'Point Inaccessible' en route. All this is a crammed programme. Obviously we must get started very quickly and make up for lost time by rushing the process of reacquaintance. First we must celebrate our Expedition Christmas: we ordain that 'Christmas Day' will be the day after tomorrow, 16 February.

That decided, I go out like a light. Our tent is bedded on soft blocks of moss lifted out of the nearby carpets. It is lovely, comfy and warm, and there is no condensation on the tent floor. I vanish into bottomless, dreamless, beautiful black sleep. I am absolutely exhausted.

15 February   It is a beautiful day for laziness. The sun shines quite often, and there is just a little wind. Elephant Island has so much better weather than Gibbs!

Nick, Dave, Chris B, Len and Gordon are building a stone house for the Christmas feast, hacking down a floor with pick and sledge hammer and building thick walls of flat scree stones filled with rubble. By the end of the day the walls stand shoulder high around a 4-m square.

John Highton goes off with Chris H, Mike and Andy to climb one of 'The Triumvirate', none of which has ever been climbed. They ski off across the glacier until they vanish as black motes over the col where Crispin Agnew's party were avalanched in 1971. This time the snow is in perfect condition, having thawed and refrozen, so that all the glaciers are showing their crevasses clearly and the slopes are holding firm snow, or ice.

I potter about talking, to the Clarence Islanders in particular, to find out what each wants to do, or must do, trying to fit them to the overall plan, and trying to blend the details of the plan to suit as many people as possible. A number of points emerge:

a. Both the Clarence Island cine cameras have been broken and ours went to the Hut. Dave wants to get the one from the Hut as quickly as possible, and then to concentrate on cinefilm. Chris Hurran's aerial photos of Walker Point are also at the Hut.

b. Frank prefers a three-man fishing party to four.

c. Nigel and Andy have earned places in the Pardo Ridge party.

d. No one really wants to do more canoeing!

e. Food. We have ample, here and at the Hut, whatever we do.

f. Skis. We have ten pairs here plus all sixteen skins; the other skis are at the Hut. With this good hard surface now, parties should get to the Hut on foot soon to return on skis.

g. Canoes. We have enough at Walker Point and the Hut to cover each their own needs.

h. Tents. At Walker Point we have six Vangos, three Ultimate Pyramids, two Arctic Guineas and two Survey tents from *Endurance*. At the Hut we have three naked Arctic Pyramids and two Arctic Guineas. Jem pitches one of the Survey tents this afternoon. It turns out to be an Edgington Windover tent, similar to the Arctic Pyramid. It looks a very good base camp tent. We can give Frank spare tentage for safety.

In the afternoon the sun really breaks through. It is too good to miss, though I am desperately behind with my journal. Four of us ski into the upper level of Stadium Glacier to look at the mountains surrounding it, and to check some likely cliffs for Snow Petrels. We find none.

John gets back from 'The Emblem'. Chris and Mike were turned back by some steep ice slopes. Andy and John got on to the ridge and part way along, before they found themselves on a great wafer of a ridge leading to a bad step. It was then quite late, and they turned back. 'The Emblem' is even harder than it looks. Andy is exhilarated by this day. Worried that the Clarence Islanders would be far fitter, he had set a very fast pace skiing over.

This evening Mike and Chris H tell me about the bird work they have done on Clarence. They have evidently counted breeding birds very thoroughly and

This docile ball of down is a young Antarctic Prion taken from its burrow in the mossy scree of Walker Point. The only known breeding colonies further south are on the other side of the Antarctic. (70/71 George Bruce)

have done more than me measuring Chinstrap chicks. They also did a traffic count on a colony of 12,000 Chinstrap nests over a twenty-four-hour period, and collected as many penguin stomachs as I have too. All in all, they have done an excellent job.

At midnight there is no wind at all. I go out to show them the prions and Black-bellied Storm Petrels. They have not seen any on Clarence, but think they may have heard them. On this unusual still and starlit night we can hear from the camp the 'chuzzing' of Wilsons Storm Petrels and the occasional 'wheee' or 'pip peep pip' calls of the Black-bellies from the lichened cliffs away on the point. I can also make out the underground murmur of the prions. We walk over to the prions' breeding area which I know from 1971 in a moss-grown scree slope. The murmurings get closer and closer then fade. Suddenly they are calling right under our feet, in a little outcrop of rock. We crawl around shining our torches into every cranny. Finally we catch sight of one adult prion, close to the surface, largely hidden by the rock, but with its bill and head unmistakable. After this, we go up to the top of the cliffs. We hear Black-bellies calling only a few metres away, but it is now so dark that I cannot even see whether the silhouettes of storm petrels rushing silently past have the white flashing tummies of Black-bellies or not.

16 February   Today is 'Christmas Day'. The weather remains sunlit; gentle zephyrs chase blue cloud shadows across the glacier below. It has been in sympathy with my mood of joy at being here among the wide horizons and separated hills of Elephant. As the days pass my heart and soul uncoil from their hunched Spit posture and bask in pleasure.

We all get into the Christmas house for lunch. They have put in a table and roofed it all with a tarpaulin held up by a pole in the middle. As we eat, I outline the programme over the final weeks of the expedition. I have decided on three three-man parties leaving for the Hut tomorrow: Frank's party will go on to fish at Rowett; John Chuter's will help them ferry gear south from the Hut, and then return here; Chris Hurran's will fetch the cine camera, and the aerial photographs of Walker Point, and come back here quickly. The six of us left at Walker Point will press on with botany and climbing and will sledge the canoes over 'Hell's Gates' ready to repeat Shackleton's boat journey, from Cape Valentine to Point Wild. The plans beyond that are vague, but the general aim is to move west in two weeks' time. The nine leaving tomorrow will have quite a rush, especially Nick and Dave, who are decorating the house, cooking, and compering today's Sods Opera. No one objects to the proposals, which is grand, as I know that some of them would not have chosen their allotted roles.

After Christmas cakes comes the Sods Opera, first the Clarence Islanders' acts then ours: a hilarious fantasy story; an ode to the hydrographic equipment; performing maggots; snow dancers; and a Vicar's sermon competition, won by Jem.

The climax of the day's festivities is the evening feast in the dry-stone Christmas house. We bring presents for each other. Some have made great efforts to produce really worthwhile things. Frank has cut, ground and polished

Official Christmas – 16 February. The Clarence Islanders sit outside the dry-stone Christmas house, while Nick leads the Gibbs Islanders' choir. On the tops of the skyline ridges lie the deepest moss beds in Antarctica. (ND)

a sizeable block of green serpentine rock to make a lovely ashtray for Len. Chris Brown has made a leather box of Gibbs geological specimens for John Chuter. Mike Wimpenny has given Andy a candle holder made from a chunk of granodiorite rock from Cornwallis, sparkling white with black bits scattered like raisins in a duff. Jem has whittled a beautiful paperknife for Dave, the handle carved like a fish swallowing the blade. The girls in the food-packing depot have knitted us each a woolly hat or a scarf, and we sit round wearing these as we tuck into a succession of goodies: nuts, shrimps, cold stuffed pork roll, asparagus, celery hearts, then hot Christmas pudding, followed by toffees, crackers, silly hats and sparklers. We have a bottle of brandy which is used first on the Christmas pud, then divided up. It fires the throat and rises behind our nostrils, so unused are we now to alcohol. We also have a bottle of whisky, which is passed around to lace our coffees; it goes around and around, most people just pass it on without drinking any. With the laced coffee, we pass round presents from home, sent last June. I get letters from the middle of a Kentish heatwave. It is lovely to think of them, of Faye and home. Faye has sent me a super watertight plastic box filled with goodies. Gradually, around midnight, we steal away to our tents. Christmas is over.

17
'The Triumvirate'

On rare occasions there were fine, calm, clear days when the glow of the dying sun on the mountains and glaciers was incomparably beautiful.
SIR ERNEST SHACKLETON

17 February Most of us wake late after that blowout. I feel sorry for the nine packing up this morning, but the glaciers will be nice and hard, and the air is clear though a chill wind is blowing. I go up to the main camp to chat with the parties before they leave, particularly, Frank, Nick and Gordon in the fishing party, whom I won't see until March. They are travelling on foot, and will keep near Chris Hurran because Frank has done no glacier work before. John Chuter, Mike and Tim leave. Tim insists on wearing his climbing helmet to walk 20 km across glaciers. He suggests that he needs it in bed! Finally Chris Hurran, Dave and Chris Brown leave after twelve on foot. All three parties plan to camp at 'Sailor's Cache' tonight, and cross Endurance Glacier to the Hut tomorrow.

This afternoon the sun shines as it has not shone for a month. Looking west, Rowett and Gibbs, Aspland and O'Brien are all now clear and beautiful in sunshine. John Highton and Nigel go across to 'Hell's Gates'. I watch their two black figures out across the glacier. Later I spot them on the shoulder of 'The Necklace', and reaching its little snowlick top.

Andy is fixing skins for his skis. Len helps Jem try the glacier corer on the big moss bank out on the point. We found this bank in 1971, but our botanist was not very interested. It is 3 m deep at its downhill edge, where it forms a brown cliff of dead fibrous roots. Apparently it is the deepest moss bank in Antarctica. Some debris taken from the bottom last time was carbon dated and found to be over 1800 years old. The moss may have been growing there when Jesus Christ was alive. After we got back in 1971 BAS were very interested in these big moss banks. There are some at Signy Island, but not quite as big. Jem plans to take cores, make a detailed map of the surface, and mark the various moss banks on the big aerial photos. This afternoon he suffers sad disappointment; the corer jams and the icy moss will not travel up the flutes. Jem is already tinkering with the brace and bit, hoping to bodge up a smaller drill to measure depths at least.

The Clarence Islanders set up the camp here; so the domestic arrangements follow their pattern. They have the boxes round the outside like fortifications. Anyone can go to boxes and help themselves. This free and easy approach is new to us, as both our dumps have been down below on beaches covered with tarpaulins to keep the penguin guano off. They have dug a gashpit and made a

John and Nigel are dots on top of 'The Necklace'. This photograph was taken from Walker Point, using a 400 mm telephoto lens. (CF)

commodious spot for a bit of contemplation in the morning, sitting on a hydrographic boatstave looking out over Walker Point to the southern sea, protected from behind by a dry-stone wall, with a Union Jack.

Two things I copied from Malcolm Burley's 1971 expedition have proved excellent in every respect. The first is having no alcohol; no one really misses it. The second is holding Sunday prayers. The Clarence Islanders have liked this just as we have. John has taken it most Sundays himself but with others choosing hymns and readings. One thing outside Malcolm's pattern was my making everyone keep a journal to produce material for this book.

John and Nigel return across the glacier. They have looked through the twin rock pillars of 'Hell's Gates'. The 300-m slope down to the sea the other side is steeper than I remembered from six years ago. Most of it is now brown ice, and the beaches at the bottom appear to be covered at high tide. So I abandon my plan to sledge the canoes over that way; instead I aim to sledge them east across the glacier to 'Pickup Point', and from there paddle around to Cape Valentine before following Shackleton's route to Point Wild.

I am very glad that I chose Walker Point to be our dump at this end of the island. Although it is an exposed campsite, its position facing the superb hills across this lovely Stadium Glacier is unbeatable. In the last two days of fine weather we have had many clear views of the 'High Peak' ridge: its snow mushroom crest is like a great white bannister rail along the top of the wall. At the east end there are the three lower but more intricate and unclimbed hills of 'The Triumvirate': 'The Emblem', 'The Mask' and 'The Baron'.

18 February   When we peer out at breakfast the weather is fine, partly blue, with only a breeze. John's normal routine is to go up to the camp at about ten, and collect a group of people to go out and do something. The Clarence Islanders' routine is very much centred about John, requiring him to stir the others daily to action. This is very different from ours, where I leave it to individuals to plan their own programme. Today we arrange to leave at eleven. Len, Nigel and I will go over to Cape Valentine; John and Andy will come with us, and then turn up the ridge at the far side of 'The Emblem'. At eleven no one is ready. Apparently this is the normal Clarence situation, which seems ridiculous to me. Finally at midday, we get away and ski across the glacier.

I love this skiing across a wide expanse of snow to reach a mountain. It is similar to the far north-west of Scotland, tramping across wide moors to reach isolated hills. The three unclimbed hills at this end form the eastern extremity of Pardo Ridge: somehow they have a special individuality and character. Today it is sheer joy to move in the sun. I ski beside John, on our separate ropes. As we reach the foot of the valley glacier, which wends down from the col between 'The Baron' and 'The Mask', the cloud comes in and the hills around us recede from sight. We reach a big errant ice block sitting on the middle of the glacier, and stop to change from skis to crampons in its peaceful lee. We have lunch, hoping that the cloud will clear and thinking of alternative plans; with this weather and late start, the Cape Valentine trip is too long.

We decide to attempt 'The Mask', up the ramp behind us. This is a corridor of ice, about 100 m across, running up 200 m height nearly to the top, with its left-hand side against rock cliffs and its right-hand side itself a diagonal icecliff. Nigel changes on to John and Andy's rope. He should manage this, whilst it is probably a little beyond Lennie and me.

NIGEL DAVIES

The ice wall looked quite steep and uninviting, but in fact it turned out to be gentler than it looked, although it made my calf muscles tremble before I had finished front pointing up. The total height of the wall was perhaps 150 m at an angle of 40-45°. Andy led off and asked me to belay him below the first ice wall. I spent a couple of minutes trying to get my iceaxe into the snow but the depth over the underlying ice was too shallow. I tested one belay: my axe flew out and the adze cut me across the bridge of my nose. Fortunately it was a small cut but it made my eyes water! We moved up over the first ice bulge and into a shallow snowbowl. This was fairly easy walking upwards for about 20 m. Then it started to steepen up. The last 100 m was 40-45° ice, which Andy led. John was wandering up and down the ice like a fly on the wall. He climbed past me to the left and gave me a psychological belay whilst Andy got over the top of the bulge. John Highton absolutely radiates confidence when climbing, though sometimes I sense that he does not feel it.

Skiing across the Stadium, Len pauses to look at his old home 35 km away on Clarence Island. The Ravelin Ridge shows through the island's own complete weather system. (CF)

I felt slightly uncomfortable on the climb as we were moving together and at no time was a proper belay used. I kept feeling that if I slipped I would drag them both off. I am afraid that to me the risk is not justified. The climb was at the limit of free movement technique for me so I started to concentrate harder on kicking and placing my feet and axe so that I wouldn't slip. Concentrating on doing this I started to slow down. I kicked twice where once would have done. I was longer on the wall and I got tired more quickly than I should. No matter: we got up; John led up the last slope to the summit. Coming down was easier than I thought it would be, with John giving me a couple of belays from above on two of the steeper ice pitches. John had thoroughly enjoyed his climb and had a contented puff at his pipe in the shelter of the ice block.

After one of Lennie's cramps breaks, he and I go over the col to spy out the route to Cape Valentine. Sloping snowfields lead to the Cape Valentine ridge. The traverse is dominated on the right by the ridge of 'The Emblem', the chaotic icefalls of 'Jumble Glacier' fall to the sea on the left. There seems to be a reasonable route. We head back to the snowblock.

The other three are on their way down, moving quickly together. They have been successful: even the sun has come out to celebrate. Andy is especially delighted to have made this first ascent, and we ski back gently in the sun to camp. Jem arrives from his mosses and we have a brew crowded into his tent.

19 February   Unbelievably we have yet another gorgeous day. Across the Stadium 'The Triumvirate' are crystal clear, against a rich blue sky. We six decide to climb in two parties. John and Andy will attempt 'The Emblem' again by the same airy snowcrest while the rest of us will climb 'The Baron'.

John and Andy ski on ahead. We sort out skis and then follow. Len and I lead, stopping to take photographs, so Nigel and Jem catch us up. One day of this crystal blue place is worth three months of foul weather. At the foot of the snowslope which spills from the valley on to the open glacier plain we take off our skis and put on cramps. As we walk on up to the col, cloud covers the hills and swirls down to us. Beyond the col we take off our packs and dig them into the snow so that they won't blow away. Each stop takes longer than it should. All we do now is remove packs and don climbing gear. Apart from rope, iceaxe and crampons I have only my chest harness, two slings, a couple of prussiks, a couple of icescrews, a deadman and several krabs, and these have been hanging clanking about me the whole way. Yet it takes half an hour to get all of us ready while the wind gets up, blasting over the col from the west. Occasionally the cloud lifts or parts briefly, then we see John and Andy traversing across a steep ice slope towards 'The Emblem'.

Ready at last, we stomp off up a lovely clean névé slope which takes us half-way from the col to the top of 'The Baron'. We collect in a big snowy schrund, and as we leave it get on to a slope with great hummocks of snow like giant white ready-sliced swiss rolls littered about in some confusion. This is just my standard of hill, and I enjoy myself wending about a little, keeping mostly on snow on the easiest route. One steeper little chute of ice gets us round the only step that looked difficult.

Len and I reach the summit mushroom first. These great mushrooms of sugary snow dominate the tops of these islands. None of us has seen them elsewhere; we suppose they must be the product of wet maritime winds rising and then depositing icy snow on to the tops. Now Len and I stand on a terrace of snow and the face of the mushroom bulges about 4 m above us.

Nigel and Jem have not appeared. We shout. Snow deadens sound completely. No answer comes. One route looked from below as if it might be possible, along the south face where a filled schrund runs like a road to a notch in the overhanging mushroom 10 to 20 m above. When I get to the notch I find it is high and bulging far over the steep face: there is no way I can get up there. We return to the little terrace, where Jem and Nigel have arrived. I decide to have a go on the north side where the mushroom blends on to the vertical edge.

There is quite an awesome feeling of exposure, despite the clag hiding a lot. This northern side is topped by a long mushroom, or snow bannister. I can see its profile clearly lower down the ridge, a round bulge like the head of an overflowing glass of Guinness, or a white cat's paw, but 10 to 20 m deep. It is raked by vertical melt fissures which accentuate its shape. I am standing on the top of a similar bulge: the snow steepens at my feet and disappears about 4 m below me. I glimpse through cloud a black rock crest 200 m below, but 700 m directly below and to the right of me I know is the sea, hidden by the swirling clag. The summit mushroom slides down over the edge.

With Jem's ice hammer I gingerly traverse around. My head bangs the icicles as I lean in as far as I can. When I get there, it is of course much more difficult than it looked, bulging over the vertical and made of rotten sugary snow ice. After I have been hacking a precarious ladder up this for twenty minutes Nigel pokes his head round the corner and shouts that they have got a tunnel. Thankfully I traverse back on to the terrace. While I was frightening myself, Nigel had started tunnelling up through the mushroom: there is a hole like a chimney above us. Jem's feet are just visible and bits of snow keep dropping down past them. I look at my watch; it is past four o'clock. Len takes a turn digging up. I am the lucky one whose iceaxe breaks through into the sky above. Nigel enlarges the hole, and one by one we scramble up through it like a white chimney twice the height of a man. Two ropes' lengths above, we stand on the summit. It is a great feeling, a first ascent, and we are delighted, but sad that all we can see is cloud. The outlooks from here would have been something of rare beauty and grandeur.

We drop back through the tunnel and down to our packs, taking them over the col to the ice block. We leave a message and some food on John's skis: he and Andy may bivouac out tonight. With this wind and cloud they will get pretty

Len waits while Jem ropes up at Walker Point. 'The Baron', 'The Mask', 'The Emblem', 'Pickup Point' and Cornwallis Island are ranged behind them. (CF)

wet and cold on the climb, so we hope they don't have to. There is no doubt that 'The Emblem' is the prize of these three eastern hills, in fact probably the prize peak in the whole of Elephant.

We ski back to Walker Point. A lovely pastel sunset is lighting Clarence, so I grab my camera and go over to the point. When I get back John and Andy are taking off their skis and winding up a long day. John is knackered and for once willing to admit it. They have had quite a climb and both been pushed to their limits: that ridge had proved frightening.

ANDY SIMKINS

The ridge was razor sharp with a steep ice wall of 80° to the south, and a steep snowslope of 65°-70° to the north. Occasionally the cornice would lean over to the south, then the north, eventually reaching the headwall of the summit finger, which presented a huge corniced ice bulge to us.

I said I would do as John decided but would ask to turn back if it became too difficult. Deciding to give it a try John said to have lunch first. Picking as windless a spot as possible, we sat down in the cold for a bite to eat, with the nagging thought of the difficulties ahead. Knowing my apprehension, John led off the slope leading to the ridge and then led along the ridge proper. The movement was not graceful but was effective, making steps for the feet 1 m below the crest and using the iceaxe and ice hammer along the top. We were able to make fair progress with John always leading off. The aspect was superb. With occasional difficult steps we arrived at a large cornice with only a rope's length to the base of the summit mushroom.

John moved off again. Looking back he told me to move quickly down from my belay, which I did without question. He gained the base after crossing difficult ice, and put in two icescrews. As I followed I looked back at my belay, to see that I had been a metre out over the cornice! On reaching the stance, we changed over for John to go for the summit, hoping that the rope's length would be sufficient. To get on to the mushroom was no mean task as it overhung all around our side. After much hacking, John made slow progress upwards. From then on he was out of sight, and the rope moved very slowly. My belay became cold and uncomfortable, with driving spindrift and wet feet and backside.

The rope came to an end. There was a jerk, then even slower movement downwards. Eventually John's boots appeared, and John's voice said that he felt a little insecure. I talked him down and he regained the stance. He had reached the summit up difficult ice, and freely admitted that it had scared him silly.

We changed over on the belay, removing my pack. I attacked the ice wall and gingerly made height. The ice didn't relent and it was hard work all the way up, contending also with a hard cold wind from the south. About 3 m from the edge the rope became taut. Without hanging about I started back down, which proved more difficult because it was not always possible to see my feet. John talked me down the ice. Together back at the stance we congratulated ourselves, and then wasted no time in retracing our steps along the ridge. We were both very tired and were relieved finally to reach the skis. A bar of chocolate, a rest and a pipe for John were most welcome. We skied down the valley (me falling over only about five times), then began the flog across the glacier. Fantastic views of the summit of Clarence, with pink clouds over the mountains and an incredible sky, made the journey more bearable despite my tiredness. It was a superbly satisfying day.

Top: *Elephant Island, 'Nelly Point' from south* (CF). Bottom: *The Stadium from Walker Point* (CF).

Below: *Sunset on 'The Emblem'*; opposite, *'The Baron'. Telephotos from Walker Point* (CF).

Top: *Walker Point, looking north-east* (CF). Bottom: *Cornwallis Island and iceberg from south-west* (DM).

18
Prodigal Brothers

Elephant Island – what a grim place: it scared me just to glimpse it through the fog rifts.
DAVID LEWIS

20 February   The morning looks reasonable and I decide to go over to 'Nelly Point', partly to count Giant Petrels, partly to meet Chris Hurran's party and partly to give Andy more practice on skis. Four of us go off in mucky weather. It takes two hours to reach 'Chinstrap Camp', moving slowly and going first below and then above the best line; but today we can spare the time. 'Chinstrap Camp' is only half-way to 'Nelly Point', and it is now two o'clock so we decide to stop here. The weather has deteriorated, and we are getting wet and cold from the sleet. Andy is pretty fed up with me and my weather today. He began a new diary with yesterday's exhilarating ascent of 'The Emblem'; now this!

Nigel and I investigate the boxes left in 1971 when we had a dumpsite here. Then we had pitched three Pyramid tents on a lovely bed of moss on the upper fringe of 26,000 Chinstraps' nests. The moss bed was being rotted by the traffic of penguins and we wondered then whether it would disappear in time. Now, as we walk around, I see the answer. The little stack of surplus boxes stands on the site of our old camp, but the site is unrecognisable. Of moss there only remain a few bits of dead brown turf. The whole area is now a dirty mess of guano and stones. Chinstraps are now increasing their world range and density, possibly because the destruction of whales has released more krill for penguins. Here is evidence of an increase. Compare this ruined vegetation with the rich areas on Walker and 'Nelly' points on each side. The three points were presumably once all rich in mosses and lichens; the other two are still rich because penguins have barely encroached on their slopes. Further, compare those two points with the remainder of Elephant, and the other islands: why should they be so very rich? At Walker Point we walk about on firm springy moss like the bounciest turf on Skye, lichens grow almost like bushes on the scree and the mosspeat banks are 3 m deep. Why was Gibbs so bare? Why is the rest of Elephant so bare? These are south coast points, away from the sun, closer to the cold of Antarctica. Why are they most verdant?

'Chinstrap Camp' is certainly no longer verdant. We break open three of the boxes covered in penguin muck. Inside we find climbing rations. We scoff a bar of Wholenut chocolate and demolish a pot of Sunny Spread (recommended price 1s 6d special offer 2½d off), like bears at the honey. We have lunch, getting wetter and colder with sleet. We load our packs to take back climbing rations, and a big tin of biscuits. Andy will lead us back, to practise choosing the best route for skiing, and to keep him awake.

As we start back a wind seems to rise from nothing, blasting over the ridge from our left. It bowls Andy over with the first onslaught. After he gets up we move on. Then another blast knocks Len sprawling. The wind is bringing with it fine, damp snow, but we can still see nearly a kilometre ahead. We make very slow progress, because everyone just stops in the blasts to brace themselves against it. It is such a short distance to camp that there is no danger. Once Andy stops after being blown over and I go up to see if he is all right. He is fine, though not enjoying it. 'Keep moving,' I say, 'there's no need to stop for the wind.' At that moment a sudden howling gust knocks both of us down! It is flat snow and I have a tremendous struggle to get up as my top-heavy pack holds me down then takes charge and throws me over as the wind grabs it. As we plod on towards Walker Point I get knocked down again, which is salutary. It makes me realise how much effort the others have to put into it. I suppose I am feeling smug that skiing is something at which I am still better than the others!

We get back to find the blow has hit the camp hard. It blew up suddenly an hour after we left, battering the tents unexpectedly from the north-east. Jem had to evacuate the Arctic Guinea, whose weak point is the open-fronted flysheet. The wind simply got inside it, flattening the inner tent on to Jem and lifting the rocks off the fly, which soon tore badly. John and he then lashed it down, and left it to shield Andy's Vango, which was threatening to take off. Mike and Chris's Vango had been standing empty; the zip chose this moment to fail, so they collapsed the tent before the flogging flysheet did itself or the poles an injury. One radio mast has been blown down; they took the other down before it fell on the tents. Nigel and Len's ridge pole breaks as we get back, so they dive in quickly and collapse the inner tent, which gives them space to work, lashing a pair of ski sticks along the ridge as a splint.

I am worried about Chris Hurran's party. They were due to reach here this evening, and the plan had been for them to leave their tent at 'Sailor's Cache'. With this drenching snow melting as it lands there is no possibility of effecting any reasonable snowhole. They would have to spend a miserable night huddled in survival bags if they were caught out. We discuss it, and decide that Chris is competent to manage, whatever happens. These conditions are the nastiest, and most dangerous for exposure. Sleet is far worse than cold snow; it breaks down insulation. In this vicious wind it is easy for someone to die of exposure in an hour or two. Still, that is what we have trained to avoid, and I am sure Chris will do the right thing.

21 February   We have not missed anything by waking late; it is grey and snow is falling. Jem lies half asleep between us, and John gently sits his mug on his chest. Jem lies peacefully looking up at it, wondering how to drink it. I decide to help by holding it. I swing round, knocking his elbow. Scalding tea flies up his nose and over his face. Jem merely says quietly that he is OK. The rest of the tent is soaking too and all our bags are shining wet. Later in the forenoon a weak sun peers through and it stops snowing.

A faint ski-track leads from Walker Point toward 'Chinstrap Camp'. Beyond, foreshortened by the telephoto, are Rowett Island and the lower slopes of Mount Pendragon, nearly 30 km away. (CF)

NIGEL DAVIES
Chris Furse came around at 1200 looking for something to do, and told us it would be a day around camp. Andy and I were having a laugh about his statement yesterday. After a little niggle about setting off in those conditions Chris came out with the phrase which threatens to be a stock one if we go out again in bad weather. 'It'll be good for you!' Andy and I have been running around all day wringing out our longjohns and shouting 'But it'll be good for you.' Chris had unintentionally contributed another bit of Elephant Island humour to the expedition.

John spends a long day removing the zip from a shredded Vango flysheet and sewing it into the Ultimate. The results of yesterday's blow have tipped the scales in my mind. We need to take these two Windover Pyramids to 'Hut Bluff', for the last two weeks and the best way to get them there is by canoe. I abandon my plan to canoe from Cape Valentine to Point Wild. Instead we will sledge the canoes to 'Chinstrap Camp', lower them to the beach, then seize the first reasonable opportunity to take the two tents along the coast to 'Sailor's Cache', and later sledge over Endurance Glacier to the Hut.

This evening Andy gets in contact with Signy. *Endurance* plans to land Alan Milne here tomorrow. We also talk to John at the Hut. Chris Hurran left the Hut only yesterday for 'Sailor's Cache', and planned to stay there today if the weather was bad. So my worries evaporate. At nine, the six of us pile into our tent for a summit brew, and go on talking until midnight, mostly about cars and soldiering. It is faraway. To me it is not nearly as exciting as this lovely island, wrapped in its foul weather. How lucky I am to be here in this cold, wet, miserable tent!

22 February   I wake with the tent walls banging to and fro in a big wind. Three of the four guys have gone, which allows the walls to flap furiously. John lights the primus and I reach out to gather snow. There is a drift against the tent; spindrift is whirling past up the slope. We will not sledge the canoes today and resign ourselves to festering. The days are slipping by far too fast; each day of foul weather is another lost. Chris Hurran's party will not be moving today. They have plenty of food and fuel at 'Sailor's Cache', but I hope their Vango survives. The worst is that Alan Milne will not be able to get ashore from *Endurance* so we won't see him until we leave. I go out to mend our broken guys and find myself in a proper Antarctic hooligan with dry spindrift instead of the beastly rain we have been getting. I forget Alan's plight in the sheer pleasure of fighting this wind. All our gear outside is drifted over, but we each know where our own things are piled so there will be no problem. I leave everything safely buried in snow, except the snow shovel.

Andy and I take the radio masts down in case they blow down. The dismal howl of wind in their rigging stops, but the hooli is still ferocious. We have to fight each step back up to the camp where we rock down the boxes more securely. Apart from the drifts around Andy's tent, the Arctic Guinea, and behind the zariba of boxes, there is little snow in the camp area. The wind has torn it all away and it lies in miniature ridges of perfect dry snowball snow stretching 10 m down the leeward slope behind each little rock. This weather is true Antarctic weather. My trousers are dry and my stockings only have dry snow on them from the drifts. Yesterday I would have been soaked in this time. I think Andy is enjoying it as much as I am.

I get back to our tent at eleven, after two hours pottering about the camp. John and Jem have kept me a pot of porridge and a brew and are sitting up in their maggots engrossed in a game of Scrabble. There is an unspoken agreement amongst all of us: not all to pile out at once if something needs doing. That would simply mean everyone getting back to the tent in wet clothes at once; it would be a nuisance rather than a help. The man outside shouts if he does want help. Otherwise those inside assume he is happy. We spend the day writing, scrabbling, talking, cooking and eating, sitting up with our nether halves in our blue maggots. The day draws towards suppertime, and the light fades.

Suddenly there is an alien noise, John and I look at each other wonderingly. Simultaneously we recognise it: 'Helicopter!' We scramble into our boots and rush out. *Endurance* is flying Alan in. The aircraft comes in, drops a smoke flare and hovers. Peter Burgess puts up five fingers and away they go to the red dot far out at sea. Now the chopper comes back. Peter Burgess looks aghast at our ravaged campsite, inside the box walls. It now holds one erect Vango, one snowed-in Arctic Guinea, two flattened Vangos and two empty platforms! Alan wombles out in his immersion suit, grinning from ear to ear.

ALAN MILNE

One week on Endurance. *Today was my only chance of rejoining the expedition. It began with no let up in the bad weather. The ship continued to heave and roll on the heavy seas, the combination of a very big, regular swell, and an erratic, wind-whipped tumult of white crests. Visibility now good, now scarcely 100 m as a squall of snow drove horizontally across the ship. After a restless night (due to excitement rather than the motion of the ship) I was called at 0630. The lurching of the sick-bay around my comfortable gimbal-mounted bunk, and the odd thump of spray on the scuttle confirmed there had been no change in the weather. No point in packing my rucksack yet. I went up to the bridge.*

Same scene as yesterday. Dismal but yet majestic as the red-hulled ship smashed, rolled and struggled through the unrelenting sea. I glanced at the anemometer; 30 knots, gusting 45. No change there. But the barometer was rising, quite dramatically. After a while on the bridge I went for breakfast.

It was now that I had to contend with something I had refused to acknowledge before. I began to think of the ship's journey south: Bransfield Strait, Neumayer and Lemaire Channels; possibly Adelaide, Marguerite Bay. I had avoided discussing the ship's programme south, but now I experienced a desire to continue with Endurance *to the Peninsula. I had not considered the prospect before. My only hope and anticipation had been to join the fellows on Elephant. But my refusal to think of the alternative had really been a defence against this wish to remain with the ship.*

There it was. I finally recognised it and had to accept it. I wanted to go south. I felt my disloyalty keenly.

I spent most of the day on the bridge, gazing out at the bleakness and storm, too ashamed to confess these conflicting thoughts. Most had accepted that the transfer would be impossible today but the Captain hadn't! He decided the ship could afford to wait a few hours. At 1700 the wind dropped. Simultaneously the sea lessened; the mank cleared; a watery sun appeared in a bluing sky. I was going to be landed! I packed my rucksack; said my farewells with especial thanks to the Captain and, armed with a bag of mail for the fellows and freshly baked bread in a paper bag, stepped into the helicopter. I landed at Walker Point to be greeted by Chris F and John H, who helped me out of the 'once only' survival suit.

The helicopter was off, and I was back with the JSE. No matter my earlier thoughts; it was good.

Now here is Alan with the six of us in our Pyramid catching up on all that has been happening: the epics on Clarence; the Christmas party here; the fine weather; and the foul; and where everyone is. He has seen across the Stadium the bases of the clouded hills, and already he is pleased in this lovely place. Alan's enthusiasms and delights are so intense, enveloping and infectious that all around must join him. Now he cannot stop grinning. It is a great day.

23 February   Alan's first day on Elephant dawns in flawless fashion. It is perfectly calm; the tent hangs silent and peaceful. The sun is shining on all the hills, across the Stadium and around to the Cornet. Even Mount Irving 30 km away on Clarence is crystal clear. Alan is rapturous. 'This', he says, 'is real Antarctica. When can I start climbing?'

John H, Nigel, Andy, Len and I are sledging two canoes over to 'Chinstrap Camp' today. By the time we have my Mischief and the James K. Caird on the glacier, with us ready in the traces, it is one o'clock. The first pull up over 'Biscoe Ridge' is a real slog: first fifty double paces at a time before a three-minute rest and pant and then repeat; then with our hands on the snow in front of us we heave and heave but can scarcely move the canoes; or so it seems, until at last we gain the col after an hour's hauling.

Today is my first day in shirt sleeves, it is so hot and still. As we stand panting on the col, the layer of cloud along the bottom half of Clarence thins out: the lower 700 m can be dimly seen in gloom, while sunlit above float the pillared white upperworks of the whole of Ravelin Ridge and Mount Irving. We pick up a good route in the sun, and an hour later the two canoes are at 'Chinstrap Camp'. There we separate them. We put the engine into Mischief and attach two climbing ropes to lower her down the penguin ladder to the beach. John belays, holding most of the weight on the rope, while Lennie and I ease her down over the scree. When we reach the end of the ropes we set her sideways on the scree and untie. Lennie stays to hold Mischief, while I walk up to help John. Andy and Nigel are easing James K. Caird down the scree and some stones are trundling downwards. Nigel shouts and I look down.

Mischief is accelerating down the hill with Len hopping behind her. She speeds away from him; bounces; rolls over; hits the snow and bounces high and broadside to the hill, somersaulting as she goes, and dropping things out of the cockpit. She hits the snow, killing two penguins, and slithers on downwards, until miraculously she comes to rest just above the icecliff. After that shattering run I'm afraid my poor old canoe will be thoroughly split and bashed: Len has reached her and slumps discontentedly as he looks. John lowers Jimmy Caird and we walk down. My anger must be obvious. Bristling in defence, Andy tells me that Len was tending the canoe, but a bloody great rock hit it which Len could not stop. So it wasn't Lennie's fault; it was mine for not putting her out to one side. It was quite a spectacular tumble for a canoe. We lower the James K. Caird down three pitches to the beach among the big brash ice blocks piled up by the storm. On the glacier John and Lennie turn Mischief over and find that she is surprisingly little damaged. Tough boats these Tasmans! The main seam has sprung amidships for a metre; there are two athwartship cracks and the forward cockpit has cracked on one side. The engine's propeller was sticking above the cockpit coaming, it must have stopped her like an iceaxe but

Len and I lower Mischief down the penguin ladder to the beach below 'Chinstrap Camp'. She has just bounced and somersaulted from the snowpatch 100 m above at the left skyline. (AS)

damaged the engine. Anyhow, we lower her to the beach beside JC.

Nigel sets to work patching up Mischief with the Ultraviolet repair kit. He also tries the little Johnson engine: it looks in a sorry state with half its top casing and frame broken off, but finally and gloriously it starts. Engine Bravo has been swamped twice and avalanched once and still works like a dream! We think the drive shaft must be bent, but if it can get the Windover tents to 'Sailor's Cache', who cares?

At six we walk back across the glacier. John and I leave first on one rope, tramping across in companionable silence, each wrapped in his own thoughts and looking at the livid purple cloud now smothering Clarence. When we reach camp Alan looks out and chats about his day, happy just to be here and also itching to climb something. Jem has a brew on, which goes down like nectar. It has started to rain as well as blow: misery again! I warn Nigel that he and I may have to head west for a third day looking for Chris Hurran's party. It's nearly midnight and I am getting worried about them again. We will leave at 0930 tomorrow, heading for 'Sailor's Cache' with the Ultimate tent and a Hjelper sledge hoping to meet them. 'Hello in there,' comes a voice through the flapping tent. 'Hello. Who's that? What do you want Andy?' I shout. 'It's Chris,' says the voice. Gosh! I untie the tunnel with fumbling cold fingers. Chris crawls through and flops in the corner, glistening with rain and exhausted. Jem puts on a brew for him and we ask him how he is. 'Knackered,' he answers. 'Knackered and wet.' He goes on to tell us of his six days, since they left here on 17 February. They had arrived without incident at the Hut on the second day, to find it chock-a-block with 1970 rations. They quickly found the cine camera and the aerial photographs, the main *raison d'être* of their journey, but the weather prevented them from leaving until 20 February. That afternoon late they reached 'Sailor's Cache', but could not find shelter of any kind. In the wind and sleet movement became impossible.

CHRIS HURRAN

I make the decision that we will go into survival bags. We quickly fashion a shallow grave with one end roofed by skis and the flysheet. We line the floor with the tent and two karrimats. Dave and Chris B move in first, sharing a polythene survival bag. I check the anchoring of the flysheet before joining them in my survival bag. Then follows a cold and very wet night spent eating almost continuously in order to stay warm, with just one period of sleep from 0330 to 0730. The most unpleasant things are the puddles of cold water which accumulate under the hips and around the knees. Peeing proves difficult and has to be done in a can inside the sleeping bag. Despite the conditions we all stay in remarkably high spirits.

21 February   *Whatever the weather today, we are not in a fit state to move on. After a slow and awkward breakfast I make the first move at 1100. I dress quickly, standing in the wind under the overcast skies, and am horrified by the amount of water in my survival bag. I pour a cupful from each boot, then go for a run around the beach to try and warm up.*

I find a reasonable spot on the beach for a tent, but we must build high protective walls (from both wind and Elephant Seals). I start digging hard to keep warm: before long three ramparts are taking shape. By 1400 we are ready to erect the tent. The wind is now increasing again with snow showers and it takes all our willpower to do the job properly. We finally get inside after 1500. The tent is really well erected. The rest of the day is spent with the stove going full blast as we try to dry out. The important thing is to eat and sleep well today and try to dry boots, socks and gloves as top priority. Tomorrow we can head off for Walker Point. It will be most unpleasant if we have to bivouac another night.

22 February   *We are all awake by 0630 but the prospects for a move look bleak. There is no improvement in the weather, and at 1100 I decide that we will not move today. We continue drying out. For the first time I have a look around 'Sailor's Cache'. The beach is 100 m long and 30 m wide. It is a real dumper and has a 10-m belt of enormous chunks of brash ice all along it – hardly a suitable place for canoe landings. In the big seas today the smallest pieces of brash have been thrown very close to our tent at the back of the beach and the flysheet has been coated in salt-spray. Our neighbours are fifteen Elephant Seals, including one enormous bull. By evening the weather is really superb with magnificent views towards Mount Elder and Mount Pendragon, so we retire at dusk with high hopes for tomorrow.*

Luckily for them the next day did indeed dawn fine and clear, and they were able to make it in twelve hours back to Walker Point, arriving after dark, long after I had given up hope of seeing them.

19
Shipwreck

The foam of the breaking sea surged white around us. We felt our boat lifted and flying forward like a cork in a breaking surf.
SIR ERNEST SHACKLETON

24 February At breakfast, we have another lovely day beginning, calm and clear. John, Andy and Nigel set off to do 'High Peak' and Alan and I finally get off at midday to tramp across the slushy glacier to 'The Necklace'. This head of snow, with its eyebrows of rock and its necklace of bergschrund, is beautifully placed in the gap between the end of 'High Peak' ridge and the eastern 'Triumvirate' of hills we climbed last week. As we walk up its easy west ridge, we see three specks climbing up through the icefall of 'High Peak'. The setting is beautiful beyond speech, and I wish I had my good camera. Alan is ecstatic.

We eat our lunch a little back from the prow of the 500-m top, which juts forward over the sea cliffs in a mushroom bulge, whilst on either side there are square cornices like thatch. Alan loves to sit in great places and talk. Now he talks of rejoining us, feeling at first almost an alien among us, particularly because of the different character of the Clarence party.

By four cloud is pouring over the cols each side of 'The Necklace', up from the sea and down into the Stadium, where it gathers in a great lake of formless white without a beginning or an end. We walk down into the cloud and then traverse around to 'Hell's Gates'. This is a truly heroic gateway, between two monoliths 15 m high which stand on the col between the Stadium and the northern sea cliffs. Now the cloud pours gloomily through the gateway where a deep windscoop has been blasted in the snow. I cannot see the sea 400 m below us in the cloud, and we do not linger. Tramping back across the glacier to Walker Point we emerge from the cloud, and enjoy the plod across the spacious plain, each wrapped in his own thoughts at his own end of the rope.

Back at camp there is a clank of ironmongery outside the tent. John H has arrived back from 'High Peak' with Andy and Nigel. For the two hours since Alan and I returned it has been raining. John is soaked, from the rain, and from the wet snow up there, which was treacherous. They were pushed out on to the precipitous north face 900 m above the sea and could not force up through the rotten, rubbishy, wet mushroom snow to the summit. Coming down, the snow conditions were getting quite dangerous with the thaw. Apart from that, they each fell once, sliding less than 15 m but enough to make them think very hard. John does not intend to climb again until there has been a decent hard frost.

At half past nine it is dark and still raining. Without warning Mike

Wimpenny puts his head through the door! The three of them have arrived from the Hut, soaking wet and tired after their two-day journey. I go to find Tim and Mike moving into the Vango we put up this morning, and John Chuter settling in with Nigel and Len.

25 February   It rained throughout the night. We stay in the tent through the morning, Jem drying mosses, and John writing up Clarence, while I work out who will be in which party going where, when. The next set of moves crystallises:

a. John H, Andy, Mike and Nigel will be the ridge party leaving here on 27February and getting to the Hut by 2 to 3 March.

b. Alan, Len and I will be the canoe party, leaving here on 27 February and getting to the Hut as quickly as possible.

c. Jem, Chris B and Tim will leave here on 28 February to reach the Hut on 2 March with Chris H, John C and Dave following a day later. Once gathered at the Hut we will sort out again depending on whether Frank's party is still there or not.

I find Mike and Chris B ensconced in their Vango with rocks from Cornwallis scattered between them. The granite is very striking indeed, white with black currant-sized bits in it, the youngest granite known in the whole world. Mike is the first qualified geologist to visit the island, and his quick survey may relate it to the metamorphic rocks of Elephant and Clarence.

As the day wears on, the wind gets up, but the rain continues. I can put off no longer mapping the birds breeding around Walker Point. I aim to mark the skuas' nests on to the enlarged aerial photograph; the positions can then be transcribed on to the 1/10,000 maps Chris will make. The chicks are now on the verge of flying and some have probably flown already. By six o'clock it is blowing a full gale, gusting hurricane force; all the skuas creep about in the shelter of little rocks, most unwilling to fly, and unusually difficult to see. I'm afraid my skua census will not be as good as I had hoped.

We have all grown to love these bomber birds. They are the eagle of the Antarctic in looks and manner, though they scavenge dead penguins and take eggs and chicks. They are almost identical to the Great Skua or bonxie of the Arctic, big brown birds with white flashes in their wings, with joyful strong flight, ripping the wind apart as they soar and then dive in twos and threes, like racing cyclists coming down off the banking. They are always noisy: their hoarse long calls are given with the wings aloft, either on the ground or in falling flight. When they are mildly disturbed they will waddle away sideways, quacking quietly. Earlier in the season, one could gently lift them off their eggs. There are two species of these skuas in the south and the northern bonxies

Alan pauses on the way up 'The Necklace'. The sharp peak in the centre is 'High Peak': the three climbing the icefall beyond are only visible with binoculars. (CF)

Top: A dark Giant Petrel, probably a yearling. (70/71 George Bruce)

Bottom: In 1970/71 we found a few Snow Petrels nesting at 'Nelly Point', the most luxuriant spot in the whole group. This may be the only colony in the South Shetlands. (70/71 Stuart Allison)

evolved from southern skuas who strayed to the north millions of years ago after wintering in the tropics. The northern and southern birds still mix in their winter quarters, and I suspect that young birds sometimes change hemisphere.

On Elephant we have flowers also. Two. On the other islands we found only mosses, lichens and more primitive plants. At Walker Point are a few little patches of the only Antarctic grass, *Deschampsia antarctica*. One patch is bigger than the floor of our tent! This evening I find a tuft with some seeds near the prion colony. On the same steep slope, I also find the only other Antarctic flowering plant, the pearlwort, *Colobanthus quitensis*. This nestles in tight rounded clumps, like pincushions 5 cm across, neatly ensconced in the moss with minute pale green or white flowers which are now turning to whitish seed heads.

1 March After four miserably wet days, the weather is good enough for the canoeing party to set off. In the afternoon we head off. Jem and Tim follow, each with a Windover tent on a packframe. We say goodbye and good luck to the six staying at Walker Point, and to John's ridge party who will leave in a couple of hours. At 'Chinstrap Camp' we choose a platform in the moss turf slope. Here there are very few penguin chicks left: I see one being fed by an impatient adult, but most have gone to sea. The colony and its fringes are now occupied by thousands of moulting adults; their shed curled feathers blow like snow on the wind, and accumulate everywhere that is wet and dirty. The moss turf is a beautiful mattress. I am ashamed to say that we hack out great lumps of spongy, springy turf 20 cm thick, and spread them over the platform. Jem is aghast at this mutilation, but accepts that we are only pre-empting the penguins by a year or two. We put the Windover up, and Jem and Tim go back.

The three of us are on our own to talk and eat and sleep ready for tomorrow. I love these separate forays far more than the crowded feel of a base camp. It is like a holiday. We have been living in the base camp at Walker Point for two weeks now.

2 March The weather looks good for canoeing, overcast but with a hint of sun and hardly a breath of wind. The barometer has scarcely moved since last night. We have all had a wonderful sleep on our great thick bed of moss lumps. It is the best night I have had on the islands. We will go as soon as possible.

After we have eaten, we pack our rucksacks. Just then it starts raining. A bank of rain blots out Endurance Glacier in the west. While waiting for it to pass I take the second tent down to the beach, partly to save time later and partly to get a closer look at the sea. From 150 m above, the calm look can be deceptive. There is some surf on the beach, but not very heavy: it seems to build up just as it enters the bay and the swell outside is imperceptible. The rain passes through, and I can see the icecliffs of Endurance Glacier again 12 km away at our destination. I go back up for a swallow of coffee. Then we pack the tent. We all three go down the penguin ladder with our packs. Lennie and Alan stay to raft up the canoes and check the engine while I come back up for the tent. When I reach the beach again, they have proved the engine and the two canoes are on the beach. Lennie is standing looking out to sea and not saying anything. Obviously he is having a mood of the miseries. Alan and I get on with rigging the rafting board and engine. We lash the skis fore and aft between the forward pair of rafting poles, giving a useful platform and allowing us to poke lumps of brash through if they get stuck between the two canoes.

As we start loading the tents and packs on to the rafting board Len finds that the fibreglass repairs on Mischief are tacky and loose. They look unsafe. That decides Len: he definitely does not want to go! However, now that we are this far committed, I don't want to give up. Lacking a proper repair kit, I decide to change dispositions in the boats: Alan and Len were to have been in Mischief on the port side with me in the James K. Caird. Now Alan and Len will be to starboard in the James K. Caird with me on top of the rafting board and packs; Mischief will be filled up with buoyancy bags and simply used as a pontoon, filling up a bit but not too much, where she leaks. To make baling easy I throw away Mischief's seats. I also mount the Whale Gusher pump on the forward cockpit lashed down for easy use. Len is still not happy, but agrees to go.

LEN HUNT

Ever since finding out I would be on this canoe trip, I had a feeling of uneasiness and foreboding about it. I didn't want to go, but I kept it to myself. The day that we left for 'Chinstrap Camp' I told Chris and John how I felt. I was scared. I suppose this surprised Chris; it surprised me, because I enjoy canoeing. It was too late to back out anyway. Before we set off from 'Chinstrap Camp' in the canoes this feeling of fear was at its highest. I have been frightened a few times through the course of my life, as I'm sure most people have, but what I felt at that moment was so acute that it was with a conscious effort that I forced myself to go, against everything that I felt. As I climbed into the raft I wanted to tell Chris that I wouldn't go; but I went, probably due to them, with their lighthearted but solid confidence.

I have discarded all thoughts of going around Endurance Glacier. I am aiming to reach Muckle Bluff, which is a better helicopter recovery site than here at 'Chinstrap Camp'. If all goes well, then we may push on to 'Sailor's Cache'.

Finally at two o'clock we haul her to the water. Lennie and Alan get in and sort out their spraydecks. I give a last push, and jump on. We paddle through small surf without trouble. The engine starts like a bird, and we are away through the swell at the entrance. It has started to rain but the weather still has that steady, dependable, slightly miserable cast about it. The only thing that worries me is that the engine doesn't like full throttle, so Alan keeps her at three-quarter speed and we plug on at three knots. Still, that is faster than we would go walking and relaying tents. I lift Mischief's spraydeck off but there is no sign of water. Better than I had expected. In fact Mischief is riding very high. The James K. Caird on the other hand is pretty low, with Alan getting lots of water in his lap, and the stern actually under water.

We reach 'Nelly Point' and get a lumpy sea as we round it. Now we can see Muckle Bluff ahead of us: we head straight for it. Sitting on top of the packs I can see further than the others with their backsides at water level. As we slowly advance I begin to feel uneasy. There seems to be big surf creaming in across the reef to smash on to the icecliffs; it looks as if it is running across the beach inside the reef also. Muckle Bluff should be a really safe beach with a south-westerly swell. I cannot understand why there should be such a surf: there was little at 'Chinstrap Camp', and I can't discern any swell out here even low down in the canoes.

Alan is sitting with his pipe upside down in his mouth, with one bare hand steering, and the other on his spraydeck. He says his hands are all right, but later I see him clenching and unclenching his free hand, which is shaking with cold. His gloves are in his cockpit, and he can't reach them as the water is slopping about over his spraydeck. Luckily I have a pair handy in my anorak pocket. Now we are committed at sea, Lennie is fine, not saying much, but cheerful and positive. He has a couple of home-made anti-Leopard Seal thunderflash bombs tucked into his hat over his ears; the striker hangs out of his mouth instead of a cigarette. We would have to go nearly a kilometre broadside to the rollers if we were to go into the beach up the channel between the reef and the icecliff. So I tell the others we will look beyond the point.

It is now three o'clock so I start to refuel the engine. It is a tricky process, spilling petrol from the five-gallon jerrican into a half-pint compo tin, shutting the jerrican, opening the engine fuel tank, pouring fuel in from the tin, trying to use my other hand as a funnel, but spilling a lot as I lie over the rucksacks and the canoes work about in the seaway. Blessedly the engine does not catch fire with the petrol pouring down over it. When I have got three cans in, we sight a hopeful looking gap between two rocks in the reef. I stand up to get a better view, steadying myself on the packs. There is a gap 50 m wide between two prominent rocks. With our slow progress, and this nasty surf running, I want to get into shore as soon as possible. So I tell Alan to turn in and head for the gap, shouting above the engine noise, to let Lennie know in the bow. Then I sit up on the packs to get a good view ahead, pointing my paddle in the direction I want Alan to steer. First I bring him up to the left, nearer to the conspicuous rock with the two penguins on it; then I glimpse the brown hump of a rock awash to the right of it, in our path. The reef is still 100 m off, giving us time: I point my paddle to starboard and Alan brings the boat round, heading for the gap.

Suddenly, dreadfully, the bottom of the sea seems to drop under our bows and there below us is a whole line of whaleback rocks, sucking and grinning at us. Lennie and I see it at the same time, and shout: 'Back!' and start desperately paddling backwards. Lennie shouts to Alan to reverse the engine.

I look over my shoulder and, thinking that Alan has not been able to, dive back over the packs to do it. He had already done it. All my interference does is somehow to stop the engine altogether. 'Paddle!' yells Len again.

While he and Alan desperately back-paddle I now paddle forwards. Mischief and Jimmy Caird swing sweetly round and the raft slowly heads away from those horrid jaws of death.

I cannot remember how close those rocks were; my brain refuses to record it. They were certainly underneath our bows, not in front of us. Alan thinks it was 15 m. Len thinks 7 m.

We head out. Alan gets the engine going and we circle and go on westwards. I see another likely gap in the rocks, but none of us is willing to repeat that fright. Alan suggests we go on to 'Sailor's Cache'. I have been wanting to do that since I saw the surf on Muckle Bluff and seize his suggestion with delight. We should get progressively less surf as we get into the lee of Endurance Glacier. So we head on past Muckle Bluff. I go on fuelling the engine: it takes another ten minutes but it's a good feeling when I have finished.

The stern of the James K. Caird really is pretty low, and water is lapping over on to Alan's spraydeck, which is full like a pond. He thinks he is wet from the spraydeck only, so we do nothing. The weather ahead begins to lower down a bit. It starts to snow gently, on a westerly breeze. We can no longer see Endurance Glacier through the cloud. Icecliffs run all along this coast for 6 km from Muckle Bluff to 'Sailor's Cache'; the only beach is at 'George's Rib', which is fouled by rocks, so we *must* reach 'Sailor's Cache'.

There are a few bands of brash along tide slicks. We go through these at their narrowest; even so they crunch, and crash, and crack on the sides of the canoes. We wince, thinking of the patches on Mischief. I have another look in her cockpit; there is a little water now, but not much. I pump a little with the whale pump: it is getting mostly air, which is hopeful.

The engine stops. Alan tries to get it going, to no avail. Len and I start paddling. It sounds as if it is trying on one cylinder. After a bit, Alan stops trying on the engine. We paddle on. It is slow work with the heavily loaded raft. We make two knots. If we keep that up we should reach 'Sailor's Cache' in two hours, too long for comfort with the way weather changes here. Alan diffidently mentions again that he is sitting in water.

LEN HUNT

Shortly after this Alan told us he would have to bale out the canoe, as it was filling up through a hole in his spraydeck. I looked over my shoulder. I was horrified to see Alan quite happily sitting with the sea lapping around his waist, and the aft end of the canoe submerged.

I had shifted two packs over to port already. Now I put the bagged tent on to the aft cockpit of Mischief, shift one pack over to port forward and lash it down a bit better and jettison the petrol jerrican, which floats off astern. Alan's cockpit top is still only just above the waterline. Obviously we must do something about it pretty quickly. First I think of the pump, but that will take time to move over and rig. So I get ready to put the spare spraydeck on and bale. Alan leaps out as quickly as possible, and scrambles over to paddle from port forward. Luckily the James Caird lifts so that water does not slop in. There is 10 cm of water in the bottom and I get most of this down quickly with the baler. Then Alan gets back in.

We paddle on. The little iceberg, which was inshore of us when the engine gave up, is now a kilometre astern. There is still a long way to go to 'George's Rib', and already I can see a big surf travelling into the beach there. I simply cannot understand this surf arising out of nothing and hammering against the shore, and I am a bit frightened of it. But we have no choice but to press on.

Behind us is only Muckle Bluff, which was bad even with the engine; 'Chinstrap Camp' is now further than 'Sailor's Cache'. Mischief has more water in her, and I pump occasionally. I am hoping this is just slops through her after spraydeck, but we are going through belts of brash and some of her patches may have been scraped off.

I ask Alan to give the engine another try. We crash through the next belt of brash and find calmer green glacier water inside. The engine putters and dies. Then it fires and keeps going! It is only on one cylinder but that is good enough to push us cheerfully along at 3 knots! With the engine going, our spirits quickly rise again, and we putter on, gradually getting closer in under the icecliffs as we get nearer and nearer at last to our goal. It is five o'clock, and it has been a pretty harrowing three hours' journey.

As we get near, we can see a fair surf running on to the beach: but at least there are no rocks to bother about. There is brash just outside the breakers. We head towards the lane between. When we are just 100 m off, the engine fails again. Alan tries it a couple of times but we are now too close in, so he gets a paddle and leaves the engine. We need its power in the surf more than at any other time, so this is quite a blow, but we are so close now that there is no time for regrets. All Lennie's miseries and forebodings are forgotten when the danger is actually on us. As at Muckle Bluff and along the long unfriendly coast, he is now all positive thought and action.

We have first to get further along to a wider bit of the beach, in the narrow passage between the breaking waves and the necklace of brash outside them. Then we must turn in at right angles to the beach and wait for our chance to go in behind a big wave, on a smaller one.

We manage to get lined up, and immediately find that there is a strong set along the shore. We are drifting sideways away from the beach area toward the icecliffs. So we have to go in quickly. We let a big one reach us, and then start paddling as fast as we can, as it lifts our bow and passes. I look behind: the 'small one' we wanted is beginning to hummock up already 50 m behind us. I hesitate, but there is absolutely nothing we can do now, we are committed and too far in to reverse.

One hundred m from the beach we are lifted up as if by a great hand and start hurtling towards the shore. I am still perched up on top of the packs with my head way up. Below me I can see the bows of the two canoes overhanging the wave; the backwash of the previous wave 3 to 4 m below them. The canoes are travelling true as an arrow at a frightening speed, and I feel immense exhilaration rather than fear, perched crazily 6 m above the shore on to which we must surely be dropped and annihilated at any second. Miraculously our stern drops and the spent wave thunders up the beach ahead of us. Now suddenly we are in danger of being sucked back down the sloping mush of white water to disappear under the next wave. My job is to leap out with the bow rope and hold the bows straight up the beach. The raft is starting to slew to the right as she loses momentum and I leap off to the left. Instantly I am in trouble. As the backwash whips my legs back I scarcely touch bottom, in water that is already above my waist. Now I cannot help the canoes, and am in danger of drowning in the undertow myself. I hang on to the bow rope and fight to get up the beach. Suddenly the raft careers away forward as the next wave engulfs me. I hang on desperately to the bow rope, which now pulls me up the shore. The wave recedes.

Incredibly we seem to have achieved what seemed impossible only moments before. Lennie and Alan are out of the raft, which is right at the top of the beach 10 m above me. The wave is receding and the water is only knee deep. Lennie yells: 'Are you all right?' and I shout back, 'Yes, OK,' as I wallow up the beach. The gravel is so full of water that it is like a quicksand, but I reach the canoes before the next wave comes. Both canoes are swamped full of water and immovable, but it doesn't seem to matter. In fact the weight will keep them there while we unload on to the ice beyond. We have made it just on to the extremity of the beach, as it meets the glacier ice. But the next breaker roars up the beach. The canoes take charge again, lifting and moving as the wave comes on forever up. They lift almost to my waist as the wave goes on up the beach on to the ice. Now the water starts to recede. Now suddenly we are fighting desperately to hold them as the suck-back begins. Alan and Lennie are heaving up on the bows; I brace my legs in the gravel to prevent the bows coming back down.

Two canoes full of water and with a topload of packs and Pyramid tents bear down on my thighs as I stand in the water holding them uphill. Then suddenly I am no longer standing, but have fallen and am pinned down to the beach on my back under a welter of water. Drowning! I can't move. One canoe lies across my stomach. I try desperately wriggling my legs, I try heaving up on the boat. I have no purchase here with my head downhill. When is the next wave coming? How long will I have to hold my breath? Desperately I clutch with my left hand at the deck of the canoe and shove my right hand back into the gravel. I can see Alan and Lennie heaving at the bows. When is the next wave coming? Then Lennie runs over to me. He holds my body up so my head is level with the canoes. Oh Lennie, that is such a wonderful relief. Now at least I feel I can survive a wave or two, and perhaps in that time they can heave these canoes off me. Behind over my shoulder I can see the next wave coming. It is not a very big one, a white broken-down crest above my head. I take a deep breath, to last as long as possible. Miraculously the canoes lift off me. I am free, and scramble to my feet. I should have realised that any wave big enough to drown me would be big enough to lift the canoes.

The wave that frees me sweeps Lennie away, until he manages to grab on to the bows. The canoes charge back up the beach, knocking Alan over; he only just escapes being caught like me. We are now in dreadful trouble. The only thing is to save as much kit as possible, as quickly as possible. My lovely knife is out in a flash, and I start cutting away the lashings on the packs. A climbing rope, a karrimat and an iceaxe are thrown up on to the ice; then one by one our three packs; then I cut free the Windover tent, which is just folded together, and we get that clear. The next wave grabs the swamped raft as if it were a toy and drags it down the beach sickeningly under the crash of another dirty, khaki-coloured breaker. We start towards it as she careers back up the beach. Suddenly we realise that the packs are still on the beach. We stagger with them up on to the ice. They seem very, very wet and heavy. That done, we look round. Poor Mischief and James K. Caird are now totally swamped, down the beach near the danger spot where the breakers fall upon the shore.

In the minute we have taken to cache the packs, the raft has been carried another 50 m along and is now below the icecliffs. The ski tips and bows stick out of the water. The hulk is swept to and fro. 'I'll just try to get the karrimats,' I shout. 'You stay with the packs.' 'If you're going, we're bloody well coming to look after you,' they both yell, and follow me along the beach. The raft is too far down to risk going to it. As if by magic, two karrimat rolls pop out of the wreck and career up in the froth to my feet with a few buoyancy bags. Then the raft charges back down again and is engulfed in the maw of the next dumper. We are now under the icecliff. It is useless to think of saving anything else. We run back to the packs.

I look over my shoulder one last time. My beloved Mischief and the James K. Caird are travelling away from us along the glacier snout, being swept in and out by the surf. They will be smashed against the icecliffs in a few minutes. Now there is just one aim. We must put the tent up, get into it and start getting warm. We have our three packs with all the essentials for survival, plus the tent. My feet and legs are freezing now. It is six o'clock, four hours since we left 'Chinstrap Camp'.

Inside the tent is chaotic, with Polybags and gear everywhere. But it is beautifully warm. Steam is rising. Lennie produces a brew, and it is a time for talking, reliving the day, and easing away the knot of tension. Len produces cigars and I have my first smoke for two years. It is wonderful. The smoke climbs up to the apex of the tent, where Alan has rigged a drying line. Lennie falls asleep in his maggot. Alan has been wondering what hit him to cause the ache up by his right ear. He realises at last: throughout the three-hour journey from 'Chinstrap Camp' he was clenching his pipe in his mouth with a grip of iron; now his jaw muscles ache! After we got ashore, we were laughing and overflowing with relief; I asked him then whether he had thought he might be a gonner, and he said: 'Never.' Now he admits that, yes, he had thought he was going to die. I had never felt that, except when the canoes were on top of me.

Now I look out of the tent door. The sea is terrifying. Still there is no wind, and the tent walls hang silent. Yet the surf has grown even bigger. What chills me is that now there is thick brash covering the sea for a kilometre out from the shore. On the beach are great chunks of rounded brash ice, many as big as cars. The surface of the sea is a dirty brownish-yellow porridge of small brash ice pieces, with bigger chunks floating in it. The whole dirty surface is heaving and churning. Offshore, succeeding swells are clearly visible as rivers of ice moving alternately right and left. Inshore, the rollers lift the ice up, up, and up, and slowly even further up until vertical walls of floating ice 5 m high hang poised above the beach, and then fall upon themselves in a ghastly welter of gnashing ice blocks which charge up the beach to fling dirty, khaki spray high into the air. The big blocks on the beach wobble and bounce and move in a ponderous dance, as if they were as light as polystyrene tea chests. No boat of any kind could live in that sea, let alone get ashore.

20
The Hut

It is impossible to describe accurately the violence of the atmosphere of Elephant Island; the screech of the wind and the driving storms, the cannon-like reports of the glaciers calving . . . Nor is it any easier to convey how nerve-wracking was the sense of being pounded and struck at ceaselessly by forces which one could not grapple with.
FRANK WORSLEY

3 March   I wake at four, cold and wet. Just outside an Elephant Seal is belching and snuffling noisily, as if blowing wet floppy bubbles through its pendulous nose, fetid breath coming up through metres of blubbery guts. If any of the seals got over our wall, they would fall on to the tent and that would probably flatten us. Two big bulls on the beach last night were fifteen boots long, their circumference was probably over 3 m and their weight over 3 tonnes, over thirty times my weight. The thought of being rolled on like a piglet is unpleasant. But that does not keep me awake. What does, is the clammy cold of wet gear. I doze and wake fitfully until eight when Alan lights the primus to put on purple porridge. He too has had a miserable night. When Len's head appears he says the same. It is dank outside, so we stay in the tent gradually getting things drier, with the primus going full blast. We all three try to write up our journals, but talk instead. These journals have caught their imagination: yesterday both Alan and Len seemed more relieved to have saved their journals than their sleeping bags!

In the afternoon the sun shows faintly as a little wind springs up and we take everything out and lay it around to dry. In two hours most of our gear is almost dry, which would have taken two days inside the tent. Our blue maggots are the most important items. They dry wonderfully quickly. We have with difficulty evicted some young Elephant Seals from the moat outside our wall. Now Len sets up a Benghazi Burner in this ditch with petrol from the cache. The resultant fire burns for half an hour and we stand around waving our hands over it.

We are worried that the swamped raft may drift right along the coast and be seen by the Walker Point parties. There is little we can do except to leave our news in the message tin when we go. However we decide to go to 'George's Rib', which might get flotsam from the wreck. We rope up and set off with our one communal iceaxe at the front. Alan is in the middle because he is the only one with a waistbelt now. The way is over a glacier in lovely condition for walking. It takes an hour, which dries us off well, and when we get to the ridge and look down on the beach we see a hundred Elephant Seals. While the others search unsuccessfully for wreckage I have a look at the Gentoo and Chinstrap

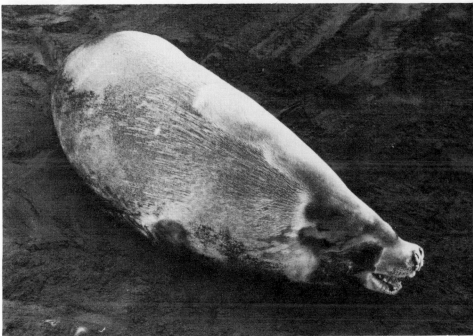

Top: A big bull Elephant Seal comes ashore. He is over 5 m long and weighs over 2 tonnes; really big ones reach 6½ m and 4 tonnes. (GT)

Bottom: The little Crabeaters are probably the most numerous seals in the world: they live in the pack ice and only a few reach these islands in summer. (NM)

Seven small Elephant Seals doze in line. So far as I know the world record for running over their backs is twelve by Dave Burkitt (without crampons) in 1970/71.(FM)

Penguins moulting on the scree platform. The Gentoos outnumber the Chinstraps still, but the latter seem to have increased a bit since 1971. When we get back to 'Sailor's Cache' it is time to cook supper.

Elephant Seals lie snoozing, farting, dozing and burping on the beach and tend to cluster together, often in disordered circular huddles called pods, but sometimes in lines. If you have the nerve you can run over these lines. If a seal senses your coming, it rears up its head and front half as when fighting. If two head-to-tail rear up, there is very little room between. As you run over the first ones they rear up and complain, which disturbs the others. So the longer the line you choose, the more dangerous it is. The record in 1970-71 was twelve by Dave Burkitt. Len determines to practise on the two huge bulls along the beach; they lie head-to-tail, one reddish brown and tatty still in his old coat, the other brownish grey and smooth, having moulted. Len stands for ten minutes or more. Each time he flexes his knees, one of them opens a bloodshot eye, or rotates its head so that both eyes peer up myopically at Len, one each side of its quivery proboscis. Then, in a flash, Lennie nips over the two of them, leaping from the back of one to the other and off, and away before they move. He is chuffed as ten.

The tent is a dry place compared to last night. We all feel a great deal better for the walk. Tonight I think we will sleep well. We plan to move off at eleven tomorrow.

4 March   It is snowing gently but is calm. We set off at eleven. By then the snow has stopped, and the clouds are lifting, even showing a few golden breaks. We are taking the Windover with us. The whole point of the canoeing was to get two Windovers to 'Hut Bluff'! Alan takes the inner and I lash the outer with the poles across the top of my pack. It is an ungainly load but there is no wind and I reckon it could bridge a crevasse and stop me dropping too. Alan is in the middle again with our one iceaxe; I go in front with Mischief's double paddle; Len at the other end of the rope has the single paddle we salvaged.

After walking up the glacier behind the beach, we set off across the wide expanse of snow and ice. Today it is in perfect condition for us, firm ice underneath a light dusting of snow which provides a grip for our cramponless boots without hiding the crevasses. The big paddle is a grand crevasse probe. As we walk, the cloud base lifts to 600 m and we can see the sky dark beyond the level ice-shed at the head of the glacier. There is a great sense of space and wide horizons on this gently undulating white expanse. At the end of each hour we sit on our packs, spaced out on the rope, for a smoke. Alan lights his pipe each time and revels in the sense of open freedom. I am very much hoping that we will find Frank, Gordon and Nick at the Hut. If they have canoed down to Cape Lookout, the expedition's plans will be hamstrung until they get back, even if we abandon the canoes (and I don't think I could just abandon the eighth and ninth of our ten canoes!).

It takes four hours to cross Endurance Glacier. We have our last smoke on the rubble moraine scattered on the glacier surface half a kilometre from the Hut. At four o'clock as we move on to the final icy crevassed section we sight figures outside the Hut! They are still there! It is a tremendous relief. They walk on to the glacier to meet us.

We drop our packs beside civil engineering works that would have made General Wade proud. They have built a series of dry-stone walls to shelter tents. Then we all crowd into the little Hut for a brew. Alan and Gordon have not met since last December. It is over two weeks since Len and I last saw them when they left after our 'Christmas' party. The three of them have had a frustrating time, but seem in very good heart. They have been unable to fish even once. At first this was due to high winds. In February they averaged 40 knots here, they were often over 60 knots with gusts estimated at 100 knots. Then recently they have had calm weather, but the bay has been full of brash with a south-easterly swell running big surf in.

They have spent their days building these great walled enclosures. The site now looks like a ghost village in the Highlands of Scotland, with roofless crofts and byres. This work will prove invaluable, saving our shrinking tentage over the last ten days. However we may have a lot of digging to do as snow starts drifting over the tents behind the walls! The Hutmen say this is the most exposed site they have met. But they have clearly enjoyed being here, just the three of them, isolated from the rest of the world and living together in the comparative comfort of the Hut.

I wander up the bluff and look down the cliffs to the beach. It is rather like coming home after six years away. I find two or three of our old marker flags lying about the slopes where the storm petrels nest, and there are chicks in our two old skua territories.

We spend the evening chatting in the Hut. They have painted a sign, The Happy Haggis Café, with prices in oatmeal blocks. I think they are glad to have more company now. When you are static in one place as a small group, it is difficult to maintain impetus. They have done very well to keep lugging away at the enclosures and particularly Frank as leader. It is a lovely feeling, sitting on a box, leaning against a wall, with a mug of coffee in your hand. Here also we have the grand white light of a Tilley lamp; we take one back to our tent. It lights the whole tent, and warms it too.

The clouds disintegrate as the evening wears on, leaving the lovely range of Pardo Ridge sharp white against the leaden sky beyond. It is the first time that the three fishermen have seen the hills laid out for inspection like this. 'Moby Dick' dominates the ridge; beyond it are the cluster of tops backing Muckle Bluff, which we hope the ridge party will have cracked. We are looking at 20 km of snowy mountains, which belong to us, and are staggeringly beautiful. Proud above our backs is Mount Elder, its steep eastern snowface broken by a crumpled icefall. The dark sky makes the white hills stand out with kukri-sharp edges. Clarence is 50 km away, couched clear on the eastern horizon; most of Ravelin Ridge is clear, and the 2-km-high southern cliff, blue-shadowed, stops a band of pastel green sky. The whole panorama is breathtaking.

I feel very happy to be here, and lucky to be seeing this sight whose beauty had faded in my mind over the years. Len and the others, seeing it for the first time, exclaim their pleasure too. Later there is a glorious moon, the clear sky darkens to indigo; a great bank of ghost white cloud rolls over Pardo Ridge, with the moonlit and shadowed snowslopes casting up weird shapes below. Tomorrow I will be going up Mount Elder with Alan and Nick, who leaps at the chance as if bottled up.

5 March　A fine morning with very blue patches of sky behind blowing clouds. Alan and I spend the forenoon fitting new crampons to our boots. Finally we set off to climb Mount Elder. A little way on to the glacier one of Nick's crampons snaps across the joining link. He has another pair at the Hut but by the time he is ready again it is two o'clock, so we decide to go by the easier north-east ridge, the right-hand skyline from the Hut. Nick leads. On the way up there are the most glorious views, but finally we are in cloud as Nick triumphantly plants his iceaxe in the snow at the summit. In 1970-71 we climbed this second highest peak on Elephant eight times, but no one ever got a view from the top because of cloud; so we called it 'Misty Mountain'. Its official name is Mount Elder (after John Elder, our surveyor), but I still call it 'Misty' and today we are the ninth group to get a good eyeful of cloud from the top. We walk down, wending between the formless white mushrooms in the white-out of cloud.

After half an hour we are down out of the cloud. Walking back towards Endurance Glacier, bits of blue show and disappear behind the clouds. Clouds are going in two directions at once: some are boiling up into veiled cauliflower heads coming very slowly from the east, whilst most is mountain cloud sweeping over the top in the westerly wind. Sometimes as they pass the sun the cauliflower heads are rimmed by faint rainbow edges. It is a lovely delicate effect. We feel very happy. Walking back from climbing a mountain is a great time of satisfaction, relaxation and contentment. At one stage I nearly turned back when Alan seemed tense and tired on a steeper bit at the top. What a

A Tilley lamp inside the little 'Refuge Hut' silhouettes an occupant. Snow has cased the stores outside. Our way up Mount Elder is near the skyline on the right. (GT)

tremendous difference it makes to have reached the summit! If we had turned back we would not have thought it a good day, despite the fun of wending among the mushrooms in the clouds. What a disproportionate importance that last 50 m bears, in a mountain of 940 m.

As we draw near the Hut moraine we can see figures and two extra red dots. I think that they are Vangos from Walker Point; Alan that they are the ridge party's Ultimates. He is correct. John Highton's party was beset by cloud and white-out on the ridge, but they have had a great journey since they left Walker Point. Andy tells me that these days out in the mountains have been the best five days of the expedition for him.

ANDY SIMKINS

1 March   *My rucksack weighed about 35 kg. It contained the Ultimate tent, four days' rations, clothing, met books and climbing gear. I was on a rope with Mike, leading off across mucky ice about 10 cm thick with water beneath. As we turned the corner into the upper glacier we got hit by progressively heavier gusts of wind. The long haul up to 'Doddler's Gap' took several hours. It was sheer hard work. My back ached with the rucksack; my crutch ached with skiing. It was treadmill repetition. My mind would wander occasionally, then be brought back with a jolt. Knackering. It's as if I could just drop down in the snow and say I wasn't going any further. Up and up we climbed. The angle became steeper; it became more tiring. The wind got up and I had to stop occasionally as a hard gust tried to knock me off my feet. Then: thump. I was on my back; and couldn't get up. I had to remove my sack to stand up. I fell over again.*

It is now 2340 in bed and relaxed. We are camped in shelter at 'Doddler's Gap' just below the bergschrund and it is gently snowing.

2 March   *Over the top we set off on skis down the other side. I found it hard work, especially as the heavy pack made balance difficult. With crampons we started up the slope beyond; it became very hard work. It was now a bright day and extremely warm. John had to break a trail into deep snow. It was very sweaty and he found it difficult to see with the salt running into his eyes so our progress was slow. There were occasional steep parts with large crevasses and ice bulges. Soon the mist closed in and it started snowing. We came to a large mushroom which we supposed to be the summit mushroom, but there appeared no way up it. With poor visibility John decided to camp so we hacked out a platform for the two Ultimates under the eave of the mushroom at 750 m. We have not seen the ridge, except a glimpse of frequent mushrooms suggesting very slow going indeed in cloud. The White Company may well be too far. Anyway, although the trogging is hard work, the whole venture is good fun and a bloody good experience.*

3 March   *John set off down the slopes into the mist and we all followed on one rope of four. There were occasional steep parts which required front pointing, but within forty-five minutes we had dropped 250 m and started heading west along an undulating glacier at about 500 m. My rucksack was too heavy. After half an hour it started to hurt my shoulders; at the end of an hour I was nearly dropping. The weight was overwhelming; it drained me completely. I tried putting my thumbs under the straps, which helped a little; but the weight was always bearing down. Nigel in front was having the same problem. Whenever John* *stopped Nigel would bend down to relieve his shoulders. I became a timekeeper, saying that I would go for another ten minutes . . . Luckily John stopped when I reckoned I could last another five. Strangely the agony goes within seconds of taking off the sack, and all thoughts of failing fade. Odd how easily suffering is forgotten.*

The next forty-five minutes' walk wasn't so bad, because the route was more interesting. Then we moved into a crevassed area with a slope up to our left. John decided to camp here: so we found a fairly flat platform, dug ourselves in and were very comfortable there too. I went off up the hill to see if I could see anything but the cloud enveloped us.

4 March *Still snowing. We started on skis, but found it hard down the steep slope as it was fresh snow on top of ice. Nigel and I fell a few times but we persevered on skis, didn't fall over again, and stayed fairly close on the heels of Mike and John. I don't know anything about snow conditions, but we certainly got up quite a speed. After crossing a flat glacier we caught up with the other two, who were pausing to check the map. They agreed that we had just crossed 'Big Wave Glacier'. There we cramponed up and headed uphill, a long slow slog, but with my lighter sack (no tent, but stove and billies) it was not too exhausting.*

We reached a col at 600 m and were given a marvellous view of the mountains ahead. We paused to eat and considered the route ahead. We had to descend a long way before heading up a ramp which would bring us to a high col. We discussed how long it would take. I said one and a quarter hours. We set off, dropped rapidly then started the long, tiring plod uphill: surprisingly, within half an hour we were at the top of the col! It had been 100 m down and 130 m up. We didn't stop, but plodded on downhill again, to reach another uphill slope that went on and on. It was tiring but satisfying. After an age John reached the top and Mike followed.

I came up and saw the most fantastic sight. Endurance Glacier spread out beneath us, between Mounts Elder and Pendragon away to the south and the White Company to our right. It was spellbinding and we were all taken aback. We sat and gloried in the scenery for a long time. Then I said I wanted to climb the mountain to our left rear. Mike told us it was called 'Flat Top'. We quickly raced up it, to get a panoramic view of the south coast, of 'The Flukes' (a narrow summit on the ridge with a bulging mushroom on top), and the whole of Pardo Ridge right along to 'The Emblem'. We could also see Clarence and Gibbs Islands quite clearly. We then headed north-west along the ridge, climbing the next summit in easy time. This was 'Pic de Gaulle', so we had climbed two peaks in an hour.

By this stage we were all very tired and headed downhill to find a campsite. Into the tent for a brew and food, after a truly satisfying, tiring, worthwhile day. A memorable day.

5 March *Mainly downhill on our skis, over a col and then down the side of the glacier – all very exciting stuff and not at all tiring, though my shoulders now ached from the five days of carrying and my heels were developing blisters. After three hours crossing that vast glacier, we finally reached the last icy slope leading to the campsite. Skis off and 200 m up to the campsite and the Hut, the Hut I have heard so much about, all forlorn and peeling paint.*

John and Mike were already in there brewing up, so we quickly joined them. A mess inside – lots of food and kit, paint off the wooden walls, radio equipment in the corner, two pictures of Brigitte Bardot nude, shelves and a bench seat. We sat for an hour eating, drinking, talking. There was a note from Chris saying that three had gone to climb Elder and three to the beach.

21
Last Days

. . . the mystical value of moments which are the unique reward of the solitary climber, moments when the mountains throw off their reserve and admit you to a communion . . .
SIR ARNOLD LUNN

6 March   Mike Wimpenny and I will go along the shore to 'Crab Beach' today. He hopes to find some pink marble which Richard Roxburgh collected in 1970. It is interesting because it seems to consist entirely of calcite and garnets. I will look for the whale vertebrae we found there last time, to search for graffiti by the whalers or sealers of last century, and to carry one back for Lennie. Traversing 'Hut Bluff' beach, Frank and Gordon join us, because the wind is too much for fishing. They are both greatly disappointed over the fishing on Elephant but bear it so well that I too easily forget to comfort them. Today was to be their last attempt to fish.

We cross 'Hut Glacier' on two ropes. The far side is fun, with shattered bridges wiggling across crevasses, but hard frozen and safe. One piece higher than me is shaped like a wine glass with a stalk only 20 cm across: the others each leap down on to it from the ice wall above, then each in turn realises what he has landed on. The wine glass holds.

As we walk along the shore to 'Crab Beach', it starts to sleet. When we get there, it gets worse. The only vertebra there is over a metre across, smothered in penguin filth, and has no graffiti. It can stay there! It is now four o'clock and it is windy, wet and miserable. By the time we have walked back along the shore, up the loose scree, cramponed up, crossed the glacier, down the snow, removed crampons, along the shore, up the penguin colony, up the side of the glacier, on to the moraine, and reached the camp, it is seven o'clock, and we are all bloody wet, and bloody miserable.

After supper we meet in the Hut. First we have a service, singing Jerusalem from varied memories. Crowded into the Hut I find it very moving. It may be our last service on the islands.

7 March   Today I am filled with lethargy, due to the dull weather, or to the expedition drawing to a close so rapidly. I have to crack into paperwork during this last week on the island. Apart from catching up on this journal, I now have to write the Elephant Island bit of the report, plus standard thank-you letters and advertisement letters, and magazine articles. Then there is the difficult and important job of writing reports on each of the team. I always show people their reports, so have to do them now, as there will be no time in *Endurance*. Showing this team their reports will be a pleasure, because it's always grand to tell good blokes that you know they are good.

Alan shouts that the six are in sight. I poke my head out of the tent door. Way out on the white desert of the glacier, six tiny specks are lined across a chance sunbeam. It will take them over an hour to get here. I get out to find Alan marshalling a welcome in the Hut. I remember that in 1970-71 our group returning to join the main party always felt a little deflated at coming back 'under mother's wing', after being out on our own. At that moment of arrival a splinter-group feeling can all too easily develop. The best way to prevent this is for the main party to make a real warm welcome for the returning group. They may want to coil their own ropes and carry their own packs the last few metres; they may not actually want to have a brew and talk at that minute; they may want to put their own tent up; but it is crucially important to go out to meet them, and to offer help and welcome.

The six finally arrive two hours after Alan first sighted them. For the first time on the island all sixteen of us are in the same place at the same time. We all crowd into the Hut to hear how they have fared since we left them at Walker Point a week ago. They finished their survey, and the botany and geology work in three days and then journeyed safely along the south coast. As the second and third brews get sunk and the condensation gathers on the Hut walls, we work out plans for these last hectic days. Chris Hurran wants to head for Stinker Point tomorrow and five others with him. Mike will take another five-man party south and John H will take a three-man party out on the glacier levelling. Alan and I will stay at the Hut – odd feeling, like staying on at school after the end of term, when everyone else is off on holiday. Still, I could not have a more delightful companion.

Chris Brown comes to our tent later for Alan to patch up his blistered feet. One of his Achilles' tendons has swollen hugely, and both feet are raw meat in places. He has done remarkably well to have done so much walking and skiing on Elephant; but obviously he now needs a retread rather than another expedition, to Stinker, in the morning. So the three of us will stay.

8 March   The night has been cold. This morning spindrift is being blown through the camp. With a temperature of minus 4°C the wind is very chilling, and people come to life slowly. This is more like the real Antarctic. Chris Hurran's five get away at two o'clock. Mike's five follow them up the south-east ridge of Mount Elder half an hour later. We watch them zigzagging up the first big snowslope. At intervals we can see the dot in the middle of the front rope stopping and sitting down; we know that is Lennie without crampons. Slowly they go up into the cloud.

John has trouble putting the Hjelper sledge together because it came with a stanchion and a crossbar missing: finally he uses a full tin of Smedley's Red Cherries and masking tape in place of the stanchion, and a broken tent pole in place of the crossbar. When Tim has finished sorting and packing his hydrographic gear they set off in line ahead, towing the little sledge across the glacier. The westerly is now really whipping up the spindrift.

Gordon and Mike pack up: they will go up the shoulder of Mount Elder on the right, then drop down behind 'Crab Mountain' on the left. The stone wall protects the flimsy Vango from the wind, but creates snowdrifts. (FM)

Alan, Chris B and I stand at the edge of the moraine watching them off. I'm not used to waving people off into the hills: it is better to be going oneself. Still, this Base Party feeling has a flavour of its own, and I don't envy John's glacier party. They have a very tedious job to do, marking a rockface and then measuring the surface contour of the glacier on a bearing from there to the midline near the top of the glacier. It will be used for comparison years later, to indicate whether this glacier is growing or diminishing. As the most northerly glacier on the line up the Antarctic Peninsula towards South America, this should be particularly useful.

The Antarctic climate and weather are radically different from that in the Arctic. While the Antarctic is a big land mass surrounded by water, the Arctic is the converse. The one major interruption to this simple system is the long finger of the Antarctic Peninsula pointing up to South America, constricting the circumpolar currents into Drake Passage and separating the maritime climate of the Bellingshausen Sea from the continental climate of the Weddell Sea. The glaciers along the length of the Peninsula (and in Patagonia) provide a transect of climatic conditions across the circumpolar weather systems. Coring down into them can also provide a record of past climatic conditions. The three of them plodding off across the glacier, leaning into their sledge harnesses and into the wind, with heads down and spindrift blowing waist high, make a real picture of Antarctica as we all imagine it.

The three of us go back to the Hut. We put on a brew. We sit and talk. Then as ever I settle into my papers. At five there is a clink outside, and there in the doorway is Nick. He quickly dispels fears that anyone is hurt. Soon all the Stinker Point party are crowded into the Hut. Alan passes out brews while they talk. There was a lot of hard ice, and Len was in great difficulty without crampons, having to walk on Nick's toes! When they got to the crest of the ridge, it was blowing a real hooli in their faces with virtually no visibility. Jem got blown off his feet on hard ice, and the ice slope was obviously not safe for Len. Since they still had a four-hour slog over badly mapped country which none of them knew, into the teeth of the storm, Chris and Jem rightly decided to turn back. So here they are.

As the second mugs go round, the door opens and in comes Dave. It takes me a second or two to remember that he was in Mike's southern party. One of Dave's crampons broke so he came back with Gordon, who follows him wearing his woollen headgear and goggles. I remember Gordon a year ago in the Cairngorms on a rope for the first time and gripped up. Now I watch him confident and relaxed after wandering about an icefall with one companion in a hooligan of spindrift, and am amazed. He has won physical self-confidence and well-being during this trip – that sort of personal victory makes the expedition worth it for its own sake.

The Hut is a great bothy, and a tremendous help to leadership, enabling everyone to get inside out of the wind and wet at once, to talk in comfort. Now it is full of talk and humour. We begin to think of the journey home and how to enliven it: we must all have the words of 'Hymns and Arias' to sing in the plane and in Customs. When we meet up with our 'wives and things' (my unthinking word provokes an outcry from the bachelors) in a group, we will all crane our necks and hiss like Chinstrap Penguins.

Gordon goes out. Five minutes later he returns absolutely smothered in snow, with a tale of woe that provokes hoots of mirth.

GORDON TURNBULL

As we prepared to go out to the tents for supper the wind grew fiercer and bolder with every gust. My drying out procedure was completely nullified by being caught in a spindrift whirly just outside the Hut: I was caught in mid-pee, unable to do anything about it. I just had to stand there and take it like an intrepid explorer. I walked the few steps back to the Hut absolutely covered in snow, my moustache glued firmly to my beard by ice, so that I could only mutter through closed lips '. . . a white hell . . . out there!'

Alan sends our last radio bulletin through Signy. It is a rather sad moment for me. This week is altogether a bit nostalgic.

9 March   Through the night it blows a real hooli. Chris has planned to leave for Stinker Point at 0800. There is little prospect of that today, although there are bits of blue sky above the howling spindrift. I spill the brew and comment that everyone does it some time or other. Chris says: 'Nick never spilt anything in his life, from birth.' Later Nick comes into the Hut in a cloud of spindrift. He laughs and replies: 'Timmy starts books in the middle and reads them outwards.' I think Tim is enjoying himself on Elephant. I wonder how he is faring now, out on the glacier. He will not be able to level in this wind. As I write that, there is a clank from outside.

There are John, Nigel and Tim, back from the glacier. Last night they found a good windscoop in which to pitch the Ultimate and spent a comfortable night. This morning they walked back with the fierce wind. Tim had invented a complex holdback arrangement for the Hjelper sledge, which pulled it apart (at the cherry tin), just at the moment when John's crampon broke. They were all being knocked down by the wind, so it had been difficult putting things together again and they lost a rope down a crevasse.

Alan comes down to the beach to change the tide-gauge paper. It has produced a perfect trace since he did it yesterday and he is very proud. We watch the great surf rolling in on the beach to one side of us, and smashing against the blue icecliffs of Endurance Glacier on the other side. At the snout it chucks spray up a long way, sometimes catching a stray shaft of sun to glitter whiter than snow against the leaden skies beyond. Two bull Fur Seals are loafing around the canoes: there are some on every beach we visit now, but we have not found any breeding. It is remarkably difficult to tell the sexes apart among the young Furs, and to distinguish pups from yearlings.

10 March   Chris Hurran decides to leave at midday. Chris B joins the party; his feet have recovered a bit, though they must still be very tender. I go up the slope with the five of them: Chris H, Gordon and Nick are on one rope, John C and Chris B on the other. I walk along free beside Chris B with his pack, in case his Achilles' tendon is too painful. The worst bit is the first bit, 400 m up on to the south-east ridge of Mount Elder. Patches of drift snow are scattered about the crisp névé in vague patterns: the going is good though the wind on the slope increases as we get higher. I go ahead up the ridge alone to see if I can recognise the line from six years ago, when this was our route to and from Stinker.

The wind is driving me up this slope. It is a lovely feeling and without a rope I really feel free. I put my arms out like wings and leap and flap, but it is not quite strong enough to lift me up the hill. When I get to the main south-east ridge I can see the cornice on my left. Beyond and below, dim in the blowing spindrift and cloud, is the icefall at the top of 'Hut Glacier'. The others are out of sight and I go up easy slopes on a rounded snow crest. On my left a steepening disappearing slope has replaced the cornices; on my right, whorls of spindrift are being blown vertically upwards by the wind roaring up the cliffs out of the clouded corrie. It feels exhilaratingly exposed here on my own battling the wind, but I decide that this is far enough and go down to meet

Bachelor Fur Seals, such as this one scratching himself like a dog, wander about from late December. (FM)

Chris H with all five together now on two joined ropes. They continue up and I walk back down the snow. It is seldom here that one is on snow on a hill alone, without even a rope snaking over the edge to one's partner out of sight. This howling wind generates excitement and the power and beauty is exaggerated by isolation. I go back down alone out of the cloud, exhilarated, but a bit jealous.

I go into John H's tent for a chat. As we start our coffee, Dave pokes his head in: the five are on their way back. Sure enough there are clinkings of climbing ironmongery soon after, with clumpings of boots and thumpings of rucksacks, and shouted greetings.

NICK MARTIN

Up we went. The wind seemed stronger even than last time. Twice Gordon was lifted right off his feet, very undignified for a big man. He swore indignantly at the wind. Further up than last time we struggled, spindrift lashing us from all directions, great clouds of it whirling mercilessly along the slopes. At length we reached the step in the ridge. Ahead there should only be a traverse on to the plateau. The cruel wind played its penultimate trick: trying to claw our way along the traverse into the teeth of driving snow in nil visibility was hopeless. Gusts caught you unaware and threw you backwards off balance. The wind drove us in retreat from the traverse. As we descended our retreat became a rout when the wind veered slightly and flung sleet and rain at our backs.

The days may be frustrating but the evenings are pleasantly spent. Chris comes to dinner, or perhaps we play a game of Scrabble. (Gordon tries to use the odd Scotticism, but CB and I give him fairly short shrift.) The candle flickers its dying gasp. We snuggle down into our maggots and pray for a better day in the morning.

11 March   The morning is grey, but drizzle soon vanishes leaving a calm, overcast day. Chris H, Nick, Gordon and Chris B are all still keen as mustard to go to Stinker and off they go at midday. Nigel and Tim follow them up to climb the south-east ridge of Mount Elder: they turn back because of thick clag, but first watch Chris's party safely on to the plateau. At last they have got away, at the third attempt! They are going to stay over at Stinker to be picked up from there by *Endurance*. That gives them tomorrow and half of Sunday to do some check altimetry for the large-scale map, survey the wreck and do a quick geomorphological survey of the great series of moraine ridges there. Chris H is also going to count and map Giant Petrel chicks for me to compare with our 1971 figures.

Through the afternoon the clouds disappear, leaving us with one of those lovely still clear days. It is so calm that we can lounge around outside. There are jobs to do around the camp and today is perfect for them. Alan and Dave paint the outside of the Hut, starting on the roof and working down. Most of it is dayglo red, with the door and metal brackets picked out in blue, a Mickey Mouse House. Len is busy inside the Hut, cooking goodies for a mess dinner tonight. John and I are hoping that Mike will have looked at this weather and done a Nelsonian 'I see no signal' to my instructions to return today.

The camp looks like a crofting village after the clearances, with tents pitched within walled and dyked enclosures. Tim made a garbage sanger while at the Hut last month, an imposing edifice, with dry-stone walls a metre high. Thinking back at our progress around the islands, we have left quite a series of stone buildings: Tim's observing sangers at O'Brien and Gibbs, stone tent shelters here, at Cape Bowles and above Chinstrap Cove, beach ramparts at Gibbs and 'Sailor's Cache', and the Christmas house at Walker Point. Thinking back over our time on the islands absorbs me today. The day after tomorrow they come to take us away. Knowing that, my mind and body are already running down towards that moment.

Jem is sorting out the stores boxes around the tents. We stand together looking at the scree and lichen slopes of the bluff, and the whole silent arena of glacier and mountains waiting for our departure. When we get home next month the countryside will be bursting into spring: lambs will be frolicking, flowers will be spattering lush meadows, and birds will be singing in the burgeoning trees. Here are no songbirds. But as we stand and watch, a young

Top: At Stinker Point Chris Hurran's party find these windblown Giant Petrel chicks and a wrecked sealing vessel of the 1820s. (GT)

Bottom: A pale Giant Petrel tries awkwardly to brood its chick. (70/71 George Bruce)

skua flies hesitantly around the nest site on the bluff, piping his reedy plaintive squirrelling call time after time in the empty silence. I shall miss this island.

As the day settles into evening, the sea deepens to a rich blue grey, and the snows grow whiter against leaden skies. We gather into the Hut for Len's dinner. As we eat, the calm clear evening rapidly changes to a miserable night of freezing rain. The rain comes without any warning. We still cannot predict the weather here even half a day ahead. Suddenly the door is opened and Mike bursts in, soaking wet and obviously knackered. It is eleven o'clock. It has been dark for nearly two hours. He comes in and stands just inside, with water dribbling off him. His pack fills the doorway but I can just see Frank in the wet blackness beyond. Their story comes slowly as we take their packs off and they sit down for a brew.

22
Over 'Southgate Bealach'
Frank Mogford

Nelson in high spirits led the way over the frightful chasms in the ice, armed with a rusty
musket . . .
ADMIRAL LUTWIDGE

8 March   It was decided we'd leave after lunch. Everyone seemed in a great
mood, despite the occasional flurry of spindrift. We left at 1430, Mike leading
Andy and Dave on one rope and I leading Gordon, so Dave could film us two
'stars'. As we left, the wind picked up and blew clouds of spindrift swiftly along
the ground in great streaks of white. Our first obstacle was the climb up 'Misty'.
It was steep with lots of hard ice, which made fast going, and we were up in
forty minutes. I was puffing hard soon, but got my second wind and things
became easier. On the col above 'Crab Mountain' the wind was very strong,
and unpleasant. My hat and beard became encrusted with frozen spindrift and
the stuff found its way between my scarf and hat, making my neck
uncomfortably cold.
  'Crab Glacier' was an impressive sight; the wind reduced as we dropped
down towards it in the lee of the hills. Then trouble struck: as we reached the
steep descent on to 'Crab', Dave's crampon broke. The front half fell and rolled
down the glacier. It slowed down, seemed to be stopping, but then slid slowly
into a huge crevasse. Andy burst out laughing, Dave wept. Mike searched
around but could see no sign, so Andy descended into the crevasse to look, but it
had slipped into a plug hole which went down and down. Dave had to return to
camp and Gordon went with him.
  Andy loved route finding among all the crevasses on the steep slope down.
Then he set a fair pace across the most exposed part of the open glacier, but I
managed to keep up. I am pleased with today: my recovery rate after a stiff
climb has much improved. But I expect the next few days to be tiring: Andy and
Mike are well used to the mountains and this is my first real out-of-base
expedition.

9 March   Last night was my worst night of the whole expedition. I finally got
up at 0900 and went outside. My bag was really wet, and I felt rotten. Misery is
spindrift and a soggy sleeping bag. After breakfast we broke camp and started
out at midday. The wind was already blowing huge clouds of spindrift across
the glacier and every now and then we had to stop and wait for it to pass. As we
progressed up the slope we became more and more exposed to violent gusts.
The going was good: hard ice with the odd splash of soft snow.

On the slope down to 'Crab Glacier' Frank and Dave wait, while Mike and Andy try to retrieve a crampon. The clear central moraine is half-way to 'Southgate Bealach'. (GT)

Soon the wind became even stronger, and I was caught and staggered even though I'd braced myself. Eventually it happened. One almighty gust hit me and knocked me off my feet; my pack helped to unbalance me, acting like a sail. I was suddenly sliding downhill, unable to stop. My iceaxe was in my hand but tangled in the flaming ropes, and there it stayed wrapped up like a Christmas parcel. I was half on my back, and I remember trying to turn but couldn't because of my pack. Then I was suddenly snatched to a halt. Mike had also been blown off his feet, but had fortunately managed to sink his axe into the ground, thus saving himself and me from a slide back on to the glacier far below. This was only the first of my falls today. The next was just as my leg sank into a crevasse; the wind hit me and did me a favour, picking me out of the hole and dropping me a couple of metres away! This time I got my iceaxe in before I could be blown far. Andy said that quite often he looked up to see Mike and me in front of him flying through the air.

Our descent to Cape Lookout was straightforward, with a steady slope down to the terminal moraine, where we unroped and took off cramps. The spit is a very windy spot. To windward the sea is very rough. To leeward in Cape Lookout bay it is fairly calm, but there is still a considerable swell breaking on the stone beach. I think if we had come here we would have managed to fish on the couple of calm days last week; but there is a breakneck tide rip between the spit and Rowett, a gap of 100 m. There are some strangely desolate rock pinnacles sticking up here and there. The side of Rowett we can see is completely devoid of bird life: very strange. We are camped right on the high tide line, having dug out a platform in the penguin colony and covered it with a bed of washed sand for comfort.

10 March   Despite the wind we decided to climb up the glacier and visit the 'Green Glen'. Off we set, crossing the spit under the watchful eyes of the Fur Seals. They are fascinating creatures. I've become aware of a very distinctive smell about them; a musky, ratty type of odour. The climb up the glacier was pleasant, and we crossed the rocky 'Flat Top Ridge' which runs down to the spit. Beyond was a further glacier. We had by this time entered cloud and visibility was intermittent. We saw the next ridge but were very surprised to find it towering so high above us. We eventually made our way up to find it rose to over 500 m, proving the map wrong again. By now the clouds had reached us, and it began to blow and snow. Mike decided it was too risky to go on to the 'Green Glen' in case we got stuck. We had food, fuel, sleeping bags and survival bags, but didn't fancy a night bivouac. So we headed back to the spit, the wind blowing us down. At the moraine level the snow turned to rain. We hurried to the tent, quite wet.

11 March   We set off, unsure which route we would be taking. The day was still and unusually warm, so we wore shirt sleeves. There was some cloud floating low over the hills but it was broken and we could see blue above. So Andy was raring to go, hoping to climb Pendragon, the highest mountain on Elephant, marked at 974 m. The initial climb up the boulder moraine was sweaty work, so it was nice to stop at the ice, at 160 m, to put on crampons. The climb up to 'Southgate Bealach' was fairly easy going. Underfoot we had melting hard ice. Despite the increasing slope we made good time. Just before we reached the bealach leading over to 'Crab Glacier' the skies cleared, revealing the mushroom-capped summit of Mount Pendragon. Looking at it from the east we could see the very steep south-east facing cliff offered no possible ascent route. However running up from the south was a ridge with many rounded mushrooms dotting the higher reaches. Andy and Mike fancying the conquest, we set off up towards the ridge.

   Soon the ice turned to exhausting soft drifts of wet snow. The rising climb became more interesting climbing than I had yet tackled. The snow high on the ridge was soft and melting. It was beautifully patterned with wind-formed sastrugi flowing to leeward. The climb was mostly a steep snowplod but every now and then we came to a bulging wall of snow. We then had to front point up for maybe 5 to 10 m, using the iceaxe as a handhold, driven deeply into the body of the mushroom. On we climbed, with Andy leading the way, I in the middle, and Mike bringing up the rear. By this time the cloud had enveloped us. We reached a mushroom which seemed to be the summit, and were just congratulating ourselves and discussing the route off, when we noticed that there was still another peak dimly showing through the swirling murk. This being higher we climbed it.

Then we set off to the north seeking a route off. Our only map didn't offer much information. Soon we were scrambling down walls of mushroom snow formations. They were only 5 to 10 m high and I found that I usually fell the last part of each small descent; I put this down to the rotten state of the snow. Andy went first down each step with a dead boy belay in the snow where we waited. On two occasions we had to lower our packs first in order to make the climb down easier. Still we were in the murk. It felt uncomfortable, when I realised that we were descending into unknown country with very steep drops on either side of the ridge. The crunch came when Andy went down one face, only to be presented with a 20-m drop out of sight into the cloud below him. 'Like the last one but a lot steeper,' he shouted up faintly. Mike decided it would be best to go back over the top, retracing our 200-m descent. Andy and his pack had to be hauled up. We then started reclimbing the ice mushrooms I had fallen down, but we made swift progress. I found the climbing up easier. I had only one thought in my mind; to get off that mountain as quickly and safely as possible by a known route, whilst the weather held good, and our footprints still showed our route. I didn't fancy being stuck up on that huge dome of ice and snow and rock swirling in mist and cloud.

We were back at the summit at 1730 in very poor visibility. A good descent put us in friendly country above 'Southgate Bealach' at 1820. Were we thankful to be off that mountain! We then had time to stop for lunch. The food was just what was needed to refuel tired limbs. The crossing of 'Crab Glacier' only took us forty-five minutes. We de-cramped above 'Crab Beach' and made a very steep descent from the glacier wall to the beach, passing the first patch of grass I've seen on the expedition. Across the length of the beach and on to the shore, with its slippery green algae-covered boulders. We had thought we might cross below the snout of 'Hut Glacier', but a timely icefall and a heavy sea persuaded us to make the back-aching climb up the unstable boulder moraine to the safe route over the top. The light was fading fast and my pack was really biting into my shoulders. The glacier was a confused mass of ice contorted into a multitude of shapes, which looked eerie in the gloom. It was pitch dark when we finally made the beach. Andy got his torch out and we set off, only to be surrounded by Elephant Seals bewildered by the torch-light, rearing up all around us. We switched off the torches, and walked singly, avoiding the large rounded shapes which meant Fur Seals or Elephants. Penguins scattered in front of us, and the odd Giant Petrel flapped off into the sea unable to get airborne. It started to rain. We were soon soaked as we plodded along the beach, avoiding the waves of high tide. Finally we reached the canoes and started up to the Hut 170 m above. It seemed to take ages. Andy was now totally exhausted but we waited so we could all arrive at camp together. We finally arrived at eleven.

They were all in the Hut, having just finished a mess dinner. We were met with great warmth. Soon we were sitting with brews and cans of fruit, while Alan knocked up a meal for us, and our tale was told to one and all. Just the welcome you would wish for.

23
Farewell Hooligan

How like a winter hath my absence been,
From thee, the pleasure of the fleeting year?
What freezings have I felt, what dark days seen?
What old December's bareness everywhere?
And yet this time removed was summer's time.
WILLIAM SHAKESPEARE

12 March   It is the morning of (probably) our last day and a gale is blowing
down the moraine. But there is no rain and no spindrift, so it is quite pleasant.
At eleven, Alan, Nigel and I go to unraft the canoes and bring up Tarka. We
carry her up the bottom part of the glacier (now mostly scree with hardly any
ice showing). Then we put on crampons and sledge her up the rest of the way. It
takes nearly two hours against the wind.

At four, three of us go down to pick up the fishing gear and bring it up on our
packframes. I am last starting back, with a wide and heavy load. The wind has
risen quite dramatically. We go in the comparative shelter between the cliffs
and the moraine ridge; feathers from the penguins moulting on the scree are
flying like snow. Half-way up we have to move out of the shelter on to the edge
of the glacier itself. The slope is gentle but now the wind is blasting down the
ice. We fight our way up on the scree beside the snow. Again and again I am
blown off my feet, twisted by the load and thrown back down the scree. It is
quite fun in a way: I know that I will get there in the end, but it is taking me a
long, long time. My knees tire straining to inch me up into the wind. This is a
real Antarctic hooligan. It is gloriously dry: the surf and the white spray torn off
the waves are often sunlit. It takes me over an hour to battle up to the camp
only 150 m above.

I join the others in the Hut. The wind is off the 60 knot scale of the
anemometer all the time, and the gusts must be about 100 knots. All four tents
are battering away at their occupants. We sit in the Hut and talk. Dave has
painted in our twelve signatures on the wall, and printed the names of the four
at Stinker Point. They face our fourteen peeling signatures from 1970-71. Later
we go back to our tents: perhaps our last evening here. The green dome of our
Windover is hammering to and fro. Inside we have to shout into each others'
ears to make ourselves understood. Somehow Nigel has got the primus alight
and supper is hotting up in the big pot. The valance is fraying as it flaps
furiously, but I have no heart to stitch the material today and in this storm. I
just lie close against the tent wall. My whole body shakes with it, but my weight
on the groundsheet helps to hold it down.

The ship is due to arrive at 0900. I will go off first, John H last; the others will leave in alphabetical order.

13 March After breakfast we screw down box lids, and carry them up to the helicopter's landing area on the moraine above the Hut. We strike John's Vango and put the food boxes into the Hut and the dry-stone annex. While we are doing this, we sight *Endurance* approaching from the east, but the wind is probably still too strong. Then Dave sights a helicopter coming in high and slow against the wind.

It lands and I get into it. We lift off and away. I cannot see the camp, because we turn with me on the outside. We go slowly over the deeply broken snout of Endurance Glacier. Then we land on board *Endurance*. Through the day the others are recovered. I feel tired, sad and anticlimatic. But what a great expedition! I think we all feel the same.

NICK MARTIN
What a way to go – sudden death – quite the best. The expedition had ended.

JEM BAYLIS
Goodbye Elephant Island, goodbye grand way of life. Hello civilisation: we greet you with mixed feelings.

It is over. I cannot even go on deck to watch my islands disappear. They slip out of sight astern. Tomorrow we will begin the work of writing it up. Today we will do nothing. I will sleep. Will I dream?

Appendices

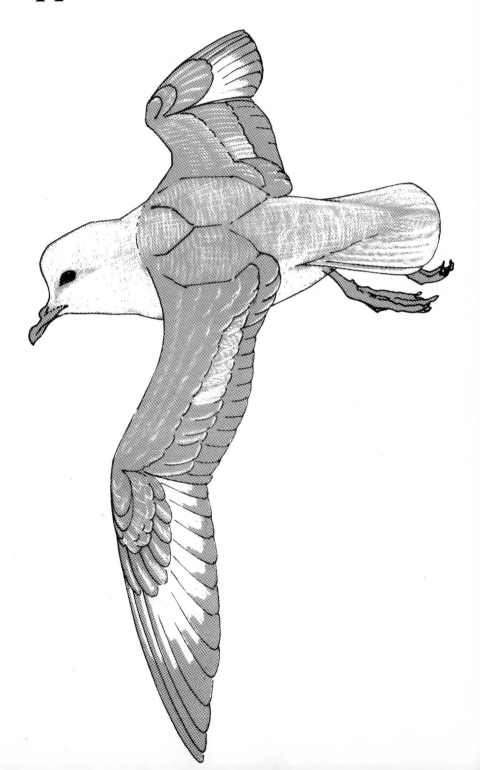

A   The Team Members

Captain Jem Baylis, Royal Army Education Corps (30) Married, 2 daughters
Botany, Report Editor
Jem grew up in the Gower Peninsula, won an Honours degree in Botany at nearby
Swansea, and did two years research on phytoplankton at Menai Bridge. Then he joined
the Army, and in 1975-76 was living in Hong Kong teaching Gurkhas. An Army Rock
Climbing Instructor with Alpine experience, but no major expeditions, Jem also proved
to be a natural canoeist. Small and wiry, with precise movements and a quiet manner,
Jem was a superb craftsman, producing lovely impressionist marquetry.

Sub Lieutenant Chris Brown, Royal Navy (23) Engaged
Geology, Paymaster
Son of a Harrogate dentist, Chris had won an Honours Degree in Geology at Leicester
before joining up as a Supply Officer. In 1975-76 he was serving in HMS *Maxton* and then
at Chatham. Of medium height and build, Chris was not a mountaineer, and walked
rather clumsily, but he enthused over potholing and canoeing, and had taken part in a
university expedition to Heimeoy. Youngest in the team, his red hair and freckles
contrasted with a hesitant manner, and an equable temperament.

Captain John Chuter, Royal Electrical & Mechanical Engineers (28) Married
Terrestrial Zoology, Communications
John came from Romford in Essex, and was a career officer. In 1975-76 he was stationed
in Germany, with a tour in Ulster. He was a climber and had been on two Army
Mountaineering Association expeditions to the Arctic, but had done little canoeing
before 1976. Of medium height and build, he marched into interview looking rather
fierce and cross, with a clipped moustache, but mellowed talking of Axel Heiberg, where
he wanted to study the ecology rather than attack mountains. John put most of us to
shame by his cleanliness, meticulous care of equipment and literary taste.

Lieutenant Nigel Davies, Royal Navy (32) Married, 1 son, 1 daughter
Canoe Equipment
Nigel hailed from Leicester and had qualified as a Clearance Diver while on a short
commission. In 1975-76 he was living in Edinburgh, diving all around Scotland while
working for an Open University degree. He had a wide range of outdoor interests
including climbing, and some canoeing, and had been to Iceland with a BSES expedition.
Tall, lean and bearded, Nigel seemed absent minded, and was usually last to arrive but his
neat rucksack held everything. His hesitant speech reflected a modest nature, and with his
easygoing outlook and ready humour, he got on well with all sorts of people.

Commander John Furse, Royal Navy (41) Married, 2 sons
Leader, Birds
I have the nickname 'Chris' in the Navy. I grew up around southern England, mostly at
my mother's farm in the Weald of Kent. Leaving Malvern College in 1953 I followed my
father into the Navy as an engineer. Since living in Arbroath in 1951 I had spent many
weeks skiing, solitary walking and camping in the mountains of Scotland, the Alps and

Norway. However, I had done little roped climbing and been on no major expeditions before I joined Malcolm Burley's 1970-71 expedition to Elephant Island. Tall, mousy haired and ungainly, I am unsociable and unable to make light conversation. My interests are mountains, the sea, birds and drawing birds: on these and my job I wax enthusiastic. I had won a Leverhulme Research Fellowship to study birds at Elephant Island.

Lieutenant Tim Hallpike, Royal Navy (30)
Hydrography
A doctor's son from West Moors in Dorset, Tim had joined the Hydrographic Branch of the Navy, and in 1975-76 was in HMS *Beagle* in the Caribbean. He had spent many of his leaves as a Temporary Instructor at Outward Bound Schools, so had reasonable experience of rock climbing, hillwalking and canoeing. Tim was a dark-haired, intense young bachelor, of medium height and strongly built. This his first expedition was a personal challenge and he was eager to prove himself.

Commander John Highton, Royal Navy (41) Married, 2 sons, 1 daughter
Deputy Leader, Equipment Officer
One of a large Yorkshire family, John was brought up in the Lakes, and after Sedbergh joined the Navy, training with me in Plymouth as an engineer. In 1975-76 he was in Fife at HMS *Caledonia* running the general and adventure training. He was a sportsman with considerable walking, skiing and climbing experience in Scotland, Norway, the Alps and elsewhere, though he had not been on a long expedition before. He was a good canoeist and swimmer, had been a Barbarian prop forward and was about as fit and tough a man as I could find. John was an extrovert without self-doubt: meticulous lists of stores and accounts were not his forte but his cheerful honesty, bluff, dogmatic manner and easy talk were of priceless value.

Lance Corporal Len Hunt, Royal Corps of Transport (26) Married, 1 daughter
Seals
Growing up in Bute, Len had joined the Army as a boy, and it was his life. In 1975-76 he was based at Catterick, a driver with 24 Field Ambulance. His mountaineering experience was solely on Army Adventure Training courses and he was not a climber, but was a good canoeist. Len was the smallest man in the team, toughly built, eager, straightforward and bouncy. Two owlish eyes peered through powerful spectacles out of a cheerful face. An irrepressible humorist and friend to all.

Captain Chris Hurran, Royal Engineers (28)
Survey
From Merchant Taylors school near his home at Northwood, Middlesex, Chris had joined the Army. After Sandhurst and a degree at the Royal Military College of Science, he was stationed at Andover in 1975-76. Although neither an experienced climber nor a kayak canoeist, Chris had already been on expeditions to Norway and the Atlas from school and had led a Klepper canoe expedition around Holland. Of medium height, slight and fit as a fiddle, Chris was a national standard orienteer and was one of those charming, cheerful and enthusiastic Army officers who successfully follow the precept that everything should be made to appear effortless.

Lieutenant Nick Martin, Royal Navy (29)
Quartermaster, Postmaster
Son of an RN Captain, Nick had joined the Navy as an Electrical Officer after leaving Stowe school. In 1975-76 he was on the staff of HMS *Collingwood* near Portsmouth. He did not actually have either canoeing or mountaineering experience but was a good piste skier, strong, energetic, and keeping himself fit playing rugger. Nick was a tall bachelor with an outgoing patrician charm, willing to try anything, and this expedition was a

challenge with a difference. History, politics and oriental civilisations were the focal points of his wide-ranging interests, which he fed by voracious reading.

Surgeon Lieutenant Commander Alan Milne, Royal Navy (37)
Married, 2 daughters, 1 son
Marine Biology, Doctor
Alan was an Aberdonian, who had spent two seasons with BAS at Adelaide Island before joining the Navy. In 1975-76 he was in the nuclear submarine HMS *Renown*. The Antarctic Peninsula remained heaven to him and second heaven was his home in Muchalls where he and Moira filled a rambling croft with three children, one dog, two cats, three in-laws and accumulating horses. Alan towered over me. A discus champion at school, he was built like a door, but surprisingly had no mountaineering or canoeing experience at all. Combining a deep sincerity with a whimsical humour Alan hated uniform and believed in the primacy of the individual over everything, which made him a most unmilitary officer and a most delightful companion.

Flight Lieutenant Frank Mogford, Royal Air Force (30) Married, 1 son
Fish, Still Photography
Frank was a fair-haired, stocky, determined Leicestershire man, who was a Navigator, serving in Germany in 1975-76. He was mad keen to further his hobby of fish, and to gain selection had spent one leave on a winter survival course, and another on photography. He had no experience of canoeing, and little of climbing except running the RAF Mountain Rescue Unit in Cyprus where he had met and married Chris. Frank did not look an adventurer and was not very forthcoming at interview, but was to prove steady, efficient and very thorough. And he was full of good surprises.

Flight Lieutenant David Monteith, Royal Air Force Regiment (26)
Cinefilm, Geomorphology
Dave was a climber from the Fylde, with a degree in Geography from Durham. In 1975-76 he was serving in Germany and around Britain. He had general outdoor experience including Alpine climbing and some river canoeing; his photographs taken in mountains were beautiful, and he was clearly most at ease and happy in the hills. He was of medium height, wiry and black-haired, with a quick, wry smile.

Lieutenant Andrew Simkins, Royal Artillery (25)
Meteorology
Andy came from Lichfield but in 1975-76 was serving with the Marines, first in Plymouth then Malta. He was first and foremost a climber, but had also done some long distance canoeing including a Devizes-Westminster race. He had not been on a big expedition before, and was new to snow and ice climbing, but Antarctica had been his life's dream. Tall, fair-haired, strong, fit and smiling, Andy was a straight-up-and-down, clean-cut young bachelor. He was always wandering off to pit his strength and skill against some rock, and was filled with curiosity and interest in all around him, as well as being a roman candle of humour.

Flight Lieutenant Gordon Turnbull, Royal Air Force (29)
Marine Biology, Doctor
Gordon had grown up in Edinburgh, joined the RAF after his houseman service, and in 1975-76 was serving first in Yorkshire then at RAF Hospital Ely. He had no experience of mountains, nor canoeing: indeed, he had seldom even camped out, and was our untried beginner. A big man, soft, with a deerstalker, a moustache, twinkling eyes and a pawky humour, he looked unfit, but proclaimed enthusiasms for rugger, and proving himself in the south. Gordon, the unworldly man of the world, liked to converse and was a delightful companion. He had won a Winston Churchill Memorial Fellowship to study plankton at Elephant Island.

Lieutenant Mike Wimpenny, Royal Marines (28)
Geology

Mike came from Yorkshire, and went to school at Uppingham, then won an Honours degree in Geology at Manchester before joining up. In 1975-76 he was in a recruiting job at Birmingham (close to the BAS Geological Department), and living in Shropshire. After three winter NATO exercises in Arctic Norway he was an Instructor in Skiing and Arctic Survival and was fighting fit. Of medium height and build, his sandy walrus moustache gave him a lugubrious expression at first sight, and he talked briefly and sparingly, but his friendliness soon showed through. A national standard orienteer, Mike really wanted nothing better than to run and ski all year, with some time for driving and maintaining rally cars.

B   History and Relics
Chris Furse

According to Rarotongan legend, in the seventh century AD a number of canoes sailed into a place of bitter cold where the sea was covered with pia (a white powder) and things like great white rocks rose high into the sky. Ui-te-Rangiora led that party, which may have been the first to discover Antarctica.

Not until April 1675 did a European follow: Antonio de la Roche, a merchant of London, sighted South Georgia when driven far off course. The belief in a vast rich southern continent persisted until Captain James Cook's great circumnavigating voyages in 1772-75 in the *Resolution*, when he crossed the Antarctic Circle, but sighted only South Georgia, where he made the first landing in the Antarctic in January 1775.

Sealers began to exploit the Sub-Antarctic islands south of New Zealand from 1784 but, apart from South Georgia, they did not reach the Antarctic. Then in 1819 the brig *Williams* en route from Montevideo to Valparaiso was driven south by storm: on 19 February the South Shetlands were sighted for the first time; her captain, William Smith, returned to land on Livingstone Island on 15 October 1819. In 1820 Captain Edward Bransfield RN in the *Williams* surveyed the strait that now bears his name, and while doing so made the first landing on Clarence Isle, at Cape Bowles.

Within a decade the sealers of Britain and New England had stripped the whole area first of Fur Seals then of Elephant Seals. (Fildes wrote of 'fur-lined beaches', but the initial annual take of 3-5 million seals soon dwindled.) There are no records of landings in the Elephant group during that time: however this was due to the sealers' habit of secrecy. (The original name was Sea Elephant Island.) In February 1821 Captain McGregor in the brig *Minstrel* anchored north of Cape Lindsey. Captain George Powell in the sloop *Dove* also visited in 1821: his chart showed West Reef (a danger stretching 10 km NW of Cape Lindsey), Table Bay (now Mensa Bay) and Narrow Island (now Gibbs). James Weddell charted the South Shetlands, after the 65-ton cutter *Beaufoy* with her crew of thirteen under Matthew Brisbane had visited Seal Islands in November 1821. Weddell's chart showed O'Briens Island, Gibbs Island (in four parts), Clarences Isle and Cornwallis, but did not name Aspland or Eadie; his grossly distorted Elephant Island was called variously 'Barrows' or 'Barrows Isle'. Passing Bridgeman Island, Weddell thought he saw smoke issuing with great violence from fissures in the rocks. By 1829 Webster reported that he saw not a single seal in the South Shetlands. Some penguins were taken as the seals disappeared and it is possible that King Penguins had bred until then somewhere in the South Shetlands, as suggested by reports of Bellingshausen, Fildes and Eights. The wreck at Stinker Point is the only evidence of sealing activities.

In the early 1830s the London oil merchants Enderbys sponsored a series of explorations, notably by John Biscoe and Balleny: but these showed no further commercial promise. Twenty years after Smith's sighting, three big national expeditions went south for science and discovery. D'Urville of France (1837-41), Wilkes of America (1838-40) and Ross of Britain (1839-43) determined the outline of much of the continent except in the ice-choked Weddell Sea. All three probably sighted Elephant, like Bellingshausen of Russia (1819-21). Like so many others, they passed its inhospitable shores without landing. Then for fifty years the scientific world forgot Antarctica, apart from the *Challenger*'s related oceanographic work, though a few sealers probably continued hunting Elephant Seals for oil. A cache of coal may exist on Seal Islands, which might suggest a sealer's visit in the 1870s, when Fur Seals briefly reappeared in the South Shetlands.

Toward the turn of the century the heroic age of Antarctic expeditions began, leading to the race for the South Pole in 1911-12. This international interest complemented the rise of Antarctic whaling. After 1890, steam driven whalecatchers and Svend Foyn's harpoon gun made it practical to hunt the faster rorquals, the Blue, Fin, Sei and Minke. In 1895 Carl Larsen's steamship *Jason* visited the Elephant Island group. Many other whalers must have worked off the islands from then until whaling collapsed in 1962-65. Some may have towed whales ashore on to the few beaches to flense. There are no records of landings. Whale vertebrae were found on beaches at Stinker Point, 'Crab Beach', 'Hut Bluff' and 'George's Rib' (all on Elephant), but with no graffiti and few artefacts.

It seems incredible, but when Sir Ernest Shackleton's 28-man team landed at Cape Valentine on 15 April 1916 they made the first recorded landing on Elephant Island. Attempting to cross Antarctica they had left South Georgia sixteen months before, but the *Endurance* had been beset at 77°S in the Weddell Sea in January 1915. After drifting north through the polar night she had finally been crushed, and sank on 21 November 1915. Camped on the ice Shackleton's expedition drifted northward until they came to the edge of the pack, where they took to their three small open boats. For seven days they sailed, through gale-tossed pack ice, hearing the blows of Killers in the leads, enduring cold 20° below freezing, weak from lack of food. Within two days of landing Shackleton sailed west past Pinnacle Rock to Point Wild, made a hut out of two upturned boats and decked over the 6½-m *James Caird*. Nine days after first landing he sailed with five companions 1300 km north-east to South Georgia. The boat journey through the vast seas of Antarctic winter took sixteen days. He followed it by the first crossing of mountainous South Georgia, non stop in 30 hours to reach Husvik. It was 30 August 1916 before at the fourth attempt he rescued Frank Wild's 22 men, who had wintered at Point Wild. They were all safe, all well; not one man had been lost in that epic of survival, which included arguably the greatest small boat journey ever. (The *James Caird* herself is now open to public view at Greenwich, beautifully preserved, immured in the basement of the National Maritime Museum.) In 1971 we visited both Shackleton sites and searched for but found no traces of their occupation.

It was the end of the heroic age of Antarctic exploration, almost. Not for forty years would anyone attempt again to cross Antarctica – not until Sir Vivian Fuchs in 1955-58.

After Shackleton, the pace of scientific exploration increased, supported by the increasing technical resources of the modern world, and by governments who made territorial claims and increased scientific research. Nevertheless, despite whalers and expedition ships passing the islands, I know of only six landings in the group between the wars, by four expeditions, none of whom slept ashore.

1922-23
Quest Expedition. Wild (deputising after Shackleton's death in South Georgia) landed parties on Elephant, near Minstrel Point and at Cape Lookout.

1928
Professor Holtedahl landed on a beach on the NE coast of Clarence (from a Christensen whaling vessel from Sandefjord).

1930-35
Sir Hubert Wilkins may have landed on Elephant at Cape Valentine from the schooner *Wyatt Earp* (but I have failed to find written support for this).

1936-37
Discovery Expeditions. On 13 November 1936 Drs Ommanney and Roberts landed near Cape Bowles. On 2 November 1937 Dr Marr landed twice on Gibbs, near the Spit.

In 1943 under Operation Tabarin, the Royal Navy established bases in the South Shetlands and South Orkneys to assert Britain's sovereignty. After the war, permanently manned bases proliferated: four nations occupied over a dozen bases on the Antarctic Peninsula and off-lying islands alone. Yet none were established in the Elephant Island group. It was too barren, too steep, and lacked beaches. Various landings were made and helicopter surveys carried out, but no one explored the islands.

In the summer of 1956-57 Hunting Aerosurveys finally managed to get strip photographic coverage of the islands from 8400 m after a month of cloud. With ground control this would enable mapping of the group to replace the vague outlines of the 1948 map. In 1964 Malcolm Burley had led an expedition following Shackleton's route over South Georgia. Later Sir Vivian Fuchs (as Director of the Falkland Islands Dependencies Survey) suggested that Burley go to Elephant Island to fill that blank on the map. Thus was born the 1970-71 expedition.

We expected to be the first to live on Elephant since Shackleton, but in January 1970 the US Icebreaker *Glacier* flew Ian Dalziel, the Scots geologist, ashore to camp five days at Stinker Point. An abortive attempt was also made then to put a small scientific party ashore on Gibbs, but it resulted in the loss of a landing craft wrecked on the Spit.

Dalziel's Lamont Doherty team again beat the 1976-77 expedition by a year, landing briefly by gemini from the Research Vessel *Hero* on all except Cornwallis and Seal Islands, at various sites (including the snout of Endurance Glacier!). A field party lived ashore on Gibbs for six weeks.

The only signs of human occupation are various stone platforms, walls and enclosures erected by the two Joint Services Expeditions and by Dalziel's shore parties in 1970 and 1976, together with the 3 m×2 m prefabricated hut erected at 'Hut Bluff' by us in 1970. Beacons have been erected at Cape Lookout (*Quest* 1923) and Cape Lloyd (*Piloto Pardo* 1976) and another is reported on 'Point Inaccessible'. Several trig points established in 1970-72 proved impossible to find in 1976-77.

C   Marine Sciences

Tim Hallpike, Frank Mogford, Alan Milne and Gordon Turnbull
supported by a Winston Churchill Travelling Fellowship

Tides (T.H.)

The 18 days continuous tide records from Gibbs are held by the Hydrographer: they will be of considerable use in predicting tides. The tidal pattern was essentially semi-diurnal; however at Neaps the tides were irregular.

Iceberg Movements (T.H.)

Between Eadie and O'Brien Islands movements were predominantly tidal. The stream flowed eastward from low to high tide, and westward during the ebb, with an hour's slack. The maximum speed of icebergs in 'The Rip' was 3.75 knots. Eddy currents caused reverse movements of bergs close to O'Brien and Aspland during the flood, but flow between Eadie and Aspland was in the same direction as the main stream.

Movements of bergs off Gibbs also varied tidally, eastward during the flood and westward during the ebb, with measured speeds during Springs of only 1.5 and 0.5 knots respectively. South and east of Gibbs there was a general northeasterly drift: on windless days during Neaps, bergs moved NE continuously.

Water Samples (T.H. and G.T.)

Five samples from 18-50 m depth off Chinstrap Cove, Clarence, on 11 January were all similar (temperature minus 0.01°C to plus 0.01°C; salinity 34.320 to 34.607 parts per 1000; pH6; Secchi disc depths 12 to 20.5 m). One sample off Gibbs Spit (south) was within these figures except warmer at plus 0.70°C.

Plankton (G.T.)

Measurements of nutrients, primary productivity, and plankton by oceanographic vessels have shown that this area is productive, but less so than east and west on the Scotia ridge.

Dr Terry Whitaker of BAS has analysed nine samples from Clarence (off Chinstrap Cove) for phytoplankton: 53 species were identified of 18 genera as follows: *Acnanthes* (1); *Actinocyclus* (1); *Amphora* (1); *Asteromphalus* (1); *Biddulphia* (1); *Chaetoceros* (6); *Charcotia* (2); *Cocconeis* (3); *Corethron* (1); *Coscinodiscus* (10); *Fragilaria* (1); *Licmophora* (3); *Navicula* (3); *Nitzschia* (12); *Pleurosigma* (2); *Thalassiosira* (1); *Thalassiothrix* (1) and *Rhizosolenia* (3).

Corethron criophillum Castracane was the most common in all nine samples.

It is planned to report these results in the *BAS Bulletin*, together with determinations of zooplankton not yet completed.

Fish (F.M)

A total of 300 fish of five species were caught using trammel nets, long lines and an Agassiz trawl from rafted canoes in inshore waters less than 30 m deep, and handlining in surf. Specimens have been provided to the British Museum (Natural History).

The table overleaf covers catches off O'Brien and Gibbs. Similar catches of the first four species were made off Clarence (near Cape Bowles and Chinstrap Cove).

Table 1. Fish

SPECIES	NUMBER CAUGHT	STANDARD LENGTH (MM) RANGE AND MEAN	WEIGHT (GM) RANGE AND MEAN
Notothenia neglecta Antarctic Cod	122	189-361 (Mean 279)	170-1430 (Mean 640)
Notothenia rossii Antarctic Cod	21	186-323 (Mean 252)	145-770 (Mean 361)
Chaenocephalus aceratus Ice Fish	4	500-557 (Mean 522)	1430-2520 (Mean 1863)
Parachaenichthys charcoti (nicknamed Crocodile Fish)	1	311	225
Harpagifer bispinis Plunder Fish	2	NR (under 70)	NR (under 50)

From a hundred sexed *N. neglecta*, otoliths were extracted for analysis of growth rates, and fin rays counted to check regional characteristics. Several of this species were caught in breaking waves around rocks. All *N. rossii* appeared to be immature. All the *Chaenocephalus* at Gibbs were ripe females; one had taken a hooked *N. neglecta* of 600 g.

Fish Parasites (A.M.)
Parasites were collected from 15 *N. neglecta*. Ectoparasites found were leeches, monogenea and crustaceans. Of interest regarding endoparasites were: (a) heavy larval infestations of the livers (b) large numbers of acanthocephola in the distal rectum (c) the absence of nematodes and the paucity of other infestations in the gastro-intestinal tract. Digenea were found in only one specimen. This parasite collection has been passed to the British Museum (Natural History).

General Littoral Biology (G.T.)
Limited collections made in 1970-71 and 1976-77 from intertidal sites showed that the invertebrate fauna resembles that of the South Orkneys and the remaining South Shetlands. The littoral zone on all these islands supports little life, which is attributed to abrasion by ice.

Turbellarians (A.M.)
In 1976-77 these free living platyhelminthes (flatworms) were searched for in intertidal sites. About 120 specimens were obtained, from O'Brien (3 sites); Aspland (2 sites); Gibbs (2 sites) and Elephant (Walker Point, no turbellarians found; and below 'Refuge Hut'; 1 site).

Tentative identifications in the field suggested there were ten species of Polyclad and Triclad turbellarians. The collection has been passed to the British Museum.

D Geology

P. W. G. Tanner, British Antarctic Survey

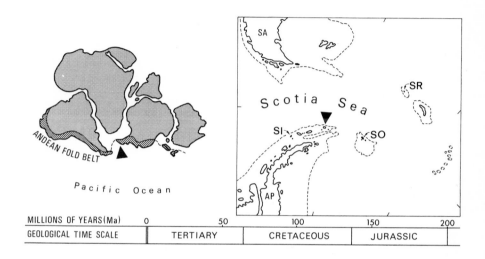

Fig 1. The postulated grouping of the southern continents around 200 million years ago is shown on the
left, with the location of the Elephant Island group marked by the bold symbol. The inset shows
localities referred to in the text, as follows: AP, Antarctic Peninsula; SA, South America; SI, Smith
Island; SO, South Orkney Islands; SR, Shag Rocks.

Some 200 million years ago (Ma) the southern continents were grouped to form a single
supercontinent, Gondwanaland (Fig 1). This landmass began to fragment 180–160 Ma
ago, and the gradual migration of the pieces to their present position is well documented.
During much of Jurassic and Cretaceous time (200–65 Ma) that side of Gondwanaland
facing the Pacific Ocean, in particular the Antarctic Peninsula, was the site of a
continuous chain of volcanoes. Lavas were poured out over the older rocks, and molten
material injected into them. Throughout this period rocks now preserved on the
Elephant Island group, South Orkney Islands and Smith Island lay to the Pacific side of
the volcanic chain, and escaped burial or profound alteration. Geological information
from these areas, and from the Elephant Island group in particular, is therefore valuable,
providing details of events which took place in the earth's crust in this region before the
Jurassic.

History of Investigation

During the Swedish Antarctic Expedition of 1903 Andersson sailed close to the islands,
and suggested that they were made of metamorphic rocks as they bore a striking
resemblance to the South Orkney Islands (Ref 1). The first geologist to land on any of
the islands was J. M. Wordie, a member of Shackleton's expedition which found refuge
on Elephant Island in 1916 (Ref 24). Tyrrell (Ref 23) summarised Wordie's findings, and
those of Douglas on Elephant Island (*Quest* Expedition 1922, Ref 10), Holtedahl on

Clarence Island (Norwegian Antarctic Expedition 1928, Refs 3 and 12) and Marr on Gibbs Island (*Discovery II, 1937*). Tyrrell made a most valuable microscopic study of rocks collected on the 1937 voyage of *Discovery II*, and recognised that the northern half of Elephant Island was made of phyllitic rocks similar to those on Clarence Island, whereas the southern half consisted of garnet- and amphibole-bearing schists, which Tilley (Ref 22) recognised as more akin to those of the South Orkney Islands.

Over thirty years then elapsed before interest in these islands was rekindled by the 1970–71 Joint Services Expedition (JSE) and by the reconnaissance by Dalziel and others from the *Glacier* and *Hero* in 1970 which established that the metamorphic rocks had undergone a long and complex history of folding. Roxburgh and Burkitt of the JSE made large rock collections, mainly from Elephant Island. One interesting result was the discovery of a biotite-granite on Cornwallis Island, which gave a surprisingly young K-Ar age of 9.5 Ma (Ref 15), making it by far the youngest plutonic body reported from western Antarctica. Dalziel *et al.* (Ref 7) reported blueschists (rocks containing a blue sodium-rich mineral) from Elephant Island in 1975, so explaining the two blueschist fragments obtained by *Discovery II* in a dredge haul south of Clarence Island (Ref 23 and Fig 2).

As geological parties from *Hero* in 1974–75 and 1975–76 had made many landings and a detailed structural assessment of the main islands, Wimpenny and Brown in 1976–77 concentrated upon collecting material for laboratory study. Data from the preliminary petrographic study of these rocks are presented here.

Table 1. Geological observations in the Elephant Island group

	ISLAND	YEAR	PUBLICATION
Ferguson	Elephant, Clarence and Cornwallis	1913	Ferguson (1921)
Wordie	Elephant	1916	Wordie (1921)
Douglas	Elephant	1921	Douglas (1923) Tilley (1930)
Holtedahl	Clarence	1928	Holtedahl (1929) Barth and Holmsen (1939)
Marr	Gibbs	1937	Tyrrell (1945)
Araya and Hervé	Elephant	1964	Araya and Hervé (1966)
R/v *Hero* cruise 70-1	Elephant and Gibbs	1970	Dalziel *et al.* (1970)
Joint Services Expedition (1)	general, mainly Elephant	1970/71	Rex and Baker (1973)
R/v *Hero* cruise 74-1	Gibbs	1974/75	Dalziel *et al.* (1975) De Wit *et al.* (in press)
R/v *Hero* cruise 76-1	general	1975/76	Dalziel (1976) Dalziel (in press)
Joint Services Expedition (2)	general	1976/77	

Main Features of the Geology

The islands are largely made up of steeply inclined and contorted grey and green metamorphic rocks, with an ultramafic intrusion (dunite and serpentinised dunite) found on Gibbs Island (Fig 2). Similar metamorphic rocks occur on the South Orkney Islands and the suite is known collectively as the 'pre-Jurassic metamorphic complex'. The rocks may be divided into three main groups:

1. Blueschist and associated phyllites on Clarence Island and northern Elephant Island.
2. Hornblende- and garnet-bearing schists with thin marble bands on Gibbs Island and southern Elephant Island.
3. The dunite complex on Gibbs Island.

As the igneous rocks such as the Cornwallis Island granite (Ref 15) and the dunite complex (Ref 9) have been fully described, attention is focused here upon the metamorphic rocks of groups (1) and (2).

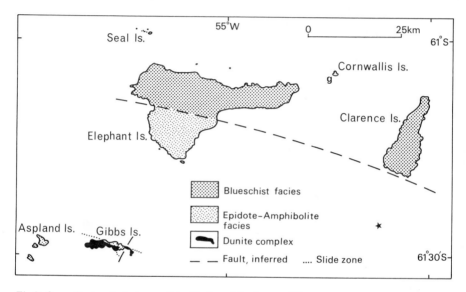

Fig 2. Generalised geological map of the Elephant Island group. The asterisk marks the location of the 1937 Discovery II *dredge haul. g=granite.*

1. The Blueschist Facies

The blueschists and associated grey-green schists are finely banded and contain epidote, albite, muscovite, calcite and chlorite with some actinolite. Small garnet crystals are present in several of the assemblages. A blue amphibole, probably crossite, occurs locally and stilpnomelane is reported for the first time. Pumpellyite occurs in one specimen, together with stilpnomelane and albite. The rocks are generally graphitic and have a phyllonitic texture, the result of intense cataclasis.

There is no evidence bearing directly upon the age of these rocks but as they show the same degree and sequence of deformation as the epidote-amphibolite facies rocks to the south (Ref 8) they are thought to be pre-Jurassic. Radiometric dating has yielded unexpectedly young ages of 99-30 Ma on phyllites from Clarence Island (Ref 13) and of 100 Ma on mica from albite-schist on Cornwallis Island (Ref 15); they relate to a young thermal or tectonic event (uplift) and not to the time of metamorphism.

Microfossils (acritarchs) of Precambrian affinity have been reported from the phyllites on Clarence Island (Ref 14). However these results need to be independently confirmed as the fragile, heat-sensitive, spore-like bodies are apparently preserved in rocks which have undergone (a) extreme cataclasis (they are phyllonites) (b) three superimposed episodes of folding and (c) recrystallisation in the upper greenschist facies.

The only other blueschist facies rocks reported from Antarctica occur on Smith Island (Fig 1, Refs 16 and 17), but albite-stilpnomelane-actinolite-chlorite schists from Shag Rocks (Ref 18) are closely similar to the stilpnomelane-bearing schists associated with blueschists on Elephant Island.

2. The Epidote-Amphibolite Facies

These grey and green banded schists contain albite, biotite and epidote and less common chlorite, white mica, actinolite and calcite with accessory tourmaline; some are rich in garnet and hornblende. They are coarser grained than the blueschists and do not show a cataclastic fabric, although evidence of this may have been destroyed by subsequent recrystallisation. Albite porphyroblasts are common and preserve fine-grained inclusion trails, largely of graphitic material. Small tight folds are sometimes preserved within individual porphyroblasts and predate the widespread crenulation cleavage seen both in hand specimen and thin section. De Wit *et al.* (Ref 9) described garnet-biotite-albite-muscovite-bearing rocks with tourmaline, and hornblende-, actinolite-, albite-greenschists from Gibbs Island, which are similar to those in the southern part of Elephant Island. Tyrrell (Ref 23) also reported chloritoid from a garnet-bearing schist on Gibbs Island.

As recognised by Tilley (Ref 22) the rocks in the southern part of Elephant Island petrographically resemble those in the South Orkney Islands. Other features in common include the presence of distinctive garnet-quartz bands, thin marble bands and albite porphyroblast schists. The metamorphic assemblages have been described in detail by Thomson (Refs 19 and 20) and indicate that the main prograde metamorphism was of medium-high pressure type (Ref 18) probably of epidote-amphibolite facies.

The only radiometric data available for the southern part of Elephant Island are whole rock K-Ar determinations on quartz-calcite-amphibole schist which yield ages of 88-77 Ma (Ref 6). However comparable rocks in the South Orkney Islands give K-Ar ages on mica as old as 200 Ma, so confirming the pre-Jurassic age of the metamorphic rocks in that area.

Synthesis

Blueschists are of considerable interest as they indicate that the rocks were once deeply buried beneath the earth's surface (over 15 km) in an area of low heat flow. Such conditions are found where a slab of oceanic crust making up the floor of an ocean is subducted beneath the edge of a continental block. The dunite complex on Gibbs Island resembles oceanic crust (Ref 9) and is probably part of the pre-Jurassic floor of the Pacific Ocean. One reason for the preservation of this fragment is that during the subduction process it became detached and was thrust over the sedimentary rocks in the adjacent trench. Much of the remainder of the 'floor' in this area has long since been consumed beneath the Antarctic Peninsula. The blueschist and epidote-amphibolite facies rocks appear to represent sediments deposited between the main volcanic arc and the trench (where the oceanic plate is being subducted) and are probably separated by a tectonic break, as is usual in such terrain. Together with the dunite complex they preserve valuable evidence of processes which took place along the Pacific margin of the Antarctic continent over 200 million years ago. Future work will concentrate upon attempts to obtain more precise radiometric ages for these events, and estimates of pressures (giving depth of burial) and temperatures for the main mineral assemblages.

References

1. Andersson, J. G. 1906. On the geology of Graham Land. *Bull. geol. Instn Univ. Upsala*, *7*, 19-71.
2. Araya, R. and F. Hervé. 1966. Estudio geomorfológico y geológico en las Islas Shetland des sur, Antárctica. *Publnes Inst. antárt. chil.*, *No. 8*, 1-15.
3. Barth, T. F. W. and P. Holmsen. 1939. Rocks from the Antarctandes and the Southern Antilles. *Scient. Results Norw. Antarct. Exped.*, *No. 18*, 64 pp.
4. Dalziel, I. W. D. (in press). The early (pre-Middle Jurassic) history of the Scotia arc region: a review and progress report. (*In* Craddock, C., ed., *3rd symposium on Antarctic geology and geophysics*, Madison, Wisconsin.)
5. Dalziel, I. W. D. 1976. Structural studies in the Scotia Arc: 'basement' rocks of the South Shetland Islands. R/v *Hero* cruise 76-1. *Atarct. Jnl U.S.*, *XI*, 75-77.
6. Dalziel, I. W. D. 1972. K-Ar dating of rocks from Elephant Island, South Scotia ridge. *Bull. geol. Soc. Am.*, *83*, 1887-94.
7. Dalziel, I. W. D., M. J. de Wit and C. R. Stern. 1975. Structural and petrologic studies in the Scotia arc. *Antarct. Jnl U.S.*, *X*, 180-82.
8. Dalziel, I. W. D., D. P. Price and G. L. Stirewalt. 1970. Structural studies in the Scotia Arc: Elephant Island, Gibbs Island, Hope Bay and Livingstone Island. *Antarct. Jnl U.S.*, *V*, 100-101.
9. De Wit, M. J., S. Dutch, R. Kligfield, R. Allen and C. R. Stern (in press). Deformation, serpentinization and emplacement of a dunite complex, Gibbs Island, South Shetland Islands; possible fracture zone tectonics. *J. Geol.*
10. Douglas, G. V. 1923. Geological results of the Shackleton-Rowett (*Quest*) Expedition. *Quart. Jnl. Geol. Soc. Lond.*, *79*, Part 1, Proc. x-xiii.
11. Ferguson, D. 1921. Geological observations in the South Shetlands, the Palmer archipelago, and Graham Land, Antarctica. *Proc. R. Soc. Edinb.*, *53*, Part 1, No. 3, 29-36.
12. Holtedahl, O. 1929. On the geology and physiography of some Antarctic and Sub-Antarctic islands. *Scient. Results Norw. Antarct. Exped.*, *No. 3*, 172 pp.
13. Grikurov, G. E., A. Y. Krylov, M. M. Polyakov and Y. N. Tsovbun. 1970. Age of rocks in the northern part of the Antarctic Peninsula and on the South Shetland Islands (according to Potassium-Argon data). *Information Bull. Soviet Antarct. Exped.*, *80*, 61-63.
14. Iltchenko, L. N. 1972. Late Precambrian acritarchs of Antarctica. (*In* Adie, R. J., ed., *Antarctic geology and geophysics*, Oslo, Universitetsforlaget, 599-602.)
15. Rex, D. C. and P. E. Baker. 1973. Age and petrology of the Cornwallis Island granodiorite. *BAS Bulletin No. 32*, 55-61.
16. Rivano, S. and R. Cortés. 1976. Note on the presence of the lawsonite-sodic amphibole association on Smith Island, South Shetland Islands, Antarctica. *Earth Planet. Sci. Lett.*, *29*, 34-36.
17. Smellie, J. L. and P. D. Clarkson. 1975. Evidence for pre-Jurassic subduction in western Antarctica. *Nature, Lond.*, *258*, No. 5537, 701-2.
18. Tanner, P. W. G. (in press). Geology of Shag Rocks, part of a continental block on the north Scotia Ridge, and possible regional correlations. *BAS Bulletin*.
19. Thomson, J. W. 1968. The geology of the South Orkney Islands: II. The petrology of Signy Island. *BAS Scientific Reports, No. 62*, 30 pp.
20. Thomson, J. W. 1974. The geology of the South Orkney Islands: III. Coronation Island. *BAS Scientific Reports, No. 86*, 39 pp.
21. Tilley, C. E. 1930. Petrographical notes on rocks from Elephant Island, South Shetlands. (*In Report on the geological collections made during the voyage of the 'Quest' on the Shackleton-Rowett Expedition to the South Atlantic and Weddell Sea in 1921-22*, London, Trustees of the British Museum, 55-62.)
22. Tilley, C. E. 1935. Report on rocks from the South Orkney Islands. *Discovery Rep.*, *10*, 383-90.
23. Tyrrell, G. W. 1945. Report on rocks from West Antarctica and the Scotia arc. *Discovery Rep.*, *23*, 37-102.
24. Wordie, J. M. 1921. Shackleton Antarctic expedition, 1914-17: geological observations in the Weddell Sea area. *Trans. R. Soc. Edinb.*, *53*, Part 1, 17-27.

E   Terrestrial Invertebrates

William Block, British Antarctic Survey

The South Shetland Islands and in particular the Elephant Island group within them form an important link in the terrestrial biology chain from the southern Andes to the Antarctic continent. In addition to their location being offset from the main axis of the Antarctic Peninsula and separated from it by the Bransfield Strait, it has been suggested that they represent the biologically richest and the most ecologically favoured of the Antarctic areas for terrestrial organisms (Holdgate, 1977).

In the absence of information on the microbial components of the terrestrial communities of the Elephant Island group, the free-living invertebrates which have been recorded to date belong to the following groups: Protozoa (unicellular animals), Nematoda (round worms), Tardigrada ('bear animals'), Annelida-Enchytraeidae (small segmented worms), Crustacea-Copepoda (small crustaceans), Insecta-Collembola (springtails), Insecta-Diptera-Chironomidae (midges) and Arachnida-Acari (mites). The following is a brief account of their distribution and ecology in the Elephant Island group, much of which has resulted from material collected by the two Joint Services Expeditions (JSE) of 1970-71 and 1976-77.

Protozoa

The earliest record is that of Sandon and Cutler (1924) for five species of flagellates and three species of amoebae in a single sample of moraine material collected from Elephant Island by the *Quest* Expedition in 1922. Smith (1972) analysed 23 samples collected in February-March 1971 from Elephant Island by Walshaw, and recorded 54 species (18 ciliates; 17 flagellates, 15 testate amoebae and 4 naked amoebae). The commonest protozoans were the flagellates *Oikomonas termo* (in 23 samples), *Cercomonas longicauda* (9 samples) and *Cercobodo vibrans* (8 samples) with the ciliates *Urotricha agilis* (11 samples) and *Enchelys* sp. (8 samples) together with the amoeba *Pseudodifflugia gracilis* (7 samples). The greatest species diversity occurred in moss carpet peats, and in soil under the grass *Deschampsia antarctica*. All these species achieved their greatest numbers in one of these two habitats, whilst the moraine clays were poor in species with only a few small flagellates present. The population density of testate amoebae varied from 0 in moraine to a mean of 7700 ± 1200 individuals per g fresh weight of peat under moss carpet. The Protozoa in the moss dominated habitats of Elephant Island show much similarity both in species and numbers with such habitats on Signy Island, South Orkney Islands.

Nematoda

Spaull (1973) extracted worms from 11 samples collected in five habitats by Walshaw and recorded the dominant genera as being *Amphidelus, Plectus* and *Teratocephalus*. Generally, the nematode fauna of Elephant Island is similar in content to Deception Island further south west. A re-examination of this material by Maslen (in press), showed that 29 species were collected in the 1970-71 samples, distributed among the Tylenchida (5 species), Araeolaimida (6 species), Teratocephalida (2 species), Monhysterida (4 species), Rhabditida (2 species) and Dorylaimida (10 species). This suggests that the nematode fauna of Elephant Island is comparable in species diversity to Signy and Coronation Islands, in the South Orkney Islands, and more diverse than the 13 Antarctic Peninsula sites examined (Maslen, in press). By comparison only 13 species of worms were identified from Deception Island but these samples were mainly volcanic ash, very different from those on Elephant Island.

Tardigrada
Five samples (four from the grass *Deschampsia antarctica* and one from the moss *Drepanocladus uncinatus*) collected on the 1970-71 JSE were examined by Jennings (1976) for tardigrades. He found 316 individuals in the moss sample, and a range of 17-115 individuals in the grass samples. *Macrobiotus furciger** occurred in all the samples, whilst *Hypsibius (Diphascon) alpinus* +*H. (D.) pinguis** and *H. (D.) scoticus* were found in four samples. *H. (D.) chilenensis* and *Hypsibius (Hypsibius) dujardini** were also identified. (The forms marked thus * are very widespread in the Antarctic Peninsula and Scotia Arc.)

Enchytraeidae
These small, segmented worms have been collected from Elephant Island on both JSE, and preserved specimens are being identified. They were extracted from *Drepanocladus*, *Chorisodontium* and *Deschampsia* samples, and occurred in populations approaching 850,000 per square m in *Deschampsia* soil at a site *c*. 30 m a.s.l. and several metres inland (Spaull, personal communication). Enchytraeids were also collected from the undersides of rocks on polygonised areas (at 130 m a.s.l. on Cape Lindsey), on rocks encrusted with lichens (mainly *Usnea antarctica*) (on moraine at 80 m a.s.l. south of Stinker Point, and on a 15° slope at 180 m a.s.l. on the north side of Walker Point), and from wet moss *(Drepanocladus uncinatus)* (on a 10° slope at 135 m a.s.l. on 'Saddleback Point', 3 km west of Point Wild) during January-March 1971 by Walshaw. In addition, worms have been collected by Chuter and Baylis in moss turf and on the undersides of stones, rocks and slabs on Clarence Island, in scree on O'Brien Island and in moss turf on Aspland Island during the 1976-77 JSE. The occurrence of enchytraeids in terrestrial habitats of the Elephant Island group is of interest not only as it is the furthest south record to date for enchytraeids, but also because of the lack of ecological information on such worms in the Antarctic.

Copepoda
Several small Crustacea identified as copepods were found in terrestrial habitats on Elephant Island by Walshaw in January 1971. The sites ranged from rock surfaces encrusted with lichens, rocks near sheathbill and Wilsons Storm Petrel nests and under stones in a Chinstrap Penguin rookery south-east of Stinker Point, to a rocky outcrop almost 2 km from the nearest sea at 230 m a.s.l. north-east of Stinker Point. These specimens are being studied by specialists to confirm that they are terrestrial, creeping forms of harpacticoid copepods. If so, it may well be the first record of such terrestrial Crustacea in the Antarctic Region.

The remaining arthropods from the Collembola, Diptera and Acari groups, which have been identified from the two JSE, are listed in Table 1.

Collembola (Table 1)
Only two species have been collected, *Friesea grisea* and the ubiquitous *Cryptopygus antarcticus*. This is somewhat surprising, as the richest collembolan fauna has been reported for the South Shetland Islands (Wise, 1967).

Diptera (Table 1)
A single species of chironomid midge, *Belgica antarctica*, has been found in several locations in the Elephant Island group as adults, but mainly as larvae and pupae in soil by the JSE. It has previously been recorded on Gibbs 'Narrow Island' and on Elephant Island at 'Cape Belsham', 1 km west of Point Wild. Elephant Island is the northern limit of this species' distribution, which extends south to Cape Tuxen on the mainland of the Antarctic Peninsula (65° 27'S) and neighbouring offshore islands.

Table 1. Records of Collembola, Diptera and Acari for the Elephant Island group.

+   Species recorded.
ALP   Adults, larvae, pupae collected.
Numbers are total of each species recorded per habitat.

Habitat	Friesea grisea (Collembola)	Cryptopygus antarcticus (Collembola)	Belgica antarctica (Diptera)	Gamasellus racovitzai (Mesostigmata)	Alaskozetes antarcticus (Cryptostigmata)	Halozetes belgicae (Cryptostigmata)	Magellozetes antarcticus (Cryptostigmata)	Nanorchestes antarcticus (Prostigmata)	Rhagidia gerlachei (Prostigmata)	Stereotydeus villosus (Prostigmata)	Ixodes uriae (Metastigmata, ticks)
Gibbs											
Moss carpet		+							+		
Aspland											
Moss turf			L	+	+						
Eadie											
Unidentified moss			L		+						
O'Brien											
Scree			ALP	+	+				+		
Clarence											
Birds' nest material		+		+						+	
Moss peat		+								+	
Under rock slabs											+
Rock crevices			L	+	+				+	+	
Undersides of rocks and stones			L	+	+		+		+	+	
Moss turf				+						+	
Meltwater pool		+									
Elephant											
Moss turf Polytrichum sp.	+	+									
Under grass D. antarctica	+	+									
Under rocks near penguin rookery		572								1	8
Undersides of rocks		26	63A	18	45	8	13	2	77	20	
Lichen-encrusted rocks		2		9			54		37	90	

Acari (Table 1)

Seven species of mites and a single tick *(Ixodes uriae)* have been found on the Elephant Island group. The predatory mesostigmatid mite, *Gamasellus racovitzai*, was recorded together with three species of oribatid (or cryptostigmatid) mites and 3 species of Prostigmata. Of the last, only *Nanorchestes antarcticus* appears to be restricted to Elephant Island itself, the others being found elsewhere in the group.

Six oribatid mites were listed by Wallwork (1973) from previous collections in the South Shetland Islands, including two of the three recorded here. *Magellozetes antarcticus*, previously found in Tierra del Fuego, South Georgia, the Antarctic Peninsula (Hope Bay and Base Gonzales Videla), Anvers Island (Arthur Harbour) and Adelaide Island, is a new record for the South Shetland Islands, being found on Elephant and Clarence Islands. This species has been thought of as part of the South American element in the Antarctic Cryptostigmata fauna (Wallwork, 1967) with a discontinuous distribution in the maritime Antarctic zone and with records from the southern portion only. The present record continues its distribution north from the Antarctic Peninsula area.

Other Groups

In addition to the above groups, it is very likely that representatives of the Rotifera ('wheel animals') and the Platyhelminthes (flatworms) will be found in wet moss and freshwater pools of the Elephant Island group in the future.

There is much scope for further terrestrial study not only of the Elephant Island group in particular, but also of the ecology of the South Shetland Islands as a whole.

In conclusion, the South Shetland Islands and especially the northern Elephant Island group possess a rather richer than expected fauna in number and diversity of invertebrate groups in comparison with the Antarctic Peninsula and the South Orkney Islands. The area is well worthy of further detailed investigation as regards enchytraeid worms, nematodes, mites and the probably terrestrial harpacticoid copepods. Present information therefore suggests that the South Shetland Islands are biologically rich in terms of terrestrial invertebrates, and are clearly of considerable importance in establishing links between the South American and Antarctic land faunas.

References

Holdgate, M. W. 1977. Terrestrial ecosystems in the Antarctic. *Phil. Trans. R. Soc., B, 279*, 5-25

Jennings, P. G. 1976. Tardigrada from the Antarctic Peninsula and Scotia Ridge region. *BAS Bulletin No. 44*, 77-95.

Maslen, N. R. (in press). Additions to the nematode fauna of the Antarctic Region with keys to taxa. *BAS Bulletin No. 51.*

Sandon, H. and D. W. Cutler, 1924. Some Protozoa from the soils collected by the 'Quest' Expedition (1921-22). *J. Linn. Soc. Zool., 36*, 1-12.

Smith, H. G. 1972. The terrestrial Protozoa of Elephant Island, South Shetland Islands. *BAS Bulletin No. 31*, 55-62.

Spaull, V. W. 1973. Distribution of soil nematodes in the maritime Antarctic. *BAS Bulletin No. 37*, 1-6.

Wallwork, J. A. 1967. Cryptostigmata (oribatid mites). *Antarctic Research Series, Vol. 10*, 105-122.

Wallwork, J. A. 1973. Zoogeography of some terrestrial micro-Arthropoda in Antarctica. *Biological Reviews, 48*, 233-259.

Wise, K. A. J. 1967. Collembola (springtails). *Antarctic Research Series, Vol. 10*, 123-148.

F   The Terrestrial Vegetation

R. I. Lewis Smith, British Antarctic Survey

The Elephant Island group lies in the maritime Antarctic biological zone which extends from Bouvetøya, the South Sandwich and South Orkney Islands southwards to the South Shetlands and from the west coast of the Antarctic Peninsula to Marguerite Bay. In this zone vegetation is locally abundant and varied, and is much more luxuriant than elsewhere south of 60°S (Ref 6).

Nevertheless, the macroscopic flora is impoverished and comprises mainly lichens (c. 150 species) and mosses (c. 75 species), plus liverworts (c. 25 species), macro-algae (c. 5 species), fungi (c. 10 species of toadstools) and only 2 species of flowering plants.

The South Shetlands lie closer to a temperate continent than any other part of Antarctica (Tierra del Fuego 600-800 km north). Yet the vegetation of this archipelago is no richer than elsewhere in the maritime Antarctic. There are two principal reasons for this impoverished flora. First, all regions south of the Antarctic Convergence experience a climate which becomes progressively colder and drier with increasing latitude. Although the climate of the maritime Antarctic is modified by westerly winds and oceanic influence, the summers are short and cold with mean temperatures for the warmest month only just exceeding 0°C, and snowfall and frost are frequent. In the South Shetlands sunshine is limited by the predominantly cloudy conditions. This summer climate is very unsuitable for flowering plants to grow and complete their reproductive cycle, whereas the mosses and lichens are more hardy and can reproduce by vegetative means, especially by fragments breaking off to blow away and colonise new sites. Secondly, the stormy Drake Passage with its strong west to east winds and currents is an efficient barrier to the dispersal of seeds and spores from South America. Such harsh growing conditions restrict those plant groups and species which can become established in the Antarctic. The development of communities is dependent on the extent of summer snow-free ground, and on the availability of water. The favoured habitats for extensive stands of vegetation are moist, sheltered, north facing and low.

The Elephant Island group is typical of the maritime Antarctic, and its predominantly moss and lichen flora and vegetation is characteristic of the South Orkney-South Shetland-NW Antarctic Peninsula complex. Prior to 1970-71 only a few landings had been made in the group, and very few botanical collections or observations. A few specimens were collected on Elephant Island by Shackleton's Expedition in 1916, the *Quest* Expedition in 1922, the British Antarctic Survey in 1961 and the United States Antarctic Research Programs in 1966. In 1936-37 the *Discovery II* Expedition collected some plants on Clarence and Gibbs Islands, and the latter was also visited by the BAS in 1961 (Ref 1). During the Joint Services Expeditions (JSE) most of the islands were investigated by Allison (1970-71) and Baylis (1976-77) assisted by Chuter and others. Most work was undertaken on Elephant, but important collections were also made on Gibbs, O'Brien, Eadie, Aspland and Clarence Islands, and the occurrence of vegetation noted on Rowett and Cornwallis Islands; plants were also collected on Bridgeman Island, 90 km SW of Gibbs. About 600 specimens have been deposited in the British Antarctic Survey herbarium. A provisional list of species is given in Table 1. The present list for the group comprises 2 flowering plants, 31 mosses, 7 liverworts, 1 macro-alga and over 56 lichens; no toadstools have yet been reported.

Allison and Smith (Ref 1) described eight main categories of plant communities on

Elephant Island of which five are locally extensive; all are widespread in the maritime Antarctic (Refs 4 and 10). Antarctic bryophytes (the mosses and liverworts) and lichens, collectively referred to as cryptogams, have no English names, so their scientific names must be used.

The two flowering plants occur sporadically at several sites, but are nowhere abundant. Small swards of Antarctic hair-grass *(Deschampsia antarctica)* up to 2 m², with scattered individual plants and associated mosses and lichens, occur in moist sheltered habitats in seven localities on the south and west sides of Elephant Island, and at one on Rowett Island. The Antarctic pearlwort *(Colobanthus quitensis)* occurs as scattered cushions with *Deschampsia* at only two locations on Elephant Island. Neither species was seen below 60 m, and both grew at *c.* 200 m, the highest altitude at which they have been recorded in the Antarctic. This is an unusual altitudinal distribution as elsewhere in the maritime Antarctic they seldom grow above 60 m.

The most widespread communities comprise various associations of short compact cushions and turves of mosses and bushy, leafy and encrusting lichens. They cover large expanses of dry, windswept, stony ground ranging from scree slopes and moraines to plateaux, ridges, nunataks and rockfaces which are not protected by deep snow in winter, thereby exposing the plants to desiccating winds and very low temperatures. The principal plants include cushion-forming species of *Andreaea, Bryum, Dicranoweisia, Grimmia* and *Tortula,* short turves of *Ceratodon, Pohlia* and *Pottia,* bushy (fruticose) species of *Himantormia, Ramalina* and *Usnea,* leafy (foliose) species of *Umbilicaria* and *Parmelia,* and an 'understorey' of many species of white, grey, brown and greenish crustose lichens on the rocks *(Buellia, Lecidea, Lecanora, Pertusaria, Rhizocarpon,* etc). Many of these, and other species also, grow in rock crevices and on ledges. The continuity of this cryptogamic tundra 'fellfield' vegetation is often broken by polygons and stone and soil stripes caused by frost action. Although often sparsely distributed, the wide variety of mosses and lichens often creates a mosaic of colour. These communities are common on all the islands, particularly on Gibbs Island and on Elephant Island, notably around Emma Cove and above Walker Point; dense stands of *Usnea* spp. occur at some of these sites.

Some of the most colourful scenes in the Antarctic environment are created by a variety of encrusting lichens and occasional other growth forms on sea cliffs and on boulders used as bird perches. Here, the marine salts deposited by the spray, and organic compounds from bird droppings, provide a favourable habitat for salt and nitrogen tolerant lichens. These include orange and reddish species of *Caloplaca* and *Xanthoria,* yellow species of *Haematomma, Catillaria* and *Ramalina,* white and grey species of *Buellia, Lecanora, Lecania* and *Physcia,* and black and brown species of *Acarospora* and *Verrucaria.* These lichens often occur in zones above high water mark related to the salt deposited up the cliffs. Bird rocks are often clearly visible from a distance by the splash of nitrophilous orange lichens. All these lichen communities are widespread throughout the group. A single salt-tolerant moss, *Orthotrichum crassifolium,* was recorded near sea level on Aspland and Eadie Islands.

There are three major types of moss-dominated community, distinguished by the growth-form of the principal species as carpets, cushions or turf. Areas inundated by melt water during summer and margins of pools and streams are usually colonised by one or more species of carpet forming mosses. Continuous stands of *Drepanocladus uncinatus* covering up to 1000 m² occur on Elephant Island on moist or gently sloping ground; smaller patches were noted on most of the islands. Smaller stands of *Calliergidium austro-stramineum* are less frequent around pool margins and only on Elephant (notably at Stinker Point) while *Calliergon sarmentosum,* common in the South Orkneys and elsewhere in the South Shetlands in such habitats, was rare. Moist ledges, sloping rockfaces, melt stream margins and wet areas close to penguin rookeries are commonly colonised by large golden cushions of *Brachythecium austro-salebrosum,* together with *Bryum* spp., *Drepanocladus uncinatus* and *Tortula excelsa,* but this community is seldom extensive. In moist areas which are stony and well drained there are occasionally small patches of the turf forming moss *Polytrichum alpinum* with associated lichens and other mosses.

The most interesting feature of the vegetation of the island group is the development of deep banks of moss peat formed exclusively by the tall turf forming *Chorisodontium aciphyllum* and *Polytrichum alpestre* with various lichens growing on their surface; they were found only on Elephant and Clarence Islands. While many banks are only 20-30 cm deep there are some above Walker Point which are dome shaped and exceed a metre in depth. There is permafrost below 20-25 cm. One exceptional bank reaches 3.4 m in depth and is the deepest accumulation of peat known anywhere south of 60°S. Identical banks occur, generally below *c.*80 m altitude, in the South Orkneys, a few of the non-volcanic South Shetlands and some localities on the NW Antarctic Peninsula, but this deep and extensive bank lies at 180 m above sea level. Several radio-carbon dates have been obtained for peat samples at varying depths close to the vertical eroding edge of this bank. The oldest sample, from near the base, was 2125-2345 years old (in 1978). Another, taken from only 30 cm deep, was 1364-1444 years old. A bank on Signy Island, South Orkneys, less than half the depth of the Walker Point bank, is almost twice as old (Ref 3). The Walker Point bank is almost certainly much older than the dating suggests, since the samples were taken near the edge of the eroding peat face where slumping would have caused younger layers of peat to over-ride older layers. Nevertheless, the date indicates that this part of Elephant Island has been deglaciated for at least 2000 years and that vegetation has been established for that period.

The leafy green alga *Prasiola crispa* forms crinkly mats in wet muddy habitats, especially around penguin rookeries, Giant Petrel colonies and on ledges occupied by nesting Cape Pigeons. It is the only plant which can tolerate the trampling and concentrations of nitrogen and phosphorus from the guano (Ref 1). Late in summer when the surfaces of the icefields are melting, areas of firn snow are sometimes coloured red by dense aggregations of unicellular snow algae; less commonly other species develop 'yellow' and 'green snow'.

A feature of insular floras, where the environment imposes considerable stress, is that many species are capable of exploiting most of the limited range of habitats. This is conspicuous in the maritime Antarctic, where competition for space, water, nutrients, etc., from flowering plants is minimal or non-existent. Many of the plants of the Elephant Island group grow in most snow-free habitats. However, there are a few species which occur only where specific conditions prevail, particularly where the concentration of certain mineral elements is high. (The distinction between communities of calcium-demanding and calcium-avoiding species is best seen on Signy Island, where amphibolite and marble outcrop through the schist.) The base-rich serpentines and associated soils of Gibbs Island, unfortunately, did not support a flora much different from the other principal rock type, the relatively acid schist. However, the large black lichen *Himantormia lugubris* and black cushion moss *Andreaea gainii*, which always avoid base-rich rocks, were found only on the schist, while the lichens *Ramalina terebrata* and *Physconia muscigena*, typical of less acid substrates, occurred only on the serpentines; the small moss *Distichium capillaceum* is a useful indicator of basic rocks, and its sole collection was from a crevice in serpentine rock.

The flora and vegetation of the Elephant Island group is in no way unusual for the maritime Antarctic, but it is comparatively rich considering the harsh climate and shortage of snow-free ground. There are no endemic plant species in the group. Most species which occur elsewhere in the South Shetlands and South Orkneys and northern Antarctic Peninsula are present. Notable exceptions include the mosses *Polytrichum juniperinum*, *P. piliferum*, *Psilopilum trichodon* and *Racomitrium austro-georgicum*, and the lichens *Alectoria minuscula* and *Umbilicaria decussata*. Several species reported in Ref 1 as not occurring in the Elephant Island flora were collected by Baylis. Several species have been found in single localities in the group, but probably have a wider distribution. The highest record for plants was at 465 m where *Chorisodontium aciphyllum*, *Placopsis contortuplicata* and *Usnea antarctica* were collected; another 12 species were recorded at over 400 m. Elephant Island is the farthest south locality for the lichens *Alectoria nigricans* and *Cladonia mitis*, the former being common in the South Orkneys (Ref 7) and the latter previously known only from a single site on South Georgia (Ref 9), although both occur in Tierra del Fuego. The mosses *Dicranum oleodictyon* and *Pohlia inflexa* have not been reported from farther south, but probably do grow there; *P. inflexa* has been described as endemic to South Georgia (Ref 2) but it is now known from Signy and Elephant Islands. Several of the liverworts are also not known farther south, but as yet the only taxonomic study of Antarctic liverworts is Ref 5.

Collections and ecological notes made by the two JSE have revealed a much more diverse flora in the Elephant Island group than was previously suspected. At a few localities, notably above Walker Point, the extent of the plant communities is exceptional, considering the high altitude and windswept nature of the terrain. The comparatively poor floristic composition and scattered distribution of vegetation on some of the smaller islands is due to a scarcity of suitable snow-free habitats, water, soil development or shelter from the wind; also, less time was available for botanical investigation at Eadie, Aspland and Bridgeman Islands so those plant collections were not comprehensive. Taxonomic revisions of the collections will reveal further species not yet identified, particularly for the encrusting lichens. Almost certainly, additional species exist on the islands which have been overlooked.

The Joint Services Expeditions have made a major contribution to the knowledge of the flora and plant ecology in the maritime Antarctic, where similar work has been undertaken from the South Sandwich Islands (Ref 11) to Marguerite Bay on the Antarctic Peninsula (Ref 13). A classification of the plant communities of the Elephant Island group has been produced (Ref 1) and the vegetation shown to have very close similarities and affinities to that of the rest of the South Shetlands (Ref 8) and of the South Orkneys (Ref 12). The islands are clearly an important link in the biogeography of the maritime Antarctic biota.

References

1. Allison, J. S. and R. I. L. Smith. 1973. The vegetation of Elephant Island, South Shetland Islands. *BAS Bulletin Nos. 33 and 34*, 185-212.
2. Clarke, G. C. S. 1973. A synoptic flora of South Georgian mosses: III. *Leptotheca, Philonotis, Mielichhoferia* and *Pohlia*. *BAS Bulletin No. 37*, 53-79.
3. Fenton, J. H. C. and R. I. L. Smith (in press). Distribution, composition and characteristics of moss banks of the maritime Antarctic. *BAS Bulletin No. 52*.
4. Gimingham, C. H. and R. I. L. Smith. 1970. Bryophyte and lichen communities in the maritime Antarctic. (*In* Holdgate, M. W., ed., *Antarctic Ecology*, 2, London and New York, Academic Press, 752-85.)
5. Grolle, R. 1972. The hepatics of the South Sandwich Islands and South Georgia. *BAS Bulletin No. 28*, 83-95.
6. Lamb, I. M. 1970. Antarctic terrestrial plants and their ecology. (*In* Holdgate, M. W., ed., *Antarctic Ecology*, 2, 733-751.)
7. Lindsay, D. C. 1969. Further data on Antarctic Usneaceae. *BAS Bulletin No. 20*, 33-40.
8. Lindsay, D. C. 1971. Vegetation of the South Shetland Islands. *BAS Bulletin No. 25*, 59-83.
9. Lindsay, D. C. 1974. The macrolichens of South Georgia. *BAS Scientific Reports, No. 89*, 91 pp.
10. Longton, R. E. 1967. Vegetation in the maritime Antarctic. (*In* Smith, J. E., A discussion on the terrestrial Antarctic ecosystem. *Phil. Trans. R. Soc., B, 252, No. 777*, 213-235.)
11. Longton, R. E. and M. W. Holdgate. 1979. The South Sandwich Islands: IV. Botany. *BAS Scientific Reports, No. 94*, 53 pp.
12. Smith, R. I. L. 1972. Vegetation of the South Orkney Islands, with particular reference to Signy Island. *BAS Scientific Reports, No. 68*, 124 pp.
13. Smith, R. I. L. and R. W. M. Corner. 1973. Vegetation of the Arthur Harbour-Argentine Islands region of the Antarctic Peninsula. *BAS Bulletin Nos. 33 and 34*, 89-122.

Table 1. Provisional list of plants collected

* Mosses found with fruit.
R Also found on Rowett Island.
† Plants collected only by the Imperial Trans-Antarctic Expedition, 1916.

	Elephant	Gibbs	O'Brien	Eadie	Aspland	Clarence	Bridgeman
Flowering Plants							
Colobanthus quitensis	+						
Deschampsia antarctica	+R						
Mosses							
Amblystegium subvarium†	+						
Amblystegium sp.	+	+			+		
Andreaea depressinervis	+		+			+	
Andreaea gaiñii var. gainii	+	+					
Andreaea regularis*	+						
Bartramia patens*	+						
Brachythecium austro-salebrosum	+	+	+	+	+	+	
Bryum antarcticum†	+						
Bryum algens*	+				+	+	
Bryum spp.	+	+	+	+	+	+	
Calliergidium austro-stramineum	+						
Calliergon sarmentosum	+						
Ceratodon cf. grossiretis	+	+	+	+		+	
Chorisodontium aciphyllum	+					+	
Dicranoweisia grimmiaceae*	+			+		+	+
Dicranum oleodictyon	+						
Distichium capillaceum		+					
Drepanocladus uncinatus	+	+	+	+	+	+	+
Grimmia antarctici*	+			+		+	
Orthotrichum crassifolium				+	+		
Pohlia cruda var. imbricata	+	+					
Pohlia inflexa	+						
Pohlia nutans	+						
Polytrichum alpestre	+					+	
Polytrichum alpinum	+		+				
Pottia heimii var. heimii					+	+	
Tortula conferta	+	+			+	+	
Tortula excelsa	+						
Tortula fusco-viridis	+	+	+			+	
Tortula cf. grossiretis	+					+	
Tortula cf. monoica						+	

Liverworts

	Elephant	Gibbs	O'Brien	Eadie	Aspland	Clarence	Bridgeman
Anthelia juratzkana	+						
Barbilophozia hatcheri	+					+	
Cephalozia badia	+						
Cephaloziella varians	+		+				
Cephaloziella sp.	+						
Lophozia sp.	+						
Roivainenia jacquinotii	+						

Algae

	Elephant	Gibbs	O'Brien	Eadie	Aspland	Clarence	Bridgeman
Prasiola crispa	+	+	+	+		+	

Lichens

	Elephant	Gibbs	O'Brien	Eadie	Aspland	Clarence	Bridgeman
Acarospora macrocyclos					+	+	
Alectoria chalybeiformis	+						
Alectoria nigricans var. implexiformis	+						
Alectoria pubescens	+						
Buellia anisomera	+					+	
Buellia coniops	+						
Buellia latemarginata	+					+	
Buellia russa	+						
Caloplaca regalis	+	+	+			+	
Caloplaca sp.	+	+	+	+	+	+	
Catillaria corymbosa	+	+		+			
Cladonia cf. balfourii	+						
Cladonia furcata	+						
Cladonia cf. gonecha	+						
Cladonia metacorallifera	+						
Cladonia mitis	+						
Cladonia rangiferina var. vicaria	+						
Cladonia sp.	+					+	
Cornicularia aculeata	+						
Cystocoleus niger	+						
Haematomma erythromma	+		+				
Himantormia lugubris	+	+	+	+			+
Lecanora aspidophora	+					+	
Lecanora atra	+		+				
Lecania brialmontii	+	+	+	+	+	+	
Lecidea cf. atrata			+				
Leptogium puberulum	+						
Mastodia tesselata	+	+	+	+	+	+	
Microglaena antarctica					+	+	
Ochrolechia antarctica	+	+					

	Elephant	Gibbs	O'Brien	Eadie	Aspland	Clarence	Bridgeman
Ochrolechia frigida	+	+	+			+	
Pannaria sp.	+						
Parmelia saxatilis	+	+				+	
Peltigera rufescens	+						
Pertusaria sp.	+	+				+	
Physcia sp.	+					+	
Physconia muscigena		+					
Placopsis contortuplicata	+	+					
Psoroma cf. follmannii	+	+					
Psoroma hypnorum		+					
Ramalina terebrata	+	+			+	+	
Rhizocarpon geographicum	+						
Rinodina petermanii	+						
Sphaerophorus globosus	+					+	
Stereocaulon alpinum	+	+	+				
Umbilicaria antarctica	+			+		+	
Usnea antarctica	+	+	+	+	+	+	+
Usnea fasciata	+	+					
Verrucaria elaeoplaca						+	
Verrucaria cf. maura	+						
Verrucaria racovitzae†	+						
Verrucaria tesselatula			+				
Verrucaria sp.		+	+		+	+	
Xanthoria candelaria	+	+	+	+		+	
Xanthoria elegans	+	+	+			+	
Xanthoria sp.	+						

Many of the lichens, notably crustose forms, have yet to be identified and many species will eventually be added to the list. In particular, several unidentified species of *Buellia*, *Lecanora* and *Lecidea* have been collected on each island, but are not listed.

G   Ornithology

Chris Furse

supported by a Leverhulme Research Fellowship

As not all our 1976-77 field notes have yet been collated and analysed, the following is an interim report. Comprehensive lists of references are given in the reports in the Bibliography.

Our primary task was a breeding census, which covered most parts of all islands in the group, and counts or estimates of numbers of nests were made covering every area of every island. BAS holds copies of our maps at 1/30,000 covering all of Elephant Island for all species, but these have still to be updated and a further 160 maps completed to present our 1976-77 results covering all the islands. Until then final census figures cannot be compiled, but meanwhile the table lists all species recorded in the group, and shows their status on each island. The notes below indicate the salient points noted on census.

As regards breeding biology and behaviour, hatching date was the event most widely determinable by our mobile summer expedition; it is also most important ecologically, and provides a simple basis of comparison. Accordingly the timing of breeding is indicated by reference to hatching dates only. As well as recording all observations on foods and feeding (and collection of food samples from penguins) we devised some numerical sampling techniques to suit our mobile expedition, including checks on random samples of nests, 24-hour watches and traffic counts, and irregular measurements of large samples of marked chicks. Certain aspects of specific interest were studied. Normal bird watcher's logs, sketches and photographs completed our field records.

Blue-eyed Shag *Phalacrocorax atriceps*. Shags bred in scattered colonies around the whole group and were seldom seen outside those localities. One, two (and sometimes three) eggs were laid. Peak hatching was before mid-December, but there was wide variation and extreme dates may have been mid-November and 20 December (earlier than in the South Orkneys). In some mixed colonies, penguins had usurped shags' nests. I never saw these shags drying their wings like *P. carbo*.

King Penguin *Aptenodytes patagonica*. One moulting on Elephant in December 1970 was very unusual this far south. We found no sign of breeding in the group.

Adelie Penguin *Pygoscelis adeliae*. The only significant colony was on Clarence at Cape Bowles where the mean number of offspring per nest was 1.70 in December. Elsewhere some non-breeders were present until January. Hatching dates were about 13 December to about 27 December, only four to five days before the Chinstraps. The small numbers were surprising, since Adelies abound in the South Orkneys and remaining South Shetlands.

Chinstrap Penguin *Pygoscelis antarctica*. This was the dominant bird throughout the islands, nesting densely on almost all possible areas, with colonies up to nearly 300 m. On Elephant, Chinstraps outnumbered all other species combined and accounted for 95 per cent of the total biomass of breeding birds. Two eggs (often one, rarely three) were laid. Hatching was closely synchronised in each colony within a period of two weeks, after which 10-15 per cent of eggs were brooded a further two weeks and were mostly addled. Hatching dates varied no more than a week around the group, but sometimes between neighbouring areas: Elephant 'Hut Bluff' 16 December to about 31st; Clarence Cape Bowles 17 December to about 31st; O'Brien 'Camp Corrie' 22 December to about 4 January (but O'Brien NW passage four to five days earlier). A traffic count on Elephant in late December showed 2250 foraging trips of 4-5 hours per day per 1000 nests; another on Clarence in late January showed only 1450 per day per 1000 nests. Forty-nine returning adults carried up to 880 g of food, of which over 90 per cent by weight was large *Euphausia superba*.

Gentoo Penguin *Pygoscelis papua (subspecies?)*. Gentoos bred only at the six sites on Elephant where open beaches provided space for creches of chicks and were backed by gentle slopes. Elsewhere only a few non-breeders came ashore. No three-egg clutches were noted. Hatching dates varied remarkably with the peak from late November to mid-December: extreme dates estimated in 1970-71 were conservatively 18 November-16 January and more probably 12 November-27 January. Gentoos took fish as well as krill, and staggered breeding contrasted with the krill-eating species. The timing of breeding corresponded more closely with the population on South Georgia (ascribed to the nominate Sub-Antarctic race *P.p. papua*) than with those on the South Orkneys and remaining South Shetlands (ascribed to a separate southern race, *P.p. ellsworthi*). Culmen lengths of seventeen breeding adults on Elephant (mean 50.4 mm; SD 2.1) also closely corresponded with sixteen on South Georgia (mean 51.0; SD 5.0) and differed significantly from seventeen South Orkney and South Shetland birds (mean 44.0; SD 2.8). This presents interesting questions.

Rockhopper Penguin *Eudyptes chrysocome*. The one nest on Clarence at Cape Bowles contained two eggs. One hatched on 31 December, but on 25 January the chick died (probably killed by Chinstraps). This nest was visited on at least eight days: there was always one Rockhopper, never a Macaroni and this appears to be the first recorded breeding inside the Antarctic Treaty area. One non-breeder was seen on Aspland.

Royal Penguin *Eudyptes schlegeli*. One non-breeder moulting on Gibbs in January showed all the characters of Royal Penguins, which breed only at Macquarie Island and may be a race of the Macaroni.

Macaroni Penguin *Eudyptes chrysolophus*. They breed locally on most of the islands, but usually as a minority among Chinstraps and only three colonies exceeded 500 pairs. Among hundreds of nests inspected from 13 December onward, no second eggs were found. Hatching occurred in a concentrated period of ten to fourteen days within each colony: over the second half of December on Elephant, seven days later on Aspland and Gibbs and an intermediate date on Clarence. Fifteen returning adults (all females) carried up to 565 g of food; proportions of prey species differed between Gibbs and Clarence (fish, over 60 per cent to nothing; *Thyssanoessa*, under 20 per cent to over 50 per cent; *E. superba*, 20 per cent to nearly 50 per cent of different sizes). Most food was well digested, suggesting two day foraging trips (as at South Georgia) with longer range than Chinstraps.

Black-browed Albatross *Diomedea melanophris*. This species foraged regularly offshore, but only very occasionally within sight of land.

Grey-headed Albatross *Diomedea chrysostoma*. In April 1923 the *Quest* Expedition saw many on Elephant at Cape Lookout and suspected breeding. They certainly do not breed there now, and we saw only a few at sea (NW of Cornwallis in March).

Light-mantled Sooty Albatross *Phoebetria palpebrata*. All three records were at Gibbs. In

1977 one flew across the island and another along the cliffs, but there was no suspicion of breeding.

Giant Petrel *Macronectes giganteus*. Stinkers bred only on Seal Islands, and on Elephant, where two of the three colonies were counted and mapped in detail in 1971 and had changed little when recounted in 1977. Most of the single chicks hatched 10-14 January, but dates from 4-16 were also recorded and 2 and 27 were estimated extremes: these dates were the same as in the South Orkneys. Miscellaneous observations were made on plumage, displays and breeding biology. The foraging routines of adults feeding young chicks were very flexible, with durations generally less than at Signy Island and often much less than one day.

Antarctic Fulmar *Fulmarus glacialoides*. This species was distributed extremely unevenly: none nested on Elephant or Seal Islands; on Cornwallis and Clarence this species and Cape Pigeons both bred abundantly; on Gibbs, Aspland, Eadie and O'Brien fulmars greatly outnumbered Cape Pigeons. Fulmars nested up to 500 m height, with a catholic taste for sites generally steeper than the Cape Pigeons. The species has not been recorded nesting elsewhere in the South Shetlands. Hatching of the single chicks was concentrated between 15 and 24 January on Gibbs, coincident with fulmars in Terre Adelie. Circumstantial evidence of nocturnal feeding was obtained, and one food sample.

Cape Pigeon *Daption capensis*. This species was abundant on many parts of Elephant, Cornwallis, Clarence and Seal Islands, but on the south-western islands was rather locally distributed in smaller numbers. It nested up to definite ceiling heights of 100-200 m, in less steep sites than the fulmar. Hatching of the single chicks was synchronised within colonies, but varied between areas (5-10 January on Elephant, 9-17 January on Gibbs and intermediate on Clarence). The Gibbs dates coincided with those at Signy and in Terre Adelie.

Antarctic Petrel *Thalassoica antarctica*. The *Quest* Expedition saw many at Cape Lookout in April 1923, but they certainly do not breed there now. They were seen around some cliffs of Gibbs: a colony could exist there, but is unlikely, as the nearest known sites are over 500 km south.

Snow Petrel *Pagodroma nivea*. A small breeding group on Elephant at 'Nelly Point' appears to be the only one recorded in the South Shetlands, though they are numerous on the Peninsula and in the South Orkneys. Hatching was estimated to have been in early January and the chicks had left by early March, which corresponds with the South Orkneys.

Antarctic Prion *Pachyptila desolata*. Two breeding groups on Elephant are the only recorded colonies in the South Shetlands and the furthest south on this side of the Antarctic. Very few were seen elsewhere and breeding was only suspected on Eadie, although this nocturnal species is easily overlooked. Estimated hatchings were over the latter half of January, though some eggs were still attended in mid February, and a spread from mid January to mid February may occur as in the South Orkneys.

Black-bellied Storm Petrel *Fregetta tropica*. I found this exclusively nocturnal species breeding in large numbers on every island I visited myself. The Elephant Island group appears to be its centre of world population. Observed hatching dates of the single chicks were evenly spread from 27 January to 21 February, but the overall spread at marked nests and elsewhere was estimated to be 22 January to 27 February. (Compare 2 February to 16 or 26 for the tiny population on Signy.) Typically it nested in steeper screes and cliffs; most nests in flatter sites contained corpses of chicks entombed by April snowdrifts. Measurements of ten adults were all but one within limits noted by Beck and

Brown, but twelve measured eggs extended the known range. The species did not feed in sight of land, but foraging trips were probably less than the three days suggested by Beck and Brown.

Wilsons Storm Petrel *Oceanites oceanicus exasperatus*. This crepuscular species bred on all islands we visited, but was strangely localized and in several places outnumbered by *Fregetta*. The two species occupied distinct but overlapping terrains, *Oceanites* preferring the gentler screes and moraines. Observed hatching dates of the single chicks were from 16 January to 1 February, but the overall spread at marked nests and elsewhere was estimated to be 11 January to 28 February, with an ill-defined peak period over the first two weeks of February. This breeding season was about two weeks ahead of that at Signy, and corresponded closely with that on the Peninsula. This species often fed close inshore; diets of chicks included euphausids up to 30 mm long.

Brown Skua *Catharacta skua lonnbergi*. Skuas bred in many but not all suitable areas; however the only large colony found was 65 pairs and a club of 70 at Stinker Point and only two pairs bred on the east coast of Clarence. One or two eggs were laid. Hatching dates on Elephant ranged from 20 December to 13 January coincident with dates on Signy, plus one about 28 January. Scanty records elsewhere suggested later dates on Clarence (from December to after 20 January) and on O'Brien, Eadie, Gibbs (from 24 December to 28 January). Over thirteen prey species were noted among remains. Four ringed birds were seen.

South Polar Skua *Catharacta skua maccormicki*. Two non-breeders on Elephant were thought to be this species, but not certainly identified.

Kelp Gull *Larus dominicanus*. Although present and evidently resident in small numbers on most coasts, breeding was seldom proven. Hatching of the one, two or possibly three eggs was observed only in the second week of December 1970; all chicks and fledgelings seen indicated synchronous hatching over the first half of December. Observed foods included limpets, carrion, plankton and habitual scavenging after Leopard Seals. Sub adults departed after December; post-fledging movements of family parties were seen, and roosting flocks of up to 37 in March.

Antarctic Tern *Sterna vittata*. The few colonies were on typical open moraines and also scree slopes and cliff ledges, and were unevenly distributed without evident pattern or ecological reason. Cornwallis and Elephant held the only three large colonies excepting one on Bridgeman found by *Endurance*, while only one group of four nests was found on Clarence at Craggy Point. Peak hatching of the one or two egg clutches was around Christmas, but there was wide variation both within colonies and between areas: Elephant 13 December to 10 January; Gibbs from early January until after 27 January; O'Brien from 16 December, and Cornwallis until after 10 February. The staggered dates were attributed to both vulnerability to snowdrifts and fish diet: small silvery fish were the regular prey. Twenty-six eggs were measured.

Arctic Tern *Sterna macrura*. A tern in winter plumage was seen briefly at O'Brien, and thought to be this species.

Sheathbill *Chionis alba*. Sheathbills bred around all coasts. Density depended primarily on penguins: on Clarence penguin/sheathbill ratios were between 145 and 400 in every area; on Elephant most sheathbills exploited between 40 and 200 penguins, but 8 per cent were remote from any penguins and 9 per cent enjoyed over 500 (such high ratios were attributable to factors such as lack of nest sites). Clutch sizes varied from place to place: on Elephant the mean was 2.6 eggs (range 1-3), on Clarence mean was 2.7 eggs (range 1-4) and in the Gibbs group 2.4 eggs (range 1-4). On Elephant the extreme hatching dates probably extended one to two days outside observed range of 6 to 21 January; observed range in Gibbs group was 2 to 17 January and on Clarence 30 December to about 14 January. A big influx in late March was probably autumn migration from the Antarctic Peninsula.

Table 1. Ornithology: Status of species

	O'Brien	Eadie	Aspland	Gibbs	Seal	Elephant	Cornwallis	Clarence
Blue-eyed Shag	n77	n77	n77	PB77	PB70	PB	n	PB77
King Penguin						n70		
Adelie Penguin	n77	n77	n77	PB77		n70		PB
Chinstrap Penguin	PB	PB	PB	PB	PB70	PB	PB	PB
Gentoo Penguin	n77		n77	n77		PB		n
Rockhopper Penguin			n77					PB77
Macaroni Penguin	n77	n77	PB77	PB77	PB70	PB	EB77	PB
Royal Penguin				n77				
Black-browed Albatross					s	s70	s	s77
Grey-headed Albatross						n23	s77	
Light-mantled Sooty Albatross				s				
Giant Petrel, M. giganteus	n77	n	n77	n	PB70	PB	s	n
Antarctic Fulmar	PB77	PB77	PB77	PB	s70	n	PB77	PB
Cape Pigeon	PB77	PB	PB77	PB	PB70	PB	PB	PB
Antarctic Petrel	s77			n77		n23		
Snow Petrel	n77				s	PB70		n77
Antarctic Prion	n77	EB77		n77		PB		
Black-bellied Storm Petrel	PB77	EB77	EB77	PB77		PB		
Wilsons Storm Petrel	EB77	EB77	tb77	PB77		PB	EB77	PB
Brown Skua	PB	PB77	n77	PB	n70	PB	tb	PB
South Polar Skua						p70		
Kelp Gull	tb77	tb	tb77	tb77	n70	PB	tb77	PB77
Antarctic Tern	PB77	n77	EB77	PB77		PB70	PB77	PB77
Arctic Tern	p77							
Sheathbill	PB	PB	PB	PB	PB70	PB	PB	PB

PB   Breeding proven.
EB   Circumstantial evidence of breeding, but not conclusive proof.
tb   Present and believed to breed, but good evidence not obtained.
n   Present on or over land, but no evidence of breeding.
s   Observed offshore or overflying, but not on land.
p   Probably seen, but identification not certain.

23   Only noted during *Quest* Expedition, 1923 (*Wilkins*).
37   Only noted during *Discovery II* Expedition, 1937 (*Marr, Roberts*).
70   Only noted during Joint Services Expedition, 1970-71 (*Furse, Bruce*).
77   Only noted during Joint Services Expedition, 1976-77 (*Furse, Hurran, Wimpenny*).

Where no figures are shown, this status was observed on this island during two or more of these four expeditions.

H   Seals of the Elephant Island Group

Len Hunt

	Year of census	Number of seal beaches visited	Elephant Seal *M. leonina*	Leopard Seal *H. leptonyx*	Crabeater Seal *L. carcinophagus*	Weddell Seal *L. weddelli*	Ross Seal *O. rossi*	Fur Seal *A. gazella* (Totals inc. pups)	(Pups)
Clarence Island	1976-77	11	29	13	1	50	—	91	—
Cornwallis Island	1977	1	—	2	—	—	—	3	—
Elephant Island including Stinker Point	1977	16	3342	13	3	145	—	353	—
	1970-71	42	3044	26	5	166	—	254	3
Stinker Point only	1977	6	2276	—	1	—	—	74	—
	1971	6	1636	4	1	10	—	60	—
Seal Island	1970	2	100	—	—	—	—	62	16
Gibbs Island	1977	6	6	2	1	18	—	19	—
Aspland Island	1977	3	10	4	—	37	—	4	—
Eadie Island	1977	1	—	2	—	1	—	—	—
O'Brien Island	1976-77	2	1	2	—	2	—	—	—

Seal count figures

These figures are sums of the maximum counts at each beach. They do not equate to populations, except perhaps for the sedentary Weddells. (Wandering Furs and Leopards may be counted twice, whilst male and female Elephants come ashore at different times to moult so only one sex may be counted – in 1970-71 adult population of Elephant Seals on Elephant Island probably exceeded 6000.)

The figures for Elephant Island for 1977 include also the 1970-71 figures for the 26 beaches that were not revisited, so the differences shown are only those on 16 beaches visited both seasons.

Several tagged seals were sighted – 8 Elephants in 1971 on Elephant Island (one from Signy Island, the others probably all from South Georgia) and 1 Fur in 1977 on Clarence Island.

I   Equipment and Food Report

The lists below include everything we took except scientific equipment and stationery. While returning in HMS *Endurance* to the Falklands and Montevideo, we met to vote on the Quality of each item (Outstanding/Satisfactory/Poor), and on the Quantity (Too much/Adequate/Not enough). The comments in these tables show where there was net bias of four or more votes one way or the other: the absence of any comment shows there was no significant bias, suggesting reasonable satisfaction. Actual voting figures are given in the Expedition Report. Note that the votes on Quality reflect various different properties of items, including Importance (*eg* Snow shovels), Pleasure (*eg* Candles), Design Suitability (*eg* Ultimate Pyramid Tents), and Quality of Manufacture (*eg* Dolomite boots and Optimus Stoves) as well as all round outstanding Performance (*eg* Polywarm sleeping bags). Note also that votes on Quantity were influenced by uneven dumps and caches.

Clothing, Personal and Camping Equipment

ITEM	QUANTITY	COMMENTS
Balaclava	17	
Headover (woollen tube)	15	Outstanding (6)
Scarf	16	
Earband	6	
Climbing helmet	4	
Snow goggles and ski goggles	22	Poor (4)
Mountain jacket (zipped) Tisos	16	
Anorak general purpose	14	
Cagoule (110 g material)	14	Poor (5)
Duvet jacket	7	Outstanding (7), Not enough (4)
Overtrousers, proofed nylon	14	
Trousers, cotton and nylon	14	
Breeches	20	Too many (5), Poor (4)
Braces	18 pairs	
Snow gaiters (canvas, zipped)	20 pairs	Poor (4), Not enough (6)
Crampons: Grivel 12 point	41 pairs	Too many (6)
Crampons: Salewa adjustable	6 pairs	Outstanding (6), Not enough (9)
Boots: Dolomites	6 pairs	Outstanding (4)
Boots: Greenlanders	6 pairs	
Boots: Super RD, Caber, Nordica	4 pairs	Outstanding (4)
Boots: Others	13 pairs	
Gym shoes	17 pairs	
Spare crampon straps	14 sets	
Sweaters (service wool jerseys)	32	Too many (4)
Polar jerseys	5	Outstanding (5)
Shirts (service knitted flannel)	30	Outstanding (9)
Undershirts	42	
String vests	32	Too many (6)
Drawers (wool, for cold weather)	42	
Underwear, long limbed: RAF Aircrew, Damart and Helly Hansen	7 sets	Outstanding (7)

Spongebag, towel and first aid kit	16	
Housewife (sewing materials)	13	Outstanding (7)
Stockings: heavy wool submariners	48 pairs	Poor (5), Too many (9)
Stockings: Norwegian loopstitch	30 pairs	Outstanding (11)
Socks (plain wool, white)	30 pairs	Outstanding (4)
Divers, dress trousers (waders)	6 pairs	Outstanding (11), Not enough (9)
Wetsuit helmet	6	Too many (9)
Wetsuit mittens	16 pairs	Outstanding (4)
Wetsuit waistcoat	16	
Wetsuit trousers and bootees	8 sets	Poor (6), Too many (11)
Mittens, Dachstein and Helly Hansen	14 pairs	Outstanding (13)
Mittens, RM inner and outer sets	20 pairs	
Gloves, Fireball	15 pairs	Poor (7), Too many (4)
Gloves, silk and wool inners	16 pairs of each	
Seaman's knife (service pattern)	16	Poor (7), Too many (6)
Watches (waterproof service pattern)	16	
Tent: Ultimate Pyramid	3	Outstanding (10), Not enough (11)
Tent: Arctic Pyramid (secondhand)	5	Poor (9)
Tent: Arctic Guinea (secondhand)	4	Poor (12), Too many (10)
Tent: Vango Force 10 Mk 5 Everest	11	Poor (7)
Spare tent poles	0	Not enough (10)
Tarpaulins 4×4 m	12	
Karrimat 76×183 cm	18	
Air mattress	1	Too many (4)
Sleeping bag: Polywarm Base Camp	16	Outstanding (15)
Survival polybag	16	
Polythene tubing 136 cm circ.	25 kg	Outstanding (4)
Polybags 61×61 and 30×22 cm	1600	Too many (4)
Tilley lamp and spare mantles	7	Outstanding (10)
Candles	18 kg	Outstanding (4)
Torch (waterproof right angle)	20	
Torch: spare batteries	168 pairs	Too many (6)
Matches (ordinary boxes)	576 boxes	Poor (5), Too many (9)
Matches (waterproof)	5 packs	Outstanding (7), Not enough (8)
Optimus III paraffin stove	26	Outstanding (16), Too many (8)
Kerosene Grade A	1230 litres	
Jerricans and polythene bottles	80	Outstanding (4)
Snow shovels	4	Outstanding (13), Not enough (9)
Spades and hand shovels	6 each	Too many (4)
Pickaxe and sledgehammer	6 each	
Snowsaw	6	
Arctic pots (nesting saucepans)	15 pairs	Outstanding (8)
Mess tins	24 pairs	Too many (8)
Knife, fork and spoon	20 sets	Poor (5)
Plastic cup	24	Outstanding (5)
Vacuum flask	20	Too many (5)
Funnels (various sizes)	15	
Bucket (plastic)	6	
Sponge	28	Outstanding (10)
Dishcloths	60	Too many (8)
Paper towels	30 rolls	Outstanding (14), Not enough (7)
Scouring pads	100	Outstanding (4), Too many (9)
Brush sink snow	14	Outstanding (6)
Soap	60 bars	Much too much (13)

Climbing, Skiing and General Movement on Land

ITEM	QUANTITY	COMMENTS
Rucksack: Karrimor Pamir/K2 frame	16	Outstanding (6)
Rucksack: Berghaus Cyclops	1	Outstanding (1)
Rucksack: Climbing daysack	14	Too many (9)
Compass: Silva No. 2	20	Poor (4)
Altimeter	14	
Heliograph	20	Too many (15)
Whistle	14	
Miniflare kit	24	
Hjelper sledge complete with harness	4	
Touring skis (205 cm Kongsberg)	17 pairs	
Ski sticks: metal	8 pairs	Outstanding (4), Not enough (5)
Ski sticks: wood	8 pairs	Poor (10)
Sealskins	16 pairs	
Ski wax and scraper	20 sets	Poor (4), Too much (6)
Ski repair kit with emergency tips	4	
Iceaxe (70 cm long)	20	
Ice hammer, Salewa	4	Outstanding (6), Not enough (9)
Piton hammer and rock pitons	8+30	Too many (7)
Holster for iceaxe, etc	4	Not enough (5)
Climbing harnesses (chest and/or waist)	7	
Waist belts	14	Too many (4)
Descendeurs (figure of 8)	14	
Jumars	6 pairs	Too many (7)
Karabiners: Screwgate	60	Too many (5)
Karabiners: Hiatt snaplink	28	
Deadman belays	14	
Snowstake belays	0	Not enough (4)
Icescrews	20	
Rope: nylon, hawser laid No. 2 (220 m)	4 lgths	Too much (5)
Rope: nylon, hawser laid No. 4 (35 m)	20 ropes	
Slings (2 and 3 m loops, Nos. 3 and 4)	12	Too many (4)
Slings (nylon tape)	28	Too many (6)
Prussik line (22 mm nylon for loops)	180 m	

Canoeing Equipment

The following equipment proved adequate.

10 Tasman double canoes (Kirton Kayaks, Canoe Centre), fitted out
34 jointed flat double paddles (Ottersports); 6 spare blades
24 normal spraydecks; 8 blanks for empty cockpits; spare material
6 fibreglass repair kits; 6 ultraviolet repair kits (Valley Canoes)
3 handpumps (Whale Gusher and Henderson Chimp); 8 balers
3 spare rudders; 6 sets spare tiller wires, brackets, pins, etc
20 buoyancy bags (Crewsaver); 16 closed cell buoyancy aids
4 sets rafting equipment (3 poles, board, canvas dodger, line)
4 Johnson Euro 4 engines (E. P. Barrus); 2 toolkits; 8 plugs; 24 shearpins

Still Photographic Equipment (all 35 mm)

ITEM	QUANTITY	COMMENT
Pentax KM body and case	2	
Pentax SIA body and case	3	Not enough (5)
Pentax KM 200 mm lens	2	Outstanding (3)
Pentax KM 85-210 mm zoom lens	1	
2×2 Converters (Komura and Vivitar)	2+1	Outstanding (4)
Pentax 28 and 35 mm lenses	2+2	Outstanding (5)
Pentax 55 mm lens	2+2	
Pentax SIA 135 mm and 150 mm lenses	2+2	Too many (3), Outstanding (2)
Pentax SIA 300 mm lens	2	
Pentax SIA close up bellows	3	Too many (3)
Pentax screw/bayonet adaptor	2	
Olympus OM1 camera outfit	1	Outstanding (3), Not enough(4)
Rollei 35 camera	1	Outstanding (4), Not enough (5)
Calypso Nikkor underwater camera	5	Outstanding (5), Not enough (5)
Olympus RC 135 automatic camera	2	
Olympus RC 135 lightmeter batteries	4	Not enough (4)
Konica C35 automatic camera outfit	4	
Konica C35 spare lightmeter batteries	12	
Polaroid camera	0	Not enough (6)
Weston lightmeters	6	Not enough (4)
Lens hoods (various cameras)	10	Too many (7)
Spare lens caps	0	Not enough (7)
Filters: yellow (various cameras)	6	Not enough (4)
Filters: skylight (various cameras)	15	
Filters: UV (various cameras)	2	
Filters: polarising (various cameras)	6	
Flash units (each 3 spare batteries)	4	Outstanding (4)
Tripods and mini tripods	4+6	Poor (4), Too many (4)
Cable releases	4	
Lens cleaning brushes	2	Not enough (4)
Lens cleaning tissues	6 pkts	
Lens cleaning cloths	20	Outstanding (4)
Photo log books (10×10 cm)	16	Outstanding (5)
Changing bags	2	
Colour slide film: Kodachrome X (36 exp. cassettes)	100	
Colour slide film: Ektachrome X (36 exp. cassettes)	200	Not enough (4)
Colour slide film: Ektachrome X (20 exp. cassettes)	350	Poor (4), Too many (5) (20 exp. disliked)
Colour slide film: HS Ektachrome (20 exp. cassettes)	150	
Colour negative film	0	
B and W film: Kodak Plus X (36 exp. cassettes)	150	Not enough (4)
B and W film: Ilford FP4 (36 exp. packets)	150	Poor (4) due packaging
B and W film: Ilford HP4 (36 exp. packets)	50	
Spare cassettes	0	Not enough (4)

General Materials and Tools

We took the following, which was most of what we wanted, and all that we needed.

Wood; leather; rubber patches; rags; 2 toolboxes; 4 toolbags.
6 sets tent repair materials; 4 sailmakers' palms and sets of needles
36 rolls 5-cm masking tape; 5 rolls 2.5-cm insulating tape
60 m seizing wire; 4 kg twine; 400 m codline; 1440 m nylon parachute cord
20 m 1-cm plastic hose; 24 tubes Bostik clear adhesive
12 cans WD40; 3 bottles light oil; 1 kg silicone grease; 60 tins dubbin, etc
4 litres black and white paint; 40 litres dayglo paint; 16 paintbrushes
144 marker flags; 12 steel rules; 12 tape measures
4 hacksaw frames and 24 blades; 5 scissors; 2 wire brushes
6 flat chisels; 4 centre punches; 5 flat and 4 round files
2 oilstones; 72 sheets emery paper; 5 blowlamps
4 hammers; 2 small crowbars; 3 nail-pullers; nails
4 hand-drills and sets twist drills; 6 braces and bits
19 standard, Phillips and jewellers' screwdrivers; woodscrews
8 pairs sidecut and longnose pliers; 4 molegrips; 6 hand-vices; 2 adjustables
4 eyelet punches and eyelets; 2 pop rivetters and rivets
6 base medical kits; 2 doctors' bags

Bulk Rations

Additional rations to boost the Army Compo Rations from 3500 to 5500 calories per manday.
Quantities below are the total for 896 mandays.
Quantities of several items exceeded requirements. The only quoted additional wants were condensed milk, dried vegetables, salad dressing, curry powder, herbs and spices.

70 kg plain biscuits; 27 kg oatmeal blocks; 23 kg sweet biscuits
25 kg spaghetti; 112 kg flour; 14 kg milled rice
10 kg cocoa powder and Ovaltine; 10 kg orange and lemon powders
25 kg honey and golden syrup; 21 kg butter concentrate; 5 kg peanut butter
90 kg sugar; 3 kg dessicated coconut; 9 kg raisins and sultanas
3 kg peanuts; 33 kg Lyon's fruit cakes; 3 kg custard powder
12 kg egg powder; 38 kg cooking fat; 3 kg dehydrated onions
10 kg tomato paste; 1 kg ground white pepper; 2 kg curry paste
10 kg chutney; 10 kg mixed pickle; 10 kg tomato sauce; 10 kg brown sauce
1 kg Parmesan cheese; 500 g plastic Jif lemons
65 kg tinned potatoes; 130 kg each tinned carrots, beans, peas and tomatoes;
65 kg dried mixed veg.; no broad beans
14 kg tinned blackberries; 60 kg each tinned apricots, pears and peaches;
27 kg cherries; 114 kg apples; 70 kg pineapples
33 kg sardines; 15 kg herrings in sauce; 44 kg pork sausages; 44 kg luncheon meat.

Army Composite Rations (Seven menus ABCDEFG)

A largely tinned ration, in boxes each for 4 mandays.

Expedition took 896 mandays (224 boxes) (2.3 kg and 3500 calories per manday). Quantities below are per 4-manday box.

ITEM	MENU	QUANTITY	COMMENT
Breakfast			
Baked beans in tomato sauce	All	450 g	
Sausages	ACEG	450 g	
Oatmeal blocks	ACEG	5×25 g	Outstanding (10), Not enough (7)
Bacon grill	BF	450 g	Outstanding (5)
Baconburger	D	425 g	
Main meal (supper)			
Soup powders: Various	All	75 g	
Meats: Casserole steak, onion	C	450 g	Outstanding (7)
Meats: Goulash	A	450 g	Outstanding (5)
Meats: Stewed steak	G	450 g	
Meats: Corned beef	B	340 g	
Meats: Chicken curry	D	450 g	
Meats: Steak and kidney pud.	E	450 g	
Meats: Chicken supreme	F	450 g	
Mashed potato powder	ABCEG	170 g	
Rice (not pre-cooked)	DF	280 g	Poor (9)
Vegetables: Carrots	ADG	280 g	
Vegetables: Processed peas	CEF	280 g	
Vegetables: Mixed vegetables	B	280 g	
Puddings: Apple pudding	A	630 g	Outstanding (9)
Puddings: Mixed fruit pudding	C	470 g	Outstanding (6)
Puddings: Canned pears	F	680 g	Outstanding (5)
Puddings: Fruit salad	D	680 g	Outstanding (4)
Puddings: Rice pudding	BE	680 g	Outstanding (4)
Puddings: Chocolate pudding	G	470 g	
Tea (snack)			
Rich cake	B	280 g	Outstanding (10)
Luncheon ham	AD	450 g	Outstanding (4)
Hamburgers	EF	425 g	
Salmon	CG	450 g	
Jams (various)	All	250 g	Outstanding (5)
Processed cheese	All	225 g	
Margarine	All	215 g	
Chocolate bars (milk or Tiffin)	All	4×50 g	
Boiled sweets	All	100 g	Poor (7), Too many (12)
Drinks and Sundries			
Tea (15 g teabags)	All	50 g	Outstanding (5)
Coffee (instant)	All	15 g	Not enough (9)
Dried milk	All	75 g	
Sugar	All	400 g	Not enough (4)
Salt	All	25 g	
Mustard powder	All	7 g	
Jiffy tin opener	All	1	Outstanding (8)
Matches	All	1 booklet	Poor (12), Not enough (9)
Toilet paper	All	24 sheets	
Reclosure lids (plastic for tins)	All	2	
Paper towels	None		Not enough (5 and 8)

Royal Marine Arctic Rations (Four menus ABCD)
A largely dehydrated ration, in packets each for 1 manday.
Expedition took 1120 mandays (1.4 kg and 6500 calories per Manday).
Quantities below are per manday.

ITEM	MENU	QUANTITY	COMMENT
Breakfast			
Porridge (quick oats)	All	90 g	Outstanding (13)
Drinking chocolate powder	All	70 g	Outstanding (13)
Snack			
Chicken and bacon spread	C	50 g	Outstanding (4)
Beef spread	A	50 g	
Cheese	D	50 g	
Chicken spread	B	50 g	
Jam	None		Not enough (11)
Margarine	All	25 g	
Plain biscuits	All	75 g	
Squashed fly biscuits	All	75 g	Outstanding (10)
Chocolate bars (each 50 g)	All	100 g	Outstanding (7)
Chocolate caramels	All	50 g	
Nuts and raisins	All	40 g	
Dextrose tablets	All	25 g	
Main meal (supper)			
Soup powder (various)	All	25 g	Too much (4)
Curried beef granules	B	70 g	Outstanding (5)
Mutton granules	C	70 g	Outstanding (4)
Chicken supreme	D	70 g	
Beef granules	A	50 g	
Surprise dehydrated peas	All	45 g	Outstanding (10)
Pre-cooked rice	BD	75 g	Outstanding (5)
Smash potato granules	AC	50 g	
Carrots, beans, mixed veg.	None		Not enough (9)
Apple flakes	AC	25 g	Outstanding (8)
Apple and bilberry flakes	BD	25 g	Outstanding (8)
Drinks			
Coffee (Nescafé instant)	All	10 g	
Oxo	All	1 cube	
Tea (Nestea instant)	All	3.5 g	
Dried milk	All	15 g	Poor (4), Too much (4)
Sugar	All	25 g	
Sundries			
Salt	All	1.25 g	Too much (14)
Wooden spatula	All	1	
Jiffy tin opener	D	1	Outstanding (9)
Matches	All	1 box	
Paper tissues	All	1 packet	Outstanding (12)
Toilet paper	All	10 sheets	Too much (7)

Glossary

BEALACH A way over a mountain shoulder (Gaelic).

BRASH ICE ('BRASH') Loose bits of floating ice, fallen from glaciers.

BELAY One climber ties himself on to a secure belay, providing protection for his partner on the rope while the latter climbs a pitch.

CLAG Cloud

COULOIR A steep snowslope between rock spurs, a big gully (French).

CRAMPONS ('CRAMPS') Steel spikes on a frame strapped on to the bottom of climbing boots to grip on ice.

CWM A bowl formed by a cirque of rock cliffs (Welsh, as Scots corrie).

DACHSTEINS Woollen mittens made large and then specially shrunk in Austria, sold in Britain by Lawries, good for snow and ice climbing.

DEADMAN (and DEADBOY) larger (and smaller) metal plates used like spades for belays in snow.

DUMPER BEACH A beach steeper (with pebbles) at the top so that surf falls upon itself and creates strong undertows.

FESTER Slang for staying in your tent all day.

GASH Naval word for rubbish or waste.

GRP Glass Reinforced Plastic (fibreglass).

GRIPPED UP Stuck on a climb, too frightened to move up, down or sideways.

HAYSTACKS Standing waves below a rapid or tide rip.

HJELPER SLEDGE A compact aluminium and canvas kit using a pair of skis to make a 20-cm-high stretcher sledge.

HOOLIGAN ('HOOLI') A blizzard.

ICE SCREW A hollow steel screw about 25 cm long screwed into ice as a belay.

KARABINER ('KRAB') An oval steel link with a hinged gate in one side for connecting ropes and other climbing equipment.

LEUCISTIC Lacking pigments, pale but not albino.

LONG LINE A fishing line stretching between two buoyed anchors and carrying many baited hooks on short snoodlines.

MANK, MANKY Slang for miserable cloud and sleet.

NANSEN BOTTLE An oceanographic collecting bottle for water samples. Like a small torpedo.

NÉVÉ Snow which is crunchy due to thaw/freeze cycles, and firm underneath also (the nicest snow).

PACK ICE ('PACK') Ice formed by freezing of the sea; floes may be several metres thick and hummocked by pressure over years. The northern limit of the Weddell Sea pack lies well south of Elephant Island in summer, but well north in winter.

PITCH The climb from one belay stance to another is a pitch (usually as near the full 40-m length of the rope as possible).

POINTS, FRONT POINTS Two of the twelve points on each crampon stick forward from the toes and slightly down. On steep hard ice these front points may penetrate only a centimetre, yet carry your whole weight.

PRUSSIK, PRUSSIK LOOP A loop of thin line, tied on to a climbing rope by a prussik knot, which slides when loose and grips when loaded so it can be used as a ratchet.

QUADRAT A rectangular frame about 30 cm×30 cm with subdividing cross wires. To survey vegetation it is thrown down and the plants covered are 'mapped' by eye.

SANGER A small stone protection for a sniper (Indian Army).

SASTRUGI Sharp waves of packed snow formed by high winds on exposed areas, often knee height, seldom waist height.

SERAC A separate block or pinnacle of ice in an icefall, or at a glacier snout.

SCHRUND (BERGSCHRUND) The transverse crack where the top of a snowslope has slumped away from the cliff above (a bergschrund if this is a rock cliff, rather than ice or snow). The crack may be filled with new snow.

SKINS Strips of (imitation) sealskin strapped underneath one's skis with the hairs pointing backward so they act as a ratchet.

SNOW ALGAE See the Botany appendix.

SPINDRIFT Snow torn up by the wind, flying horizontally.

STANCE The place where one belays.

STORM BEACH The beach level a metre or two above high tide, thrown up by the big storm waves.

TRAMMEL NET A net with three layers, one coarse-meshed between two fine-meshed. Fish push the fine net through the coarse net, thus 'bagging' themselves.

WIND SLAB Windblown snow forms a hard pack. This may form slabs over friable snow. Thin slab gives way suddenly underfoot. Thick slab is prone to avalanche.

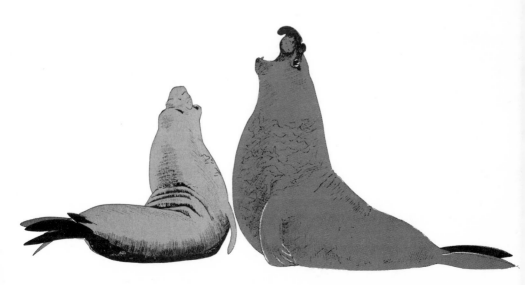

Bibliography

Imperial Trans-Antarctic Expedition 1914-17
Sir Ernest Shackleton cvo. 1919. *South, the story of the 1914-1917 expedition* (London, Heinemann.)

Results of Joint Services Expedition to Elephant Island 1970-71
Burley, M. K., ed. 1971. *Joint Services Expedition: Elephant Island, 1970-71* (London, Ministry of Defence.)

Burley, M. K. 1972. Joint Services Expedition to Elephant Island. *Geographical Journal, Vol. 138, Part 3*, 298-308.

Agnew, C. H. of Lochnaw. 1972. Elephant Island. *Alpine Journal, Vol. 77, No. 321*,204-210.

Smith, H. G. 1972. The terrestial protozoa of Elephant Island, South Shetland Islands. *BAS Bulletin No. 31*, 55-62.

Rex, D. C. and P. E. Baker. 1973. Age and petrology of the Cornwallis Island granodiorite. *BAS Bulletin No. 32*, 55-62.

Allison, J. S. and R. I. L. Smith. 1973. The vegetation of Elephant Island, South Shetland Islands. *BAS Bulletin Nos. 33 and 34*, 185-212.

Hunt, J. F. 1973. Observations on the seals of Elephant Island, South Shetland Islands, 1970-71. *BAS Bulletin No. 36*, 99-104.

O'Brien, R. M. G. 1974. Meteorological observations on Elephant Island. *BAS Bulletin No. 39*, 21-32.

Conroy, J. W. H., M. G. White, J. R. Furse and G. Bruce. 1975. Observations on the breeding biology of the Chinstrap Penguin at Elephant Island, South Shetland Islands. *BAS Bulletin No. 40*, 23-32.

Furse, J. R. and G. Bruce. 1975. Birds of the Elephant Island group. *Ibis 117*, 529-531.

O'Brien, R. M. G., J. C. C. Romans and L. Robertson. 1979. Three soil profiles from Elephant Island, South Shetland Islands. *BAS Bulletin No. 47*, 1-12.

Map of the Islands
Mapping and Charting Establishment (RE). 1972. Series D501, map sheet W61 54 (extended) part of 1:200,000 series DOS 610 (Directorate of Military Survey, United Kingdom).

Results of Joint Services Expedition to the Elephant Island Group 1976-77
Furse, J. R., ed. 1977. Joint Expedition to the Elephant Island group, 1976-77 (HMS *Collingwood*).

Furse, J. R. 1978. The Antarctic Fulmar at home near Elephant Island. *Sea Swallow, Vol. 27*, 7-10.

Furse, J. R. 1979. Crested penguins in the Elephant Island group. *Sea Swallow, Vol. 28*, 7-10.

Croxall, J. P. (in prep.). Food of Chinstrap and Macaroni Penguins at Elephant Island group, South Shetland Islands

Acknowledgements

1. General
Ministry of Defence
Foreign and Commonwealth Office
British Museum (Natural History)
British Mountaineering Council
Royal Geographical Society
Scott Polar Research Institute
British Antarctic Survey
Torry Marine Labs., Aberdeen
Lindblad Travel Inc
Williams and Glyns Bank
Universities of Glasgow, Leicester and Birmingham
Prof. G. E. Fogg
Dr S. W. Greene
Prof. I. W. D. Dalziel
Cdr M. K. Burley RN Rtd
Dr B. Stonehouse
Capt D. Dalgliesh RN Rtd
Mr C. Garrod
Mr A. Tritton
Mr A. Stephenson
Mr K. Shackleton

2. Finance
British Petroleum
Mr W. R. Freer
Boyd Line
Ellis and Everard
Homa Castors
Leverhulme Trust Fund
White Fish Authority
Peter McRae Group
Mr W. U. B. Reid
Taylor and Son
H. W. Coates Ltd
WEXAS
British Aircraft Corporation
Godman Exploration Fund
Trans-Antarctic Association
Sir James Caird T. S. Trust
Nuffield Trust
Boston Deep Sea Fisheries
Winston Churchill Memorial Fund
High Voltage Applications Ltd
Hawker Siddeley Foundation
Mount Everest Foundation
Trenchard Memorial Award Fund
Gino Watkins Memorial Fund

3. Equipment and Services
Adventure Equipment
Crewsaver
Ottersports
E. P. Barrus
The Canoe Centre
Karrimor
Ultimate Equipment
Falkland Islands Co
Wearra Shoes
Jeppeson Heaton
Teacher's Whisky
P. S. de M Ltd
Cutty Sark Whisky
Howson Devitt

4. Food
Rowntree Mackintosh
Baxters of Speyside
Fortnum and Mason
Robert A. Jewison
Lyons Bakery
Lyons Tetley
NAAFI
Graham Reid
Smiths Food Group
Whitworth Holdings
Batchelors Foods
Danoxa
Honey Boy (Jenks Bros)
Kelly of Cults
Nabisco
James Robertson and Sons
Tate and Lyle
Seagram UK Ltd

5. Subsequent analysis
British Antarctic Survey
Mr B. G. Bell
Prof. J. Redon
NERC Radiocarbon Lab., Glasgow

Index